THE 46TH ANNUAL

BRIGHAM YOUNG UNIVERSITY

SIDNEY B. SPERRY SYMPOSIUM

PROPHETS & PROPHECIES OF THE OLD TESTAMENT

Edited by Aaron P. Schade, Brian M. Hauglid, and Kerry Muhlestein

Published by the Religious Studies Center, Brigham Young University, Provo, Utah, in cooperation with Deseret Book Company, Salt Lake City.

Visit us at rsc.byu.edu.

© 2017 by Brigham Young University. All rights reserved.

Printed in the United States of America.

DESERET BOOK is a registered trademark of Deseret Book Company.

Visit us at DeseretBook.com.

Any uses of this material beyond those allowed by the exemptions in US copyright law, such as section 107, "Fair Use," and section 108, "Library Copying," require the written permission of the publisher, Religious Studies Center, 185 HGB, Brigham Young University, Provo, Utah 84602. The views expressed herein are the responsibility of the authors and do not necessarily represent the position of Brigham Young University or the Religious Studies Center.

Cover and interior design by Madison Swapp

ISBN: 978-1-9443-9422-6
US Retail: $24.99

Library of Congress Cataloging-in-Publication Data

Names: Sperry Symposium (46th : 2017 : Brigham Young University), author. | Schade, Aaron, editor. | Hauglid, Brian M., 1954- editor. | Muhlestein, Kerry, editor.
Title: Prophets and prophecies of the Old Testament : The 46th Annual Brigham Young University Sidney B. Sperry Symposium / edited by Aaron P. Schade, Brian M. Hauglid, and Kerry Muhlestein.
Description: Provo, Utah : Religious Studies Center, Brigham Young University, Salt Lake City : Deseret Book, [2017] | Includes index.
Identifiers: LCCN 2017013079 | ISBN 9781944394226
Subjects: LCSH: Bible. Old Testament--Criticism, interpretation, etc.--Congresses. | Bible. Old Testament--Prophecies. | Mormon Church--Doctrines--Congresses. | Church of Jesus Christ of Latter-day Saints--Doctrines--Congresses. | Prophets--Congresses.
Classification: LCC BS1198 .S64 2017 | DDC 221.6--dc23 LC record available at https://lccn.loc.gov/2017013079

Contents

Introduction

The Old Testament challenges its readers to understand the background and language underlying the text. Latter-day Saint students and readers of this book of scripture alike, often struggle to understand its prophetic imagery, as well as to find relevance of application for these Old Testament prophetic writings. Yet all other books of scripture in the Latter-day Saint canon presuppose that their readers have a sound knowledge of the Old Testament. An enhanced understanding of the restored gospel and its scripture is only possible with a fundamental understanding of the Old Testament. This volume aims to help modern readers by providing information and tools that help bring Old Testament prophets to light. The knowledge that is gained from the authors of this volume who contextualize the prophets will help readers understand not only the specific prophecies addressed herein, but many others contained in the New Testament, the Book of Mormon, and the Doctrine and

Covenants. Moreover, the authors model ways to analyze and apply the texts they discuss, thus providing tools that will serve the reader well in his or her broader Old Testament reading. The articles presented herein will also help the reader to see how the gospel, prophets, and Christ himself span across millennia, as well as across other volumes of scripture. The prophets are thus both timely and timeless. Both aspects are investigated in the current volume.

Beginning with keynote speaker Elder Spencer J. Condie, this book explains Old Testament prophecies in their original linguistic, historical, and theological contexts, helping us to more fully understand the Old Testament and its relevance to us individually. Prophetic books and prophets such as Amos, Micah, Isaiah, and Obadiah are contextualized. Topics include the language of prophetic imagery and naming and their interpretative usage in scripture, the original context for becoming Saviors on Mount Zion in the book of Obadiah, fulfillment of the Immanuel prophecy of Isaiah in the New Testament, and how the Old Testament is used broadly across the New Testament. Authors of this volume also contextualize prophecies of Isaiah, Micah, and Amos through the lens of those prophets, from the perspective of God, and through the reception of the community and the peoples engaged in prophetic reception. The Old Testament is also discussed within the framework of its language as it is found in the Doctrine and Covenants.

We are happy to offer this volume to students of the Old Testament. We trust that it will inspire and inform your understanding of Old Testament and provide a greater understanding of the gospel of Jesus Christ and the scriptural canon as a whole.

Aaron P. Schade
Brian M. Hauglid
Kerry Muhlestein
Beverly Yellowhorse
2017 Sperry Symposium Committee

1

"I Will Write My Law in Their Hearts"

Elder Spencer J. Condie

Elder Spencer J. Condie is an emeritus member of the First Quorum of the Seventy.

Several years ago, I served on a committee assigned to evaluate the content of the Gospel Doctrine curriculum. I was a bit surprised when someone raised this question: "Inasmuch as the Book of Mormon, Doctrine and Covenants, and Pearl of Great Price were revealed in our day, why don't we allocate more time to these modern-day scriptures and devote less time to the Old Testament?" This sincere question sparked a lively discussion highlighting the relevance of the Old Testament and why we devote so much time to its study. A few examples from Restoration scripture highlight this relevance.

First, the Lord's preface to the Doctrine and Covenants, section 1, has more than sixty footnote references to twenty-one different books of the Old Testament. Thus, from the beginning of the book, our attention is immediately directed to the Old Testament.

Second, in the Book of Mormon, the prophet Lehi considered the brass plates to be so valuable that he risked the lives of his sons to retrieve them. These plates of brass contained the genealogy of their forefathers and the prophetic words of the Lord as contained in the Old Testament (1 Nephi 3–5). They contained the covenants of the fathers (2 Nephi 3:7) and helped the peoples of the Book of Mormon keep the covenants of the Lord.

Third, on the eventful evening of 21 September 1823, Moroni informed young Joseph Smith of some gold plates which gave "an account of the former inhabitants of this continent" and contained "the everlasting Gospel." Moroni then proceeded to quote from the third and fourth chapters of Malachi, the eleventh chapter of Isaiah, and the second chapter of Joel, all from the Old Testament (Joseph Smith—History 1:30–41). The Old Testament thus became crucial to the unfolding of the Restoration.

Fourth, during the Savior's visit to the Nephites, Jesus rehearsed the marvelous message contained in the Sermon on the Mount in the New Testament, and He reviewed the words of Isaiah and admonished them to "search these things diligently; for great are the words of Isaiah" (3 Nephi 23:1). He also taught them the words of Malachi, which had not been contained on the brass plates (3 Nephi 24–25). Furthermore, He "expounded all the scriptures in one" (3 Nephi 23:14), which serves as great counsel for everyone engaged in religious education.

Fifth, the title page of the Book of Mormon indicates that the purpose of this sacred record "is to show unto the remnant of the House of Israel what great things the Lord hath done for their fathers; and *that they may know the covenants of the Lord,* that they are not cast off forever" (Book of Mormon title page; emphasis added). The Old Testament covenants were perpetuated and recorded by Lehi's descendants (see Jarom 11; Omni 26; Mosiah 3:13; 16:6; and Alma 25:15, 34:16).

Covenants

The covenants of the Lord are "an agreement . . . between God and man" in which "God in his good pleasure fixes the terms, which man accepts."[1] Covenants are accompanied by ordinances, and though we generally speak more of ordinances of the gospel, we should ever keep in mind that ordinances are an outward manifestation of a personal covenant with God.

Throughout the Old Testament, God's children had a proclivity to forget the covenants they had made with Him, but there is perhaps no greater reassurance that the remnant of the House of Israel have *not* been cast off forever than the messianic declaration found in Isaiah 49 and repeated with near exactness in 1 Nephi 21: "But, behold Zion hath said: The Lord hath forsaken me, and my Lord hath forgotten me—but he will show that he hath not. For can a woman forget her sucking child, that she should not have compassion on the son of her womb? Yea, they may forget, yet will I not forget thee, O house of Israel. Behold, I have graven thee upon the palms of my hands . . ." (Isaiah 49:13–16; 1 Nephi 21:14–16).

Through the prophet Jeremiah, the Lord declared, "This shall be the covenant that I will make with the house of Israel; . . . I will put my law in their inward parts, and write it in their hearts; and will be their God, and they shall be my people" (Jeremiah 31:33). I wish to discuss with you the covenants of the Lord and the ordinances which are associated with these covenants. We will also address the means by which the Lord continually strives to write these covenants in our hearts.

Symbols

The holy scriptures are replete with sacred symbols, tokens, rites, ceremonies, types, and shadows, all of which point to the Atonement of the Son of God, which the Prophet Joseph Smith taught is the fundamental principle of our religion "and all other things which pertain to our religion are only appendages to it."[2]

Perhaps no other Old Testament prophet was more adept in employing masterful metaphors and eloquent symbolism than the prophet Isaiah, who, speaking messianically, testified, "The Spirit of the Lord God is upon me . . . to appoint unto them that mourn in Zion, to give unto them beauty for ashes, the oil of joy for mourning, the garment of praise for the spirt of heaviness; that they might be called trees of righteousness, the planting of the Lord, that he might be glorified" (Isaiah 61:1, 3).

The prolific use of symbols is a profound means whereby the Lord teaches us lifesaving principles and helps us make and keep our covenants with Him. For example, we raise our arm to indicate that we sustain our leaders. Young children become familiar with the symbolism of the sacramental emblems and of baptism by immersion. These become foundational as we learn of entering into and keeping covenants, and they prepare us to learn of other sacred symbols in holy temples of the Lord.

The Old Testament opens up vistas of symbols, and frequent temple worship can afford an opportunity to grow in understanding according to the Lord's method of teaching through symbols. We are instructed to not try and explain in detail the meanings of all these symbols to the newly endowed, because the power and beauty of teaching through symbols is that more can be "caught" than was "taught."[3] As ancient prophets in the Old Testament teach us, learning in such a way allows the lessons to go beyond our minds and to be "put . . . in [our] inward parts, and [written] in [our] hearts" (Jeremiah 31:33).

When members receive their endowments in the temple they can be somewhat overwhelmed by the number of new and different symbols with which they are not familiar. Each time we return to the temple, we hopefully gain additional insights into the meanings of various symbols and their relation to covenants and salvation. Imposing stringent interpretations upon various symbols may actually limit the additional revelatory insights one may gain when the Holy Spirit is the teacher. President Gordon B. Hinckley taught, "The Holy Ghost is the Testifier of Truth, who can teach men things they cannot teach one another."[4]

Joseph Fielding McConkie additionally cautioned us regarding the dangers of confusing figurative symbols with literal symbols and vice versa.[5] For example, the brief biblical account of the creation of the earth has become a point of blazing contention between scientists and so-called scientific creationists. The biblical account of the Creation is described in only thirty-one verses, which hardly constitute a detailed handbook adequate for explaining, even to the brightest among us, how the earth was created. The language of the texts evokes questions concerning timing, means, and mechanisms. Despite the relevance of these issues, the scriptures focus more upon *why* the earth was created (Moses 1; Abraham 3:22–26) than upon *how* it was created and how long it took. When we understand that the purpose of the scriptures is to explain the details of the plan of salvation, we put realistic expectations on what allegorical symbols can and cannot explain, and the Old Testament and related Restoration scriptures provide this framework of God's purposes and covenants.

There are also those who believe that the sacrament bread or wafer literally becomes the body of Christ and the sacramental wine literally becomes His blood through transubstantiation. Despite good intentions, interchanging the figurative or allegorical with the literal can cause confusion and contention, and may even lead to disbelief and apostasy as the symbols lead one away from their intended use and what they were meant to teach. The Joseph Smith Translation of the New Testament explains the bread and water as symbols, and Jesus links his sacrifice as a fulfillment of the Old Testament conception of sacrifice and Passover in the form of the Lamb of God.

In this vein, the meaning of symbols is not necessarily intrinsic to the symbol and requires the application of the proper context to understand the true meaning behind the symbol. For example, if I were to write on the blackboard the letters *m-u-t-t-e-r*, most English speakers would immediately associate that symbol with complaining and murmuring. However, if you were a native German speaker, you would immediately associate that same symbol with "mother—*mutter*." The proper context is thus crucial in understanding the intent of the meaning and deciphering symbols can be quite the challenge with the Old Testament.

An example of how symbols unfold in a variety of circumstances can be seen in the Ndembu tribe in Zambia, a people who neither read nor write. They live in an area where their villages are protected by dense vegetation. To sustain themselves, they leave their jungle homes to go hunting onto the savannah plain with its tall grass where the antelope and other animals feed. Sometimes, locating their prey requires them to venture some distance from the familiar entrance to their forest homes. To ensure that they never lose their way, they cut marks on the branches and trees. In their language, these marks are called "symbols,"[6] and they are meant to show the way back home.

So it is with gospel symbols that remind us of our commitments and promises and show us the way back to our heavenly home. Elder Neal A. Maxwell assures us that we "shall probably learn later on that the number and nature of the markers are such as to maximize our growth in mortality while in the second estate. Too few, and we would be lost. Too many, and we would not stretch our souls."[7] The Old Testament challenges us in this regard, and the Lord allows us to learn and grow through symbols that stretch our spiritual understanding while simultaneously allowing us to exercise our faith. This can create within us a "new heart," or a "heart of flesh" wherein God can write his covenants and laws: "A new heart also will I give you, and a new spirit will I put within you: and I will take away the stony heart out of your flesh, and I will give you an heart of flesh" (Ezekiel 36:26).

The following examples illustrate that a given symbol may have a certain meaning in one context and another meaning in another. Take the symbolic significance of a cup, for example. In the eloquent twenty-third Psalm, David writes, "Thou preparest a table before me in the presence of mine enemies: thou anointest my head with oil; my cup runneth over" (Psalm 23:5–6). In this context, David's cup is the receptacle of the Lord's bounteous blessings and represents exquisite joy.

In Judges 7, we learn of Gideon's preparations for fighting against a mighty Midianite army. The Lord cautioned him that a large Israelite army would cause Israel to "vaunt themselves against me, saying, Mine own hath saved me." So the Lord gave Gideon counsel on how to reduce his troops from thirty-two thousand to twenty-two thousand and then to ten thousand. The final test was to observe how his troops drank from a refreshing stream of water. Those troops who lapped the water like a dog were excused from further military service, but those three hundred men who drank from hands formed in a cupping shape were retained for the battle (Judges 7:2–6). Here, these individuals who have cupped their hands become a representation of the saving and delivering power of God, and the need to rely upon him.

The cup may also symbolize extremely bitter contents as evidenced by the Savior's prayer in the Garden of Gethsemane as He prayed: "Father, if thou be willing, remove this cup from me: nevertheless, not my will, but thine, be done" (Luke 22:42). Then, to the ancient Nephites He testified: "I have drunk out of that bitter cup which the Father hath given me, and have glorified the Father in taking upon me the sins of the world" (3 Nephi 11:11). The cup in this context is brim with agony and anguish of soul.

The ritual expression of symbols may change according to a given context. For example, certain feasts were originally established in ancient Israel to keep God's love and mercy in remembrance. The

Feast of Unleavened Bread reminded them of their hasty deliverance from bondage as they fled from Egyptian captivity. The bread also reminded them of the manna that they received daily and that sustained them for forty years in the wilderness (Exodus 12:17–20; 23:15–18; Deuteronomy 16:16). The Passover feast was instituted to remind them of the command to smear lamb's blood on their doorposts so the angel of death would pass over their homes and spare the lives of their first-born (Exodus 12:7–12, 23–27; 13:15).

Eventually, these symbols would take on a very nuanced meaning focused on Christ. Near the close of his earthly ministry, the Savior gathered his twelve disciples in an upper room and began to do something with which they had been familiar since their youth. "As they were eating, Jesus took bread, and brake it and blessed it, and gave to his disciples, and said, take, eat: this is in remembrance of my body which I give a ransom for you" (Joseph Smith Translation, Matthew 26:22). After this moment, the broken bread pointed directly to Christ as the Lamb and developed a new and parallel meaning to what it represented during the Feast of Unleavened Bread—namely, Christ was the deliverer from sin and death. The bread was then meant to represent the broken body on the cross at Golgotha.

"And he took the cup, and gave thanks, and gave it to them, saying, Drink ye all of it; For this is my blood of the new testament, which is shed for many for the remission of sins" (Matthew 26:27–28). The wine no longer represented lamb's blood on Hebrew door posts; rather, it represented the blood of the Lamb of God which would be shed because the heavy weight of the sins of the world would cause Him to bleed at every pore (D&C 19:18; Moses 3:7).

A Pattern in All Things

In latter-day revelation the Lord declared, "I will give unto you a pattern in all things, that ye may not be deceived" (D&C 52:14). This pattern includes the repetitive performance of ordinances, which are an observable manifestation of a covenant or inner commitment. President Boyd K. Packer has taught us that "Ordinances and covenants become our credentials for admission into His presence. To worthily receive them is the quest of a lifetime; to keep them thereafter is the challenge of mortality."[8] In other words, we must seek to have our covenants constantly written in our hearts. Ordinances are observable to others, while covenants are kept privately in our hearts.

In the Joseph Smith Translation of Genesis we learn that after Adam and Eve had been expelled from the Garden of Eden: "Adam was obedient unto the commandments of the Lord. And after many days, an angel of the Lord appeared unto Adam, saying, Why dost thou offer sacrifices unto the Lord? And Adam said unto him, I know not, save the Lord commanded me" (Joseph Smith Translation, Genesis 4:6–7). "And then the angel spake, saying, This thing is a similitude of the sacrifice of the Only Begotten of the Father, which is full of grace and truth" (Moses 5:5–7). The repetition of the sacrifice would act as a covenant renewal and reminder of the redemptive power of Christ.

To Noah, the Lord provided the rainbow as a token of His covenant with Noah that there would never be another flood that would cover the entire earth (Genesis 9:13–15). Jehovah rewarded Abram's ninety-nine years of faithfulness by changing his name to Abraham and covenanting with him. The following excerpt outlines the promises the Lord made with Abraham:

> I will make thee exceeding fruitful, and I will make nations of thee, and kings shall come out of thee.
>
> And I will establish my covenant between me and thee and thy seed after thee in their generations for an everlasting covenant, to be a God unto thee, and to thy seed after thee.
>
> And I will give unto thee, and thy seed after thee, the land wherein thou art a stranger, all the land of Canaan, for an everlasting possession; and I will be their God. (Genesis 17:6–8)

Abraham's acceptance of this covenant was manifest by his undergoing circumcision, which the Lord described as "a token of the covenant betwixt me and thee" (Genesis 17:11). All of these examples demonstrate to us that personal covenants between God and His children are accompanied by observable ordinances attesting to the acceptance of that covenant.

The divine covenant of posterity began to be fulfilled with the birth of Ishmael, as well as with Isaac, for whom Abraham and Sarah had waited so long. But after providing them with such a magnificent blessing, the Lord commanded Abraham, years later, to "take now thy son, thine only son Isaac, whom thou lovest, and get thee into the land of Moriah; and offer him there for a burnt offering upon one of the mountains which I will tell thee of" (Genesis 22:2). This was a poignant command, given Abraham's similar experience as a sacrificial offering (Abraham 1).

Several years earlier, Abraham had sought to negotiate with the Lord to postpone the destruction of Sodom and Gomorrah (Genesis 18:26–33). But later, when the Lord asked Abraham to sacrifice his son, symbolic of an unwavering commitment to his covenants, "Abraham rose up *early in the morning*" to take Isaac with him to the appointed place designated for the sacrifice (Genesis 22:3; emphasis added). There was no time for negotiation, merely time for obedience. President Hugh B. Brown (1883–1975) said the Lord knew all He needed to know about Abraham, but there were some things Abraham needed to learn about Abraham.[9] Thus we see that in our lives, if we are to become like the Savior, we must accept the fact that "though he were a Son, yet learned he obedience by the things which he suffered" (Hebrews 5:8). The sacrifice of the Savior also seems to foreshadow personal sacrifice embodied in, and incumbent upon all, through the law of sacrifice.

The Book of Mormon prophet Jacob, referring to this account contained on the plates of brass, taught the people of his day that

"Abraham in the wilderness [was] obedient unto the commands of God in offering up his son Isaac, which is a similitude of God and his Only Begotten Son," and it was accounted unto him for righteousness (Jacob 4:5). The Book of Mormon provides a wonderful bridge between the Old and New Testaments and helps to accentuate the power of obedience and the saving power of Christ.

The Lord then gave Isaac the same blessing received by his father Abraham (Genesis 26:3–4). Isaac became the father of Jacob, and when Jacob became of age, Isaac instructed his son not to marry a Canaanite but to travel some distance to Padan-aram and take a wife from the daughters of his mother's brother, Laban (Genesis 28:1–2).

Of Jacob's experiences, President Marion G. Romney (1897–1988) taught us a profound lesson regarding the Lord's teaching through symbols:

> When Jacob traveled from Beersheba toward Haran, he had a dream in which he saw himself on the earth at the foot of a ladder that reached to heaven where the Lord stood above it. He beheld angels ascending and descending thereon, and Jacob realized that *the covenants he made with the Lord there were the rungs on the ladder that he himself would have to climb in order to obtain the promised blessings*—blessings that would entitle him to enter heaven and associate with the Lord. Because he had met the Lord and entered into covenants with him there, Jacob considered the site so sacred that he named the place Bethel, a contraction of Beth-Elohim, which means literally "the House of the Lord." He said of it: "this is none other but the house of God, and this is the gate of heaven" (Genesis 28:17).[10]

We are grateful for apostles, prophets, seers, and revelators—a pattern established in the Old Testament—who teach us, with such clarity, truths symbolically embedded in the holy scriptures.

Jacob's name was then changed to Israel and the Abrahamic covenant was renewed upon him, "and in thy seed shall all the families of the earth be blessed" (Genesis 28:14). He became the father of twelve sons, one of which was Joseph.

To me, Joseph's life is one of the greatest examples of one having the laws of God written in his heart. He temporarily paid a heavy price for offending Potiphar's seductive wife, but upon eventually being released from prison after being falsely accused, Joseph gained the favor of the Pharaoh, who perceived that the Spirit of the Lord was upon Joseph (Genesis 41:38) and who said unto Joseph, "I have set thee over all the land of Egypt" (Genesis 41:41). Joseph's obedience and faithfulness would eventually bless and save the entire house of Israel.

All of these great patriarchs sought for and received covenants with God, which allowed them to receive new hearts in which God could write his law, and to serve as symbols which teach us how to do the same.

A Tabernacle in the Wilderness

After the house of Israel had experienced a reversal of the blessings received under Joseph, "there arose up a new king over Egypt, which knew not Joseph" (Exodus 1:8). This resulted in a tragic era of Egyptian bondage for the children of Israel. The scriptures inform us that God had not forgotten His chosen people, and He raised up Moses to be His instrument in delivering the Israelites from bondage. As the exiled Hebrews were wandering in the wilderness, the Lord commanded Moses, "Speak unto the children of Israel . . . and let them make me a sanctuary; that I may dwell among them" (Exodus 25:2, 8). Jehovah then gave Moses detailed instructions for building a tabernacle. "And there," said the Lord, "I will meet with thee and I will commune with thee" (Exodus 25:21–22).

The tabernacle would, in very deed, become "a portable temple."[11] The tabernacle was constructed of the finest materials available. Fine-twined-linen curtains of blue, purple, and scarlet were held in place by clasps of gold attached to bars held up by pillars. Other curtains, made of goat's hair, provided a covering for the entire tabernacle. Boards of the finest wood were fashioned by craftsmen for the sides of the tabernacle. These boards were held together by tenens, like leaves on a dining room table held in place with tabs and sockets. In the innermost part of the tabernacle, the holy of holies, the ark of testimony, and the mercy seat were overlaid with pure gold (Exodus 25–27).

Aaron and his sons were washed and anointed and given special clothing to wear as they were consecrated to serve in the holy ordinances of the tabernacle (Exodus 28–29; 39–40). The sons of Gershon were given the special responsibility to "bear the curtains of the tabernacle . . . And the hangings of the court, and the hanging for the door of the gate of the court" (Numbers 4:22–26). As the Israelites moved from place to place, they would dismantle and then reconstruct the tabernacle after each move. The sons of Gershon were authorized to have two wagons and four oxen to assist them in moving the curtains from one settlement to the next (Numbers 7:7).

The sons of Merari were charged to transport the boards, bars, pillars, and sockets of the tabernacle, and they were provided with four wagons and eight oxen to transport their heavy load (Numbers 4:29–31; 7:8).

The sons of Kohath were given the special assignment to transport "the most holy things," the "vessels of the sanctuary"—even the ark of the covenant and its sacred contents. The sons of Kohath were provided with neither wagons nor oxen "because the service of the sanctuary belonging unto them was that they should bear [the most holy things] upon their shoulders" (Numbers 4:2–4, 15; 7:9.) This great honor and privilege of transporting the sacred vessels was eventually passed on to Kohath's son Izhar who, in turn, conveyed these sacred duties to his son Korah (Numbers 16:1).

In the evening, "the appearance of fire" could be seen above the tabernacle and a "cloud covered it by day." "And when the cloud was taken up from the tabernacle . . . the children of Israel journeyed: and in the place where the cloud abode, there the children of Israel pitched their tents" (Numbers 9:15–17).

With the passage of time, what had once been considered to be a great honor in transporting the sacred tabernacle began to seem too tedious and commonplace, and Korah and 250 other Levites began to murmur about their seemingly mundane, repetitive duties. They began to nurture false aspirations for greater, more visible responsibilities. Envious of the authority of their leaders, they one day confronted Moses and Aaron with the impertinent question: "Wherefore then lift ye yourselves above the congregation of the Lord?" (Numbers 16:1–2).

Moses was so astonished by this question that "he fell upon his face" (Numbers 16:4). The next day, having regained his composure, Moses asked Korah an extremely penetrating introspective question: "Seemeth it but a small thing unto you, that the God of Israel hath separated you from the congregation of Israel, to bring you near to himself to do the service of the tabernacle of the Lord, and to stand before the congregation to minister unto them?" (Numbers 16:9).

It is no small thing to be called to serve anywhere in the kingdom of God. Moses teaches us that there are no insignificant callings or assignments in building the kingdom. It is not important *where* we serve but *how* we serve.

In the Book of Mormon, King Benjamin taught his people that if they were to overcome the natural man, they must become "as a child, submissive, meek, humble, patient, full of love" (Mosiah 3:19). To these childlike traits I would add "a love for repetition." Little children not only endure repetition, they thrive on it! They can eat macaroni and cheese every day of their young lives, and they can hear the same stories and sing the same songs several times in succession. Oh, that all adults had such childlike faith and could thrive on the repetition of temple instruction, covenants, and ordinances performed vicariously for those beyond the veil!

It is no small thing to be set apart as a servant in the house of the Lord. Some tasks are more visible than others, and some duties and responsibilities may be more rewarding to our egos than others, but it is important to serve in the house of the Lord, or anywhere else in the kingdom. Each opportunity for service opens the heart to God and his desires.

In addition to commanding Moses to build a portable temple in which the Lord could abide, Jehovah instructed Moses to instigate several different rites, rituals, ceremonies, and feast days to help the children of Israel remember their covenants. Keeping the Sabbath day holy was a weekly reminder of sacred covenants (Exodus 31:13). All males were required to convene three times each year to participate in the Feast of Unleavened Bread, the Feast of Weeks, and the Feast of Tabernacles (Exodus 23:14–17; Deuteronomy 16:16). Over time, other feast days were added.[12]

After Moses departed from this earth, the children of Israel were led by Joshua and then by other judges, but they yearned for a king, and they also yearned for the day when a permanent holy house of the Lord could be constructed. Both King Saul and King David were denied the opportunity of building a temple, but David's son, Solomon, a wise young man of great promise, was granted the privilege of building a temple to their God.

Hiram, king of Tyre, a good friend of David and Solomon, provided the timbers for the temple from the cedars of Lebanon, the wood being floated down the coast of the Mediterranean Sea (1 Kings 5:6–10; 2 Chronicles 2:16). Hiram also provided skilled craftsmen to assist in the construction of the temple. The blocks of stone were carved elsewhere and then brought to the temple "so that there was neither hammer nor axe nor any tool of iron heard in the house, while it was building" (1 Kings 6:7). The temple contained a molten brazen sea for washing and purification which rested upon twelve oxen representing the twelve tribes of Israel (1 Kings 7:23–26; 2 Chronicles 4:2–5.) The handiwork was absolutely magnificent as the temple was adorned with gold and precious stones (1 Kings 5:17, 6:21–22).

At the dedicatory services "when Solomon had made an end of praying . . . the glory of the Lord filled the house" (2 Chronicles 7:1). Afterward, the Lord appeared to Solomon twice, and assured him, "I have heard thy prayer and thy supplication. . . . But if ye shall at all turn from following me, ye or your children, and will not keep my commandments and my statutes . . . Then will I cut off Israel out of the land which I have given them; and this house, which I have hallowed for my name, will I cast out of my sight" (1 Kings 9:3, 6–7).

Only two chapters later we learn that "king Solomon loved many strange women . . . and his wives turned away his heart. . . . And Solomon did evil in the sight of the Lord" (1 Kings 11:1, 3, 6). Upon Solomon's death, there arose a schism in Israel and in approximately 925 (930) BC, ten tribes elected to follow Jeroboam and form the Northern Kingdom of Israel while the other two tribes followed Solomon's son Rehoboam and became the Southern Kingdom of Judah (1 Kings 12:19–20).

Only eight of the subsequent forty kings of Judah and Israel did that which was pleasing in the sight of the Lord, and in 722 BC, the northern kingdom of Israel became captive to the Assyrians (2 Kings 17:23). In 587–586 BC, King Nebuchadnezzar invaded the southern kingdom of Judah and carried away "the vessels of the house of the Lord" and "all Jerusalem" to Babylon (2 Kings 24: 13–15). Thus began the Babylonian captivity. From all this we learn that as crucial as temples are to the plan of salvation, when God's children break their covenants with Him they lose their right to claim the blessings of the holy temple.

As we now live in turbulent times, it should be a source of comfort to know that God does indeed intervene in the affairs of His children and provides a way for us to keep our covenants by touching our hearts: "And I will give them one heart, and I will put a new spirit within you; and I will take the stony heart out of their flesh, and will give them an heart of flesh: That they may walk in my statutes, and keep mine ordinances, and do them: and they shall be my people, and I will be their God" (Ezekiel 11:16–20).

Around 538 BC, "the Lord stirred upon the spirit of Cyrus king of Persia, that he made a proclamation throughout all his kingdom" declaring that the Lord had charged him "to build him an house at Jerusalem, which is in Judah" (Ezra 1:1–2). And Zerubabbel "began to build the house of God which is at Jerusalem: and with them were the prophets of God helping them" (Ezra 5:2). King Darius renewed the decree of Cyrus (Ezra 6:1–3) and his successor, Artaxerxes, even helped adorn the temple and commanded that his treasurers do "whatsoever Ezra the priest, the scribe of the law of the God of heaven, shall require of you" (Ezra 7:21).

But, alas, as was the case with Solomon's temple, in consequence of the people's persistent disobedience, Zerubbabel's temple would be desecrated (Malachi 1–2); rebuilt by Herod, where the Savior frequently taught during His earthly ministry (Matthew 26:55; John 8:2); and eventually once again destroyed (Matthew 21:12; John 2:16) at the hands of the Roman army under Titus in AD 70. As important as temples are to the plan of salvation, we once again learn that God will not dwell in unholy temples (D&C 97:17).

The Temple

The holy temple is well suited for a loving Heavenly Father to write his laws upon our hearts. Through recurrent instruction and prolific symbols and the frequent renewal of covenants accompanied by observable ordinances, the covenants we make become embedded in our hearts and minds in such a way as to be unforgettable.

In a vision, the prophet Ezekiel saw the house of the Lord, and as he approached the door of the temple, "behold, waters issued out from under the threshold of the house eastward" (Ezekiel 47:1). A heavenly ministrant then brought Ezekiel through the waters until they reached his ankles and then his knees and eventually became "a river that [he] could not pass over" (Ezekiel 47:3–5).

The heavenly ministrant told Ezekiel, "These waters issue out toward the east country, and go down into the desert, and go into the sea: which being brought forth into the sea, the waters shall be healed. And it shall come to pass, that . . . every thing shall live wither the river cometh" (Ezekiel 47:8–9).

I testify that this passage, in addition to being a geological prediction, is a sacred, metaphorical, and prophetic promise that all who drink of the living waters which issue from the holy temple can and will be healed. If the living waters issuing from the temple can heal the Dead Sea, the living waters can also heal an unhappy marriage, refresh a parched testimony, restore a broken heart, and mend a strained relationship with neighbors or family members. They can give us all a new heart.

We rejoice in the healing power of the Atonement of our Savior and Redeemer. The prophet Zechariah prophesied of the Lord's appearance: "And his feet shall stand in that day upon the mount of Olives . . . and the mount of Olives shall cleave in the midst thereof toward the east and toward the west. . . . And it shall be in that day, that living waters shall go out from Jerusalem . . . And the Lord shall be king over all the earth: in that day shall there be one Lord, and his name one" (Zechariah 14:4, 8–9).

In latter-day revelation, the Lord Himself prophesied of His return:

> And then shall the Jews look upon me and say: What are these wounds in thine hands and in thy feet?

> Then shall they know that I am the Lord; for I will say unto them: These wounds are the wounds with which I was wounded in the house of my friends. I am he who was lifted up. I am Jesus that was crucified. I am the Son of God. (D&C 45:51–52; see Zechariah 13:6.)

The Old Testament is a treasure trove of symbols and teachings on the life of the Messiah. I pray that as we persist in keeping our covenants and humbly "seek learning, even by study and also by faith" (D&C 88:118), our minds will be enlightened, and the richness of sacred symbols will, in the words of the Apostle Paul, be "written not with ink, but with the Spirit of the living God; not in tables of stone, but in fleshy tables of the heart" (2 Corinthians 3:3).

Notes

1. LDS Bible Dictionary, "Covenant," 651.
2. *Teachings of Presidents of the Church: Joseph Smith* (Salt Lake City: The Church of Jesus Christ of Latter-day Saints, 2007), 49.
3. The author is indebted to Professor Chauncey Riddle for this insight.
4. Gordon B. Hinckley, *Teachings of Gordon B. Hinckley* (Salt Lake City: Deseret Book, 1997), 259.
5. Joseph Fielding McConkie, *Gospel Symbols* (Salt Lake City: Bookcraft, 1985), 205–13.
6. Victor Turner, *The Forest of Symbols* (Ithaca, NY: Cornell University Press, 1967), 48.
7. Neal A. Maxwell, "Some Thoughts on the Gospel and the Behavioral Sciences," *BYU Studies Quarterly* 15, no. 4 (Summer 1976), 595.
8. Boyd K. Packer, "Covenants," *Ensign*, May 1987, 24.
9. Truman Madsen, *The Highest in Us* (Salt Lake City: Bookcraft, 1978), 49.
10. Marion G. Romney, "Temples—The Gates of Heaven," *Ensign*, March 1971, 16; emphasis added. The Prophet Joseph Smith taught, "Paul ascended into the third Heavens and he could understand the three principal rounds

of Jacob's Ladder, the Telestial, the Terrestrial and the Celestial glories or Kingdoms, where Paul saw and heard things which were not lawful for him to utter." History, 1838–1856, volume D-1 [1 August 1842–1 July 1843], *The Joseph Smith Papers,* http://josephsmithpapers.org/paper-summary/history-1838-1856-volume-d-1-1-august-1842-1-july-1843/199.

11. LDS Bible Dictionary, "Tabernacle," 778.
12. Leaving the interpretation of symbols open-ended can be conducive to "looking beyond the mark" as described by Jacob in the Book of Mormon (Jacob 4:14). In his magnum opus *The Life of Christ,* Frederic Farrar describes the gross distortions of the law of Moses that had occurred between the time the law was given and the commencement of the Savior's earthly ministry: "The Rabbinical schools, in their meddling, carnal, superficial spirit of word-weaving and letter-worship, had spun large accumulations of worthless subtlety all over the Mosaic law. Among other things they had wasted their idleness in fantastic attempts to count, and classify, and weigh, and measure all the separate commandments of the ceremonial and moral law. They had come to the sapient conclusion that there were 248 affirmative precepts, being as many as the members of the human body, and 365 negative precepts, being as many as the arteries and veins, or the days of the year: the total being 613, which was also the number of letters in the Decalogue." Frederic W. Farrar, *The Life of Christ* (London: Cassell, Peter & Galpin, 1874), 565.

2

Ominous Onomastics

Symbolic Naming and Paronomasia in Old Testament Prophecy

Matthew L. Bowen

Matthew L. Bowen is an assistant professor of Religious Education at Brigham Young University–Hawaii.

Symbolic names and naming constituted an important part of what Nephi called "the manner of prophesying among the Jews" (2 Nephi 25:1). Recognizing how ancient Israelite prophecy and its fulfillment revolve around names and naming is indispensable to grasping the overarching messages of the prophets whose writings are preserved in the Hebrew Bible.

In this chapter I will describe how the Lord directed Hosea and Isaiah to bestow symbolic names on their children and how the meaning of those names took on thematic importance in the prophets' writings. These names become recurring symbols of divine justice and mercy—of divine destruction, gathering, and protection. Moreover, I will attempt to show that symbolic naming (including the giving of "new names") and onomastic punning—i.e., name exploitation[1] or giving an existing name new meaning—constitute salient features of the prophecies of most of the written prophets, including Jeremiah, Ezekiel, Micah, Zephaniah, and Obadiah, among others.

Isaiah: "I and the Children Whom the Lord Hath Given Me"

The first mention of a symbolic name for the first of Isaiah's sons mentioned in the text comes in Isaiah 7:3: "Then said the Lord unto Isaiah, Go forth now to meet Ahaz, thou, and *Shear-jashub* [*šĕʾār yāšûb*] thy son, at the end of the conduit of the upper pool in the highway of the fuller's field" (emphasis added).[2] Two elements comprise the name Shear-jashub: the noun *šĕʾār*, "remnant" and the third-person masculine imperfect verbal element *yāšûb* "[he/it] shall return," thus "a remnant shall return." The first part of the name, "remnant," emphasizes divine justice or judgment. The Lord will permit the consequences of Israel and Judah's covenant infidelity to overtake them and they will be largely destroyed, smitten, and scattered. However, the second part of the name emphasizes divine mercy: the opportunity for "repentance" or a "return." The Lord's covenant is thus not completely disannulled. Israel and Judah will have a remnant of the "ransomed" or "redeemed of the Lord" that eventually "*shall return* [*yĕšûbûn*] and come with singing unto Zion" (Isaiah 35:10; 52:11).

The text of Isaiah does not give full expression to this symbol in prophecy until Isaiah 10:19–22, where he prophesies concerning a "remnant" of Israel that would survive the Assyrian exile and eventually "return":

> And *the rest* [*šĕʾār, remnant*] of the trees of his forest shall be few, that a child may write them.
>
> And it shall come to pass in that day, that *the remnant* [*šĕʾār*] of Israel, and such as are escaped of the house of Jacob,

> *shall no more again* stay upon him that smote them; but shall stay upon the Lord, the Holy One of Israel, in truth.
>
> *The remnant shall return [šĕʾār yāšûb]*, even the *remnant* [*šĕʾār*] of Jacob, unto the mighty God.
>
> For though thy people Israel be as the sand of the sea, yet *a remnant of them shall return* [*šĕʾār yāšûb*]: the consumption decreed shall overflow with righteousness. (Isaiah 10:19–22)

Joseph Smith recognized the importance of the Shear-jashub theme. In March 1838, he answered "certain questions on the writings of Isaiah . . . at or near Far West, Missouri."[3] These answers were later canonized in Doctrine and Covenants section 113. The final question in this section pertained specifically to Isaiah 52:2: "What are we to understand by Zion loosing herself from the bands of her neck; 2d verse?" (D&C 113:9). Joseph's answer notably incorporated the meaning of the name Shear-jashub and the prophecy of Isaiah 10:19–22:

> We are to understand that the scattered *remnants* are exhorted to *return* to the Lord from whence they have fallen; which if they do, the promise of the Lord is that he will speak to them, or give them revelation. See the 6th, 7th, and 8th verses. The bands of her neck are the curses of God upon her, or the *remnants* of Israel in their scattered condition among the Gentiles. (D&C 113:10)

Joseph Smith evidently interpreted "the captive daughter of Zion" or "Zion" in terms of the "remnant" mentioned elsewhere in Isaiah (see hereafter). Importantly, Isaiah 52:8, the last verse used in the Prophet's explanation, employs the verb *šûb/yāšûb*: "for they shall see eye to eye, *when the Lord shall bring again Zion* [*bĕšûb yhwh ṣiyyôn*]." As John A. Oswalt notes, "The phrase 'the Lord's returning of Zion' [*bĕšûb yhwh ṣiyyôn*] can be taken as either an objective genitive or a subjective genitive: the Lord's returning of Zion or the

Lord's returning to Zion."[4] The KJV and the Book of Mormon both follow the former interpretation.

The Shear-jashub theme resurfaces in a prominent way in Isaiah 11, a text which Moroni recited to Joseph Smith three times during the night intervening between 21 and 22 September 1823 and once more the following morning.[5] Isaiah prophesied that Israel and Judah's "remnant" would be gathered from every part of the earth: "And it shall come to pass in that day, that the Lord shall set his hand again the second time to recover *the remnant* [*šĕʾār*] *of his people, which shall be left* [*ʾăšer yiššāʾēr*] *from Assyria* [*mēʾaššûr*], and from Egypt, and from Pathros, and from Cush, and from Elam, and from Shinar, and from Hamath, and from the islands of the sea" (Isaiah 11:11; cf. v. 12). The language of Isaiah's prophecy not only plays on the name of his son Shear-jashub ("a remnant shall return"), but it describes in vivid terms the nature of the remnant's return. Isaiah declares that the Lord himself will be the agent that gathers Israel and Judah and causes their "return" or restoration, which is a major theme in prophets, the Book of Mormon, and, to an extent, the New Testament.

The same alliterative paronomasia (i.e., "playing on the sounds and meanings of words"[6]) is repeated for emphasis a few verses later: "And there shall be an highway for *the remnant* [*šĕʾār*] *of his people, which shall be left* [*ʾăšer yiššāʾēr*], *from Assyria* [*mēʾaššûr*]; *like* [*kaʾăšer*] as it was to *Israel* in the day that he came up out of the land of Egypt" (Isaiah 11:16). In piling on the alliterative wordplay, Isaiah further transforms the name of his son, Shear-jashub, into a prophecy of a second exodus from a symbolic seven nations (including Assyria and Egypt) and the "isles of the sea" mentioned in verse 11.[7]

Isaiah 8 gives us a brief account of the birth and naming of Isaiah's son Maher-shalal-hash-baz. Isaiah informs us that the Lord commanded him to give his son this name, which means something like "to speed the spoil, he hastens the prey"[8] or as many modern translators and commentaries render it, "the spoil speeds, the prey hastens" (*mahēr šālāl ḥāš baz,* Isaiah 8:1–3). In any case, this symbolic name foretells "imminent destruction." The Lord then states the first event that the name symbolizes: "For before the child shall have knowledge to cry, My father, and my mother, the riches of Damascus and the *spoil* [*šĕlal*] of Samaria shall be taken away before the king of Assyria" (Isaiah 8:1–4). The name thus constitutes a divine promise of the imminent destruction of Syria (with its capital, Damascus) and the northern kingdom of Israel (with its capital, Samaria) at the hands of the Assyrians.

As with the name Shear-jashub, Isaiah withholds further prophetic exploitation of Maher-shalal-hash-baz's name until Isaiah 10, where he abruptly returns to the themes of spoil and prey. In doing so, Isaiah describes the sinful conditions that he saw pervading Israelite and Judahite society: "Woe unto them that decree unrighteous decrees, and that write grievousness which they have prescribed; to turn aside the needy from judgment, and to take away the right from the poor of my people, that widows *may be their prey* [*may be their spoil*], and that they may rob [make a prey of] the fatherless!" (Isaiah 10:1–2). The KJV obscures the link between the verbs Isaiah uses and the name of his son, Maher-shalal-hash-baz. Israel and Judah have sped to the widow as their spoil and made orphans their prey—i.e., they have exploited their societies' most vulnerable people.

Consequently, the Lord will send a commensurate punishment upon Israel in the form of Assyria: "O Assyrian, the rod of mine anger, and the staff in their hand is mine indignation. I will send him against an hypocritical nation, and against the people of my wrath will I give him a charge, *to take the spoil* [*lišĕlōl šālāl*] *and to take the prey* [*lābōz baz*] and to tread them down like the mire of the streets" (Isaiah 10:5–6). The name Maher-shalal-hash-baz thus becomes a sign of Israel's enemies speeding to the spoil and hastening to their prey—i.e., of Israel's imminent destruction. Similar allusions to

Maher-shalal-hash-baz recur throughout Isaiah: "Thy tacklings are loosed; they could not well strengthen their mast, they could not spread the sail: then is the prey of a great *spoil* divided; the lame take *the prey*" (Isaiah 33:23; see also 42:22).

One of the "sons" with symbolic names mentioned in Isaiah 7–10, the eighth-century BCE "Immanuel," may have been a son of Ahaz, a son of Isaiah, or the son of someone else. Isaiah 7:14 reports the birth of a "son" named Immanuel: "Therefore the Lord himself shall give you a sign; Behold, a virgin [*hāʿalmâ*] shall conceive, and bear a son, and shall call his name Immanuel." The name Immanuel transparently denotes "With us is God" or "God with us."

In view of this name's meaning, Matthew cites Isaiah 7:14 as a prophecy of Jesus Christ as Messiah (see Matthew 1:22–23). Matthew recognized that Jesus represented "God" (Yahweh) being "with us" (with the human family) in the flesh. Many Latter-day Saints have been content to simply read Isaiah 7:14 exclusively as a prophecy of Jesus Christ without considering the historical context of this prophecy described in Isaiah 7–10 or the prophecy's broader theological implications for the Davidic dynasty. Joseph Jensen suggests that the *ʿalmâ* "referred to is a wife of Ahaz, and the son to be born would be of a child of Ahaz; as such, he would be a guarantee of the continuation of the Davidic dynasty, to which perpetuity has been promised (2 Samuel 7) and from which great things had been expected."[9]

From a temporal standpoint, the Davidic dynasty ended with deposed kings Jehoiachin and his uncle Zedekiah in exile in Babylon. However, Matthew recognized that as a promise of divine protection for Judah and the Davidic dynasty, Isaiah's Immanuel prophecy inevitably pertained to the Messiah as David's descendant ("son of David") and thus to Jesus himself. Isaiah promised that Judah and the Davidic dynasty would not be destroyed: "And he [the king of Assyria, symbolized as the Euphrates] shall pass through Judah;

he shall overflow and go over, he shall reach even to the neck; and the stretching out of his wings shall fill the breadth of thy land, *O Immanuel* [*ʿimmānû ʾēl*]" (Isaiah 8:8). Confederates Israel and Syria would not succeed in their attempt to end the Davidic dynasty: "Take counsel together, and it shall come to nought; speak the word, and it shall not stand: for *God is with us* [*ʿimmānû ʾēl*]" (Isaiah 8:10).

The "us" in the name Immanuel evokes both the divine council "us" of Isaiah 6:8,[10] and the "us" mentioned in the birth of divine son of Isaiah 9:6: "For unto us a child is born, unto us son is given: and the government shall be upon his shoulder: and his name shall be called Wonderful, Counsellor [i.e., Wonderful Counselor], The mighty God, The everlasting Father, The Prince of Peace." These titles (or variations) are elsewhere used of the Lord himself,[11] suggesting that Isaiah envisioned a Messiah over an imperfect Davidic descendant (like Ahaz).

Isaiah's declaration "I and the children whom the Lord hath given me are for signs and wonders in Israel from the Lord of Hosts" invites us to consider the function of Isaiah's own name in his prophecies. Recognizing that Isaiah's name means "The Lord is Salvation" helps us to appreciate the distinctive "salvation" motif that pervades the writings of Isaiah as a thematic wordplay on his own name: see Isaiah 12:2–3; 17:10; 25:9; 26:1; 30:15; 33:2, 6, 22; 35:4; 37:20, 35; 38:20; 43:12; 45:8, 17, 20, 22; 46:7, 13, 20; 47:13, 15; 49:6, 8, 25; 51:5–6, 8; 52:7, 10; 56:1; 59:1, 11, 16–17; 60:18; 61:10; 62:1, 11; 63:1, 5, 9; 64:5.

Beyond the symbolic names of Isaiah and the children named in Isaiah 7–10, the theme of giving of new names prevails throughout the Book of Isaiah. This is particularly true near the end of the book. The Lord promises even those traditionally excluded from the temple,[12] such as eunuchs (emasculated males) and the children of foreigners, a "place [*yād;* literally, "hand" or monument] and a name even better than of sons and daughters," even "an everlasting name" in the temple (Isaiah 56:5). The temple would "be called an house of prayer for all people" and Zion herself would be crowned and receive "*a new name*, which the mouth of the Lord shall name" (Isaiah 62:2–3). The "new name" is really several "new names":

> Thou shalt no more be termed *Forsaken* [*ʿăzûbâ*, or "divorced"]; neither shall thy land any more be termed *Desolate* [*šĕmāmâ*]: but thou shalt be called *Hephzi-bah* [*ḥepṣî-bāh* = "my delight is in her"], and thy land *Beulah* [*bĕʿûlâ* = "married"]: for the Lord *delighteth in thee*, and thy land *shall be married* [*tibbāʿēl*].
>
> For as a young man *marrieth* [*yibʿal*] a virgin, so shall thy sons *marry* [*yibʿālûk*] thee: and as the bridegroom rejoiceth over the bride, so shall thy God rejoice over thee (Isaiah 62:4-5).

The "new names" mentioned and explained here work a lot like the name reversal in the Book of Hosea discussed hereafter in that names that were previously symbols of divine justice are renovated into symbols of divine mercy. Names that describe a felicitous covenant "marriage" relationship (an at-*one*-ment) replace names that describe a broken covenant and the consequences of covenant violations. Moreover, the wordplay on Beulah/*bāʿal* recalls Israel and Judah's illicit Baal worship (cf. the wordplay on Ishi/Baali in Hosea below). Thus, the description of the land as faithfully "married" to Yahweh uses irony to maximum effect.

Two final "new names" mentioned a few verses later drive at the same effect: "Behold, the Lord hath proclaimed unto the end of the world, Say ye to the daughter of Zion, Behold, *thy salvation* [*yišʿēk*] cometh; behold, his reward is with him, and his work before him. And they shall call them, The holy people, The redeemed of the Lord: and thou shalt be called, *Sought out* [*dĕrûšâ*], *A city not forsaken* [*lōʾ neʿĕzābâ*]" (Isaiah 62:11–12). Besides offering two additional "new names" that evince the Lord's atoning Israel to himself in mercy, this prophecy also hints at the one who will bring about this reversal. The word *yišaʿ* ("salvation") hints at the name Isaiah[13] and is the same salvation mentioned in Isaiah 63:1–2 with its puns on *ʾĕdôm* in terms of *ʾādôm* ("red") and other winepress images.

Jeremiah and the "Righteous Branch"

The Book of Jeremiah also features the re-motivation or symbolic transformation of several names. Through punning, he gives the name Tekoa (*tĕqôaʿ*, Amos's hometown [Amos 1:1]) new meaning as a symbol of impending disaster using the images of "blowing" (*tiqʿû*) a trumpet of alarm (Jeremiah 6:1), the "pitching" (*tāqʿû*) of shepherds' tents (Jeremiah 6:3), and the "disjoining" (*tēqaʿ*) of the Lord's covenant relationship with Judah (Jeremiah 6:6).[14]

Jeremiah's prophecies, however, ultimately hold out hope for the salvation of Israel through a Davidic scion or a "righteous branch."[15] Since Jeremiah's "branch" prophecies testify of a Messiah, they are arguably the most important in the corpus of his writings:

Jeremiah 23:5–6	**Jeremiah 33:15–17**
Behold, the days come, saith the Lord, that I will raise unto David a *righteous Branch* [*ṣemaḥ ṣaddîq*] and a King shall reign and prosper, and shall execute judgment and *justice* [*ṣĕdāqâ*] in the earth.	In those days, and at that time, *will I cause the Branch of righteousness* [*ṣemaḥ ṣĕdāqâ*] *to grow up* [*ʾaṣmîaḥ*] unto David; and he shall execute judgment and *righteousness* [*ṣĕdāqâ*] in the land.
In his days Judah *shall be saved* [*tiwwāšaʿ*] and Israel shall dwell safely: and this is his name whereby he shall be called, *THE LORD OUR RIGHTEOUSNESS* [*yhwh ṣidqēnû*].	In those days *shall* Judah *be saved* [*tiwwāšaʿ*], and Jerusalem shall dwell safely: and this is the name wherewith she shall be called, *The Lord our righteousness* [*yhwh ṣidqēnû*]. For thus saith the Lord; David shall never want a man to sit upon the throne of the house of Israel.

On one level, the wordplay on forms of *ṣdq* and the name-title *yhwh ṣidqēnû* echo the name of Zedekiah ("The Lord is Righteousness"), the last regnant king of Judah who was dethroned and exiled to Babylon, but pointing forward to the future Davidic Messiah whose reign would be *actually* be characterized by total "righteousness" (cf. D&C 121:36–46).

In temporal terms, the Davidic dynasty ceased as a political entity with the exile of Jehoiachin and later his uncle Zedekiah to Babylon. Neither Jehoiachin, his son Shealtiel, nor his grandson Zerubbabel reigned as king over Judah, let alone over the whole "the house of Israel." Thus, this prophecy remained to be fulfilled by a future Davidic descendant. In the years after the exile, Zechariah picks up Jeremiah's prophecy of the "branch" ("I will bring forth my servant the BRANCH," Zechariah 3:8) as a discreet way of prophesying of a Davidic restoration, this during a time of Persian hegemony.

Another dramatic example of symbolic renaming occurs after Pashur, a priest and one of the chief temple authorities, has Jeremiah beaten for his prophecies against Jerusalem:

> And it came to pass on the morrow, that Pashur [Pashhur] brought forth Jeremiah out of the stocks. Then said Jeremiah unto him, The Lord hath not called thy name Pashur, but *Magor-missabib* [*māgôr-missābîb*, "terror roundabout"].
>
> For thus saith the Lord, Behold, I will make thee *a terror* [*māgôr*] to thyself, and to all thy friends: and they shall fall by the sword of their enemies, and thine eyes shall behold *it:* and I will give all Judah into the hand of the king of Babylon, and he shall carry them captive into Babylon, and shall slay them with the sword. (Jeremiah 20:3–4)

For his treatment of Jeremiah, Pashur receives a name that constitutes a vivid prediction of his fate and the fate of his associates prior to Judah's final exile to Babylon. Jeremiah's subsequent lament alludes again to this symbolic name: "For I heard the defaming of many, *fear on every side* [*māgôr-missābîb*] Report, *say they*, and we will report it. All my familiars watched for my halting, *saying*, Peradventure he will be enticed, and we shall prevail against him, and we shall take our revenge on him" (Jeremiah 20:10).

Lastly, Jeremiah employed *Atbash*, a "cryptic code system" or method of symbolic naming wherein "the initial letter of the Hebrew alphabet (*aleph*) [is substituted] with that of the last letter (*tav*). The second letter of the alphabet (*beth*) is replaced by the letter second from the end (*shin*)"[16]—thus Atbash ("*AThBaSh*"). Using this system, Jeremiah renames Babel (*b-b-l*) "Sheshach" (š-š-*k*) and the Chaldeans (*k-ś-d-y-m*) are rebranded *leb qamay*, "[in] the midst [heart] of them that rise up against me" (Jeremiah 25:26; Jeremiah 51:1, 41).[17] These symbolic names constitute symbols of the Lord's justice overtaking the Babylonians—symbols encoded in such a way so as to mask the meaning from everyone except the initiated, which represents a different type of symbolic naming from the other types of symbolic naming discussed here.

Ezekiel: Yahweh's "Wives"

In Ezekiel 23, Ezekiel describes two symbolic wives of Yahweh in alternating segments.[18] Ezekiel gives us their names and those whom the "wives" symbolically represent: "And the names of them were Aholah the elder, and Aholibah her sister: and they were mine, and they bare sons and daughters. Thus were their names; Samaria is Aholah, and Jerusalem Aholibah" (Ezekiel 23:4). The names, however, constitute symbols in their own right—both with temple significance: Aholah (or Oholah) suggests the meaning "her [cult] tent" or "her tabernacle." The name Aholibah (or Oholibah) suggests the meaning "my [cult] tent is her" or "my tabernacle is in her."

In fact, Ezekiel's symbolic names for these "wives" deliberately recall the building of the tabernacle, the portable temple used by the

Israelites in the wilderness as described in the Book of Exodus. In Ezekiel 16, the prophet describes the Lord's "covenant" marriage (v. 8) to, and ritual purification of, Jerusalem ("Aholibah") in terms that resemble temple rites as well as the "clothing" of the wilderness tabernacle: "Then washed I thee with water; yea, I throughly washed away thy blood from thee, and I anointed thee with oil. I clothed thee also with broidered work, and shod thee with badgers' skin, and I girded thee about with fine linen, and I covered thee with silk" (Ezekiel 16:8–10).

In Ezekiel's description of the ritual clothing of Aholibah it is hard to miss the intended connection to "clothing" of the "tent of meeting" in the ancient tabernacle structure: "And thou shalt make a covering for *the tent* [*'ōhel*] of rams' skins dyed red, and *a covering above of badgers' skins*" (Exodus 26:14; see also the "fine linen" and "badger skins" of Exodus 25:4–5). Moreover, the names Aholah and Aholibah recall one of the names of the chief tabernacle builders, Aholiab ("Father is my tent," see Exodus 31:6–7; 35:34; 36:1–2; 38:23).

Hosea and His Symbolically Named Children

The Book of Hosea chronicles how the Lord commanded the prophet Hosea to marry Gomer, the daughter of Diblaim, a woman characterized by *zĕnûnîm*—a term usually rendered "whoredoms" or "harlotries." Hosea's marriage to Gomer constitutes a lucid symbol of the Lord's covenant "marriage" to the land/people of Israel ("the land hath committed great whoredom, departing from the Lord," Hosea 1:2).[19] Gomer's *zĕnûnîm*, together with the emphatic, tautological (repetitious) use of the verb *zānâ* (*zānōh tizneh*), represent Israel's repeated cultic unfaithfulness to the Lord throughout its history. Hosea, moreover, was to have "children of whoredoms [*yaldê zĕnûnîm*]" with Gomer symbolizing Israel's nearly constant apostasy from Yahweh (Hosea 1:2; 2:4).

Hosea's first child is a son, and the Lord commands Hosea to give him a specific name: "And the Lord said unto him, Call his name Jezreel; for yet a little while, and I will avenge the blood of *Jezreel* upon the house of Jehu, and will cause to cease the kingdom of the house of Israel. And it shall come to pass at that day, that I will break the bow of *Israel* in the valley of *Jezreel*" (Hosea 1:4–5). Jezreel is, of course, the name of the Jezreel valley, the scene or vicinity of several important events in ninth-century Israelite history (see, e.g., 1 Kings 21:23; 2 Kings 9:10, 30, 36–37). The Lord thus makes Jezreel a symbol of Israel's "sowing" or "scattering." Later, however, he makes it a symbol of the Lord's mercy: "and they shall hear *Jezreel* [*yizrĕʿēl*]. And *I will sow her* [*ûzĕraʿtî*] unto me in the earth" (Hosea 2:22–23 [MT 2:24–25]).

Hosea and Gomer's next child is a daughter, and the Lord again commands the bestowal of a symbolic name: "And she conceived again, and bare a daughter. And God said unto him, Call her name *Lo-ruhamah* [*lōʾ ruḥāmâ*]: for *I will no more have mercy* [*lōʾ ʾôsîp ʿôd ʾăraḥēm*] *upon the house of Israel;* but I will utterly take them away" (Hosea 1:6). This stern prophecy is somewhat mollified by a promise of mercy toward the southern kingdom of Judah: "But *I will have mercy* [*ʾăraḥēm*] upon the house of Judah, *and will save them* [*wĕhôšaʿtîm*] by the Lord their God, and *will not save them* by bow, nor by sword, nor by battle, by horses, nor by horsemen" (Hosea 1:6–7). The prophecy adds an allusive wordplay on the name Hosea (*hôšēaʿ*, "The Lord saves") when the Lord says, "[I] will save them [*wĕhôšaʿtîm*]" (cf. Hosea 13:4: "beside me there is no *Saviour* [*môšîaʿ*]").

Hosea and Gomer's third child is a second son for whom the Lord again mandates the giving of a symbolic name: "Now when she had weaned Lo-ruhamah, she conceived, and bare a son. Then said God, Call his name *Lo-ammi* [*lōʾ-ʿammî*, "not my people"]: for ye are *not my people* [*lōʾ ʿammî*], and *I will not be your* God [or, "I [am] not your *I am* [*ʾehyeh*]]" (Hosea 1:9).

A declaration of the full reversal of the symbolic names of judgment emerges at the end of Hosea 1 and the beginning of Hosea 2: "Yet the number of the children of Israel shall be as the sand of the sea, which cannot be measured nor numbered [cf. Abrahamic Covenant, seed, and 'Jezreel']; and it shall come to pass, that in the place where it was said unto them, *Ye are not my people* [*lōʾ-ʿammî*], *there it shall be said unto them, Ye are the sons of the living God* [*bĕnê ʾēl-ḥāy*] or, "children of the living God"]" (Hosea 1:10 [MT 2:1]). The Lord states his intent to reaffirm a covenant relationship with scattered Israel, playing on the name Lo-ammi. In doing so, he uses kinship terminology that expresses a closer relationship than had existed previously: "sons of the living God" vs. "my people" or "my kin."

Hosea's prophecy then fully reverses the negative implications of all of the children's names. First, utilizing a play on Israel and Jezreel, the latter name changes from being a symbol of the Lord's scattering (sowing) Israel, into a symbol of gathering, resurrection, and renewal: "Then shall the children of Judah and the children of *Israel* be gathered together, and appoint themselves one head, and they shall come up out of the land: for great shall be the day of *Jezreel*" (Hosea 1:11). Moreover, the names Lo-ammi and Lo-ruhamah lose their *lōʾ* ("not") and become emphatic symbols of the Lord's covenant relationship with Israel and of his mercy: "Say ye unto your brethren, *Ammi* ['my people']; and to your sisters, *Ruhamah* ['shown mercy']" (Hosea 2:1).

Although the Lord states, "*I will not have mercy* [*lōʾ ʾăraḥēm*] upon her children; for they be the children of whoredoms" (Hosea 2:4), again playing on Lo-ruhamah, the Lord allows mercy to temper justice. Eventually Israel's punishment is abrogated, as evident in the full reversal of the meaning of the names of Hosea's children: "And I will betroth thee unto me for ever; yea, I will betroth thee unto me in righteousness, and in judgment, and in lovingkindness, and *in mercies* [*raḥămîm*]" (Hosea 2:19); "And *I will sow her* unto me in the earth; and *I will have mercy upon her* [*riḥamtî*] *that had not obtained mercy* [*lōʾ ruḥāmâ*]; and I will say to them which were *not my people* [*lōʾ ʿammî*], Thou art *my people* [*ʿammî*]; and they shall say, Thou art my God" (Hosea 2:22–23 [MT 23–24]). Hosea's subsequent prophecies thus change the name *lōʾ ruḥāmâ* from a sign of the Lord's disfavor and repudiation of his covenant into an emphatic reaffirmation of his covenant statement about his "mercy and longsuffering."[20]

Hosea additionally uses a marriage motif to describe the Lord's justice and mercy. The description of the Lord's marriage with Israel and the land, mirrored by that of Hosea and Gomer, begins with the language of divorce: "She is not my wife, neither am I her husband" (Hosea 2:2). After the consequences of sin catch up with Israel, there is eventual repentance: "I will go and return to *my* first *husband* [*ʾîšî*], for then was it better with me than now" (Hosea 2:7). Israel did not know that all which they had "prepared [or used] for Baal"—a divine title which means "husband" or "possessor"—really had its source in the Lord. Recognizing that both Hebrew *ʾîš* and *baʿal* both mean "husband" helps us appreciate Hosea's use of double entendre: "And it shall be at that day, saith the Lord, that thou shalt call me *Ishi* [*ʾîšî* = my man/my husband]; and shalt call me no more *Baali* [my *baal*/ my owner/my husband]. For I will take away the names of *Baalim* out of her mouth, and they shall no more be remembered by their name" (Hosea 2:16–17).

Amos, Bethel, and the Exile of Gilgal

Like Hosea's, Amos's prophecies contains several outstanding examples of paronomasia (e.g., "summer fruit," and the "end" in Amos 8:1–2). One of the most important examples of Amos using paronomasia to change longstanding place names into symbols is his prophecy regarding Gilgal and Bethel: "But seek not Beth-el, nor enter into *Gilgal* [*haggilgāl*], and pass not to Beer-sheba: for *Gilgal* [*haggilgāl*] *shall surely go into captivity* [*gālōh yigleh*], and Beth-el shall come to *nought* [*lĕʾāwen*]" (Amos 5:5). Amos reinterprets the name Gilgal in terms of the verb *gly/glh* = to "uncover," "reveal," or "go into exile." He also uses a pun on Beth-el in terms of nearby Beth-On (pejoratively Beth-aven, "house of evil"). Amos's use of the tautological infinitive (the infinitival form of the verb followed *gālâ* by its conjugated cognate form) adds emphasis to the connection he forges between "Gilgal" and "exile." Moshe Garsiel believes that the prophecy of Hosea 10:5, "The inhabitants of Samaria shall fear because of the calves of *Beth-aven*: for the people thereof shall mourn over it, and the priests there of that *rejoiced* [*yāgîlû*; or, trembled] on it, for the *glory* thereof, because it is *departed* [*gālâ*; or, gone into exile] from it," constitutes an echo of Amos's wordplay[21] (cf. also 1 Samuel 4:21–22).

Joel and Judgment at Jehoshaphat

The prophet Joel utilizes the name Jehoshaphat (*yĕhô* + *šāpāṭ*, "the Lord has judged"), a name belonging to a ninth-century king of Judah, as a symbol of Yahweh's judgment upon the nations. Just as Judah and Jerusalem had historically been subject to almost-constant threats of and outright foreign conquest, events often taken as an expression of divine justice, now the nations will be subject thereto: "I will also gather all nations, and will bring them down into the valley of *Jehoshaphat* [*yĕhôšāpāṭ*], and *will plead* [*wĕnišpaṭtî*] with them there for my people and for my heritage Israel, whom they have scattered among the nations, and parted my land" (Joel 3:2). Israel's *scattering* would not only be reversed (see Joel 3:1), but the nations themselves would be gathered for destruction. Joel emphasizes the thoroughgoing nature of this reversal: "Let the heathen be wakened, and come up to the valley of *Jehoshaphat* [*yĕhôšāpāṭ*] for there will I sit to *judge* [*lišpōṭ*] all the heathen round about" (Joel 3:12). This prophecy has often been understood as one similar to the Armageddon prophecy of Revelation 16:16.

Micah of Moresheth: "I Will Bring an Heir" and "Who Is a God like Thee?"

One of the most impressive clusters of paronomasia and onomastic exploitation in the Hebrew Bible occurs in Micah 1:1–16, near the beginning of the Book of Micah. Léo Laberge describes these verses as "the most difficult of the book."[22] The dire situation for Jerusalem (see Micah 1:8–9) and these southern cities, all besieged by the Assyrian king Sennacherib, suggests the dire situation in the kingdom of Judah overall.

First,[23] Micah makes Aphrah (or Beth-le-Aphrah) a symbol of mourning through the act of rolling herself (*hitpallāš*[*t*]î, a pun on "Philistines") in the dust (*ʿāpār,* v. 10). Dust was often connected with mourning in the Ancient Near East. Second, he makes Zaanan a symbol of impotence and ineptitude ("Zaanan came not forth," *lōʾ yaṣʾâ . . . ṣaʾănān,* v. 11). As James Luther Mays suggests, "that line means that Zanaan does not come forth to face the enemy because the struggle is hopeless, or because the city is destroyed already."[24] Third, Micah creates a pun on Maroth ("bitterness") in terms of good and evil (v. 12). Fourth, Lachish (*lākîš*) becomes a symbol of "swift steeds" (*lārekeš*) required for sudden escape (v. 13). Mays writes, "The line is an ironic cry of warning that teams should be harnessed and chariots made ready—for flight."[25] Fifth, Micah's hometown Moresheth (see Micah 1:1; Jeremiah 26:18) sounds like a word for "farewell gift" (cf. the "presents" in v. 14).[26] Sixth, Achzib (*ʾakzîb*) is made a symbol of a "lie[s]" (*ʾakzāb*) or undependable temporal things upon which we as carnal people tend to rely. Seventh and lastly, Mareshah is made a symbol of "the loss of an heir [*yōrēš*] [that] means the end of life's continuity, and [thus] no future."[27] These puns stand in stark contrast to the promise of a Messiah eventually "com[ing] forth" from "little" Bethlehem-Ephratah (Micah 5:2).

Lastly, Micah 7:18 employs a wordplay on the name Micah as a sign of mercy: "*Who is a God like unto thee* [*mî ʾēl kāmôkā*], that pardoneth iniquity, and passeth by the transgression of the remnant of his heritage? he retaineth not his anger for ever, because he delighteth in mercy" (Micah 7:18). The name Micah is a hypocoristic (shortened) form of the names Michael ("Who is like El [God]?") and Michaiah ("Who is like the Lord"?). Here again, we see the prophet's name constituting a part of the prophet's message: God, not least in his mercy, is incomparable.

Zephaniah and the Philistine Cities

Zephaniah makes ominous symbols out of the names of "two of the four Philistine cities, in announcement of the divine judgment that will befall them."[28] He states, "For *Gaza* [*ʿazzâ*] *shall be forsaken* [*ʿăzûbâ*], and Ashkelon a desolation: they shall drive out Ashdod at the noon day, and *Ekron* [*ʿeqrôn*] *shall be rooted up* [*tēʿāqēr*]" (Zephaniah 2:3–4). Regarding the rhetoric of this verse, Marvin A. Sweeney suggests that "by capturing the ear of the audience in this fashion, the verse better enables the speaker to make a lasting impression on the audience and convey the message."[29] J. J. M. Roberts notes that "Zephaniah emphasizes a common element in the fate of all four cities: They are emptied of their Philistine inhabitants."[30] Just as Isaiah prophesied that Jerusalem would no longer be called *ʿăzûbâ* ("forsaken," see above), Zephaniah prophesies that Gaza will bear this name. As for Ekron, Zephaniah's use of the verb *ʿqr* ties its fate to barrenness and childlessness.[31]

Lastly, Zephaniah again plays on or alludes to his own name a few verses later in prophesying the destruction of Assyria and Nineveh: "And he will stretch out his hand against *the north* [*ṣāpôn*], and destroy Assyria; and will make Nineveh a desolation, and dry like a wilderness" (Zephaniah 2:13). Zephaniah's name becomes a sign of what the Lord will do to "the north"—namely, to the Assyrian empire and its capital. The Babylonians destroy Nineveh in 612 BCE, and the remnant of the Assyrian empire vanishes shortly thereafter.

Obadiah: Edom and Esau—Their Destruction, Their Calamity

Obadiah, the shortest of the prophetic books of the Old Testament, evidences rich wordplay on Esau and Edom and at least one Edomite cities. Obadiah begins with a condemnation of Edom and its pride in terms of Sela ("rock," thus also known as Petra): "The pride of thine heart hath deceived thee, thou that dwellest in the clefts of the *rock* [*selaʿ*], whose habitation is high; that saith in his heart, Who shall bring me down to the ground? Though thou exalt thyself as the eagle, and though thou set thy nest among the stars, thence will I bring thee down, saith the Lord" (Obadiah 1:3–4). Sweeney calls Obadiah's use of *selaʿ* here "an obvious reference to the Edomite fortress city of Sela that was conquered by Amaziah and renamed Joktheel (2 Kings 14:7)."[32] We see this wordplay on *selaʿ* or *petra* in Psalm 137:7–9 ("Happy shall he be, that taketh and dasheth thy little ones against *the stones* [*selaʿ*]") and elsewhere.[33]

Obadiah's prophecy, as we have seen with other prophets, further employs a pun on his own name (*ʿōbēd*, "servant," + *yāh*, "the Lord" = "servant of the Lord") in terms of the partially homonymous verb *ʾbd*, which in its causative stem means "to destroy": "*Shall I* not in that day, saith the Lord, even *destroy* [*wĕhaʾăbadtî*] the wise men out of *Edom*, and understanding out of the mount of Esau?" (Obadiah 1:8). A similar wordplay occurs verses later: "Neither shouldest thou have rejoiced over the children of Judah in the day of *their destruction* [*ʾobdām*]" (Obadiah 1:12).

The name Edom is used twice and Esau seven times. In decrying Esau and Edom's national treachery against Judah, Obadiah plays on the name Edom (*ʾĕdôm*) three times in terms of the expression "their calamity": "Thou [Edom/*ʾĕdôm*] shouldest not have entered into the gate of my people in the day of *their calamity* [*ʾêdô*]; yea, thou shouldest not have looked on their affliction in the day of *their calamity* [*ʾêdô*], nor have laid hands on their substance in the day of *their calamity* [ʾêdô]" (Obadiah 1:13). Obadiah effectively ties the name Edom to "calamity."

In consequence of Esau and Edom's treachery, Obadiah prophesies that their deeds will return to them in an emphatic pun on Esau: "For the day of the Lord is near upon all the heathen: *as thou hast done* [*ʿāśîtā*] *it shall be done unto thee* [*yēʿāśeh lāk*]: thy reward shall return upon thine own head" (Obadiah 1:15). *Thou* here refers to Esau and Edom. Obadiah thus directly juxtaposes the active perfect verb form in the second person (*ʿśy/ʿśh*) with the third-person masculine passive (*ʿāśîtā yēʿāśeh lāk*) to create this wordplay. Esau and Edom's punishment will be both commensurate and retributive.

Zechariah: Beauty and Bands

In addition to his iteration of Jeremiah's "branch" prophecy in Zechariah 3:8 (mentioned previously) and his paronomastic reinterpretation of Tyre [*ṣōr*] in terms of "strong hold [*māṣôr*]" (Zechariah 9:3), Zechariah records the use of symbolic naming in the prophetic object lesson of the Lord's two staves, though without wordplay: "And I took unto me two staves; the one I called *Beauty* [*nōʿam*, or sweetness], and the other I called *Bands* [*ḥōbĕlîm*, or bonds]; and I fed the flock" (Zechariah 11:7). The Lord then explains the symbolism of his staff, "Beauty": "And I took my staff, even *Beauty* [*nōʿam*], and cut it asunder, that I might break [disannul] my covenant which I had made with all the people[s]" (Zechariah 11:10). Aelred Cody suggests that this disannulled covenant may refer to the "covenant of peace" promised in Ezekiel 34:25 and especially in Ezekiel 37:26–28,[34] which comes at the end of Ezekiel's famed "sticks" prophecy.

Then Zechariah describes the breaking of the second staff, "Bands" or "Bonds": "Then I cut asunder mine other staff, even *Bands* [*ḥōbĕlîm*], that I might break the brotherhood between Judah and Israel" (Zechariah 11:14). The name *ḥōbĕlîm/bands* symbolizes "union" or "harmony."[35] Cody suggests that "the symbolism of a complete break between Judah and Israel is just the opposite of that in Ezek[iel] 37:15–19 of the two sticks joined," but this symbolism "is not explained here."[36] From a Latter-day Saint perspective, we understand that the "breaking" of the "bonds" between Israel and Judah was part of the Lord "breaking off" the natural branches in his scattering of Israel, a scattering that necessarily preceded the future merciful gathering of Israel foretold by Isaiah, Jeremiah, Ezekiel, and Book of Mormon prophets, among others.

Malachi: "My Messenger" or "My Angel"

The first line of the Book of Malachi reads, "The burden of the word of the Lord to Israel by Malachi" (Malachi 1:1). The transparent meaning of Malachi is "my messenger" or "my angel" (see Malachi 2:7, 3:1). Malachi, excoriating the apostate Levites and priests, declared that the priest was "the messenger [*malʾāk*] of the Lord of Hosts" (Malachi 2:7). The description of the priest as a "messenger" or an "angel" is particularly significant given Malachi's focus on the priesthood and temple in his prophecies.

All of this background prepares us for Malachi's most important wordplay on his own name: "Behold, I will send *my messenger* [*malʾākî*], and he shall prepare the way before me: and *the Lord, whom ye seek, shall suddenly come to his temple, even the messenger* [*malʾāk*] *of the covenant,* whom ye delight in: behold, he shall come, saith the Lord of hosts" (Malachi 3:1–2). The Savior's quotation of this same prophecy to the Nephites and Lamanites at the temple in Bountiful makes the onomastic connection even more explicit: "Thus said the Father unto *Malachi*—Behold, I will send *my messenger,* and he shall prepare the way before me, and the Lord whom ye seek shall suddenly come to his temple, even *the messenger of the covenant,* whom ye delight in; behold, *he shall come,* saith the Lord of Hosts" (3 Nephi 24:1). The Lord Jesus Christ, whom they sought, had come suddenly to his temple—and their temple—as a resurrected being and as the very messenger of the covenant to organize the church anew under the "new covenant" (the law of the gospel). His appearance under these circumstances must have made his citation of the scripture unspeakably powerful to those who heard it from the Lord's own mouth.

Malachi's prophecy was one of several Old Testament texts recited to Joseph Smith during the evening and through the morning of 21–22 September 1823 by an angel (see Joseph Smith—History 1:27–49). It was fulfilled anew in this last dispensation on 3 April 1836, as recorded in Doctrine and Covenants 110, when the Lord again—along with other angelic messengers, including Elijah—appeared to Joseph Smith and Oliver Cowdery in the Kirtland Temple.

Conclusion

Old Testament prophets regularly used wordplay and paronomasia in crafting their prophetic messages. Moreover, Isaiah and Hosea were commanded to give their children names symbolizing both the Lord's justice and mercy. Many of their prophecies thematically revolve around these names. Ezekiel extends Hosea and Isaiah's use of the marriage and atonement metaphor with symbolic names for Israel and Judah as Yahweh's wives, names that evoke temple imagery. Some of the symbolic names, like Jeremiah's (and Zechariah's) "branch," bespeak the coming of a Messiah. Isaiah, Hosea, Micah, Zephaniah, Obadiah, and Malachi all employ wordplay on their own names. Isaiah's name, "the Lord is salvation," becomes a dominant theme in his writings.

In almost all of the prophets, we find instances of the symbolic naming or the use of wordplay to give existing names ominous new meaning. All of this suggests that understanding ancient Israelite names, name giving, and name exploitation is an important tool in understanding Old Testament writings and prophecy in particular.

These characteristics constituted an important part of "the manner of prophesying among the Jews" (2 Nephi 25:1).

Notes

1. Throughout this article I will avoid the use of the unnecessarily pejorative term *folk etymology*, which has become nearly synonymous with "false etymology." The biblical writers used wordplay in order to give old names new meaning.
2. Throughout this article I will italicize certain names, words, and phrases to add emphasis. Unless noted otherwise, all further emphases are added by me.
3. See the heading to Doctrine and Covenants 113 (2013 edition).
4. See, for example, John N. Oswalt, *The Book of Isaiah, Chapters 40–66* (Grand Rapids, MI: Eerdmans, 1998), 369.
5. See Joseph Smith—History 1:29–49, especially v. 40.
6. Richard A. Lanham, *A Handlist of Rhetorical Terms*, 2nd ed. (Berkley: University of California Press, 1991), 110.
7. In addition to Isaiah 10:19–22 and 11:10, 16, see Isaiah 28:15; 37:31–32; and 46:3.
8. Compare the footnote in the 2013 LDS edition of Isaiah 8:1, which has "to speed the spoil, he hastens the prey," to the 1979 footnote, "to speed to the spoil, he hasteneth the prey."
9. Joseph Jensen, "Immanuel," in *Anchor Bible Dictionary*, ed. David Noel Freedman (New York: Doubleday, 1992), 3:393.
10. The "us" in Isaiah 6:8 is widely understood to refer to the divine council. Compare the very similar language in Abraham 3:27, which unquestionably reflects a divine council situation.
11. *Counselor*: cf. "Man of Counsel" in Moses 7:35; cf. Jacob 4:10; Alma 37:12, 37; *Mighty*: see especially Isaiah 10:21; see also Deuteronomy 10:17; Psalms 24:8; Jeremiah 32:18; Nehemiah 9:32. Everlasting Father: cf. Christ as "Eternal Father" in the Book of Mormon (e.g., Alma 11:38–39;

Mosiah 15:4; 16:5, etc.); *Prince of Peace*: used typologically of Jesus Christ in reference to Melchizedek (JST, Genesis 14:33; Alma 13:18; cf. "king of peace" in JST, Genesis 14:36 and Hebrews 7:2) and in reference to Abraham 1:2. Cf. also Zechariah 9:9–10.

12. Deuteronomy 23:1–4 lists several classes of persons who were excluded from the cultic assembly (e.g., emasculated males, children born out of wedlock, and certain foreigners). 2 Samuel 5:6–8 gives an extra-Pentateuchal explanation for the later exclusion of "the lame and the blind" from the temple.
13. Later Christian interpreters would likely see an anticipation of the name Jesus (*yēšûaʿ*) as well. Cf., e.g., Matthew 1:21.
14. Jeremiah's oracle against Moab also makes negative symbols out of the names Heshbon and Madmen: "There shall be no more praise of Moab: in *Heshbon* [*ḥešbōn*] *they have devised* [*ḥāšbû*] evil against it; come, and let us cut it off from being a nation. Also *thou shalt be cut down* [*tiddōmî*], O *Madmen* [*madmēn*] the sword shall pursue thee" (Jeremiah 48:2).
15. 2 Nephi 3:5 shows that the "righteous branch" was associated with the Messiah, but could have broader connotations in the context of Israel's scattering and gathering (cf. Jacob 5).
16. William R. Brookman, "Athbash," in *The New Interpreter's Dictionary of the Bible: A–C, Volume 1* (Nashville, TN: Abingdon Press, 2006), 341–42.
17. See Scott B. Noegel, "Atbash in Jeremiah and its Literary Significance: Part 1," *Jewish Biblical Quarterly* 24, no. 2 (1996): 82–89; idem, "Atbash in Jeremiah and Its Literary Significance: Part 2," *Jewish Bible Quarterly* 24, no. 3 (1996), 160–66; idem, "Atbash in Jeremiah and Its Literary Significance: Part 3," *Jewish Bible Quarterly* 24, no. 4 (1996): 247–50.
18. See Ezekiel 23:5–10 (Aholah); 23:11–21 (Aholibah); 23:22–35 (Aholah); 23:36–49 (both Aholah and Aholibah).
19. On the meaning of Hosea's marriage to Gomer, see Aaron P. Schade, "The Imagery of Hosea's Family and the Restoration of Israel," in *The Gospel of Jesus Christ in the Old Testament, The 38th Annual BYU Sidney B. Sperry Symposium* (Provo, UT: Religious Studies Center, 2009), 233–49; Kent P. Jackson, "The Marriage of Hosea and Jehovah's Covenant with Israel,"

in *Isaiah and the Prophets: Inspired Voices from the Old Testament*, ed. Monte S. Nyman and Charles D. Tate Jr. (Provo, UT: Religious Studies Center, 1984), 57–74.

20. Cf., e.g., Exodus 34:6; Numbers 14:18; Psalm 86:15; Alma 9:11, 26.
21. Moshe Garsiel, *Biblical Names: A Literary Study of Midrashic Derivations and Puns*, trans. Phyllis Hackett (Ramat Gan: Bar-Ilan University Press, 1991), 200–201.
22. Léo Laberge, "Micah," *The New Jerome Biblical Commentary* (Upper Saddle River, NJ: Prentice Hall, 1990), 250. *The New Jerome Biblical Commentary* is hereafter cited as *NJBC*.
23. The initial wordplay on "Gath" in (*gat*) in terms of *taggîdû* ("tell ye") in Micah 1:10 may represent a textual corruption.
24. James Luther Mays, *Micah: A Commentary* (Louisville, KY: Westminster/John Knox Press, 1976), 57.
25. Ibid., 58.
26. Ibid., 59. May cites *rāśâ* ("dowry") as a possible basis for the pun. Cf. Deuteronomy 22:23 (1 Kings 9:16).
27. Ibid.
28. Cf. J. J. M. Roberts, *Nahum, Ḥabakkuk, and Zephaniah: A Commentary* (Louisville, KY: Westminster/John Knox Press, 1991), 198.
29. Marvin A. Sweeney, *The Twelve Prophets, Volume 1: Hosea, Joel, Amos, Obadiah, Jonah* (Collegeville, MN: The Liturgical Press, 2000), 513.
30. Roberts, *Nahum, Habakkuk, and Zephaniah*, 198.
31. Something similar seems to be at work in the fulfillment of Elijah's prophecy against Ahaziah, king of Judah. Ahaziah inquired of Baal-zebub, the version of the god Baal worshipped at Ekron, regarding his precarious health and subsequently died with "no son" (2 Kings 1:16–17).
32. Sweeney, *Twelve Prophets*, 289.
33. Garsiel (*Biblical Names*, 158–59) also sees this *selaʿ* wordplay in Isaiah 15:9–16:2; Jeremiah 48:28; 49:16; and Job 39:26-27. He also links these to Isaiah 2:21; 31:9; 33:16; 42:11.
34. Aelred Cody, "Haggai, Zechariah, Malachi," *NJBC*, 358.

35. Ludwig Koehler and Walter Baumgartner, *The Hebrew and Aramaic Lexicon of the Old Testament* (Leiden, Netherlands: Brill, 2001), 287.
36. Cody, "Haggai, Zechariah, Malachi," *NJBC*, 358.

3

Obadiah 1:21

Context, Text, Interpretation, and Application

Dana M. Pike

Dana M. Pike is a professor of ancient scripture at Brigham Young University.

Latter-day Saints have frequently used the phrase "saviors on mount Zion" in relation to proxy temple work for the dead. This phrase comes from the twenty-first, and last, verse of Obadiah, a prophetic book in the Old Testament. But many people have little awareness of or experience with the previous twenty verses in the book, nor with the intriguing contextual questions those verses raise for understanding verse 21, with its phrase "saviours shall come up on mount Zion" (KJV[1]; note the British spelling with a *u*; used herein only in quotations). Furthermore, there has been little Latter-day Saint discussion of the whole of verse 21 itself, especially regarding how the passive grammar in the Greek Septuagint (LXX) should be dealt with—"those who have been saved/rescued"—as opposed to the active grammar in the traditional Hebrew Masoretic Text (MT)—those who function as saviors on mount Zion—and how the corollary "mount of Esau" impacts our understanding of "mount Zion." Thus, the brief book of Obadiah provides wonderful opportunities to discuss matters of context *and* text in relation to verse 21.[2]

The first portion of this essay provides a brief exegetical examination of Obadiah, highlighting the various challenges to understanding this shortest book in the Hebrew Bible (the Christian Old Testament), with particular focus on verse 21 in its context. This is followed by a review of how Latter-day Saints from Joseph Smith to the present have employed Obadiah 1:21 and by an analysis of how this use interfaces with that verse in its biblical context.

This study attempts to model a responsible interpretive approach to scripture and to illustrate with Obadiah 1:21 how Latter-day Saints bring something distinctive to the interpretation of this passage that is not inherently obvious in the Old Testament. I propose that this latter approach is often more about the *application* of Restoration insights to important biblical phrases and passages than it is about finding something hiding in the Old Testament that only becomes clear with Restoration insights.[3] This seems to best describe the case of Obadiah 1:21.

Introducing Obadiah[4]

After a passage of scripture has been identified for analysis, a good interpretive approach typically includes situating the passage in question in its historical, cultural, literary, and canonical context. Canonically, the book of Obadiah is found in the "Book of the Twelve," which designates the collection of twelve so-called minor prophets (minor due to the shortness of the books). Obadiah contains a prophecy of judgment against Edom, which was located south of Judah and the Dead Sea. It thus shares similarities with portions of other biblical books—such as Isaiah 13–24, Jeremiah 46–51, Ezekiel 25–32, and Amos 1–2—that also preserve Israelite prophecies against various foreign nations, including some specifically against Edom.[5] In the Hebrew Bible and most English translations, Obadiah follows the book of Amos, perhaps due to the thematic connection with Edom it shares with Amos 9:12.[6]

Broadly outlined, the book of Obadiah falls into two major sections (different scholars divide the book somewhat differently). First, the LORD's messenger announces the LORD's judgment to humble and destroy Edom, which action is presented as justifiably deserved due to Edom's violence against Judah (1–14). Second, shifting perspectives, Jerusalem and Judah will be restored at some future time and have power over Edom and their other enemies, and "the kingdom will be the LORD's" (15–21). Thus, the ultimate justice and power of the LORD are emphasized.

The brevity of the book of Obadiah combines with its lack of specific contextualizing information to make dating Obadiah's prophetic mission and the book a challenge. The introduction includes only the prophet's name, *ʿbdyh*, which means "servant (or worshipper) of YHWH / the LORD." "YHWH" represents the four Hebrew letters that spell the divine name of the God of Israel, for which English translators have traditionally substituted "the LORD." The name is usually now pronounced Yahweh. "Jehovah" is a hybrid form composed of the consonants *yhwh* and the vowels from the Hebrew word *ʾadonay*, "lord."[7] "YHWH" will be used in this paper, except in quotations.[8] There are thirteen different people named Obadiah in the Old Testament, as well as several others who are so named in Israelite inscriptions and seal impressions.

Due to the lack of historical information about Obadiah, various suggestions have been made to date the prophet and his book, ranging from the mid-ninth to the mid-fourth centuries BC (all dates that follow are BC).[9] However, it is now common to view the backdrop of the events for which Edom is judged as the conquest of Judah by Nebuchadnezzar and his Neo-Babylonian army in 586 BC. The Babylonians fully terminated the kingdom of Judah in 586, deporting its last king, Zedekiah, and destroying the temple and much of the city (see 2 Kings 24:15–25:21). Obadiah 1:11–13 contains phrases that suggest this background, referring to "the day that the strangers carried away captive his [Judah's] forces, and foreigners entered into his gates," "the day of their [Judah's] destruction," and "the day of their [Judah's] calamity." Given this assessment, Obadiah's ministry and message fits best in the 580s. So the book as we have it likely dates to the Babylonian (lasting to 539 BC) or subsequent Persian period.[10]

Examining Obadiah

The book of Obadiah opens with the phrase "The vision of Obadiah." The Hebrew term *ḥāzon*, "vision," also occurs in Isaiah 1:1 and Nahum 1:1 (and Habakkuk 1:1 includes the verbal form *ḥāzâ*, "to envision"). It is perhaps better understood here as "revelation," since in these similar contexts it appears to convey the idea of revelation more broadly; none of these particular prophetic books are *just* vision reports, although some of the prophecies they contain may be understood to have come through visionary experiences.

Verses 1–14

Following this opening phrase identifying Obadiah as the prophetic messenger or intermediary for what follows, the phrase "Thus saith the Lord God concerning Edom," establishes the authority for and identifies the recipient or target of the divine pronouncement that occupies much of this short book.[11] The recurring use of prophetic formulas—"saith the Lord" in verses 4 and 8, and "for the Lord has spoken" in verse 18—reinforces the origin and authority of Obadiah's message. Whether or not this prophecy was ever actually communicated to the Edomites themselves, it had real value for the Judahites among whom Obadiah lived, as discussed below.

The latter portion of verse 1 contains the curious statement that "We have heard a rumour [or report] from the Lord, and an ambassador is sent among the heathen, Arise ye, and let us rise up against her [i.e., Edom] in battle." It is not entirely clear who the "we" is. Furthermore, the Greek Septuagint (LXX) reads "I" instead of "we" in this verse,[12] as does the essentially same text in Jeremiah 49:14. In fact, much of the content of Obadiah 1–7 is also found in a prophecy against Edom in Jeremiah 49:7–22. It is usually presumed that one of these prophets was dependent on the other for these statements or that they both utilized an earlier source no longer extant (there are also a number of similarities between the books of Joel and Obadiah, some of which will be noted hereafter). The "ambassador" or envoy in Obadiah 1:1 is presumably a heavenly messenger (although the Hebrew term *ṣîr* can also refer to a human messenger, as in Proverbs 13:7; 25:13).

Verses 2–7 relate YHWH's words against the Edomites, as delivered through Obadiah. This portrays the biblical concept that YHWH is God of all nations and peoples, and judges them according to his expectations. Much of the message is presented in the prophetic past tense, as if these judgments have already happened—so for example, the KJV renders verse 2a as "I have made thee small among the heathen." Many modern translations render these forms in the future tense to capture the sense of what is prophesied to happen to Edom; thus, "I will surely make you least among the nations" (NRSV).

The pride and boasting of the Edomites is described and linked to their downfall: "I [will] bring thee down, saith the Lord" (v. 4). The imagery of the high "clefts of the rock" (v. 3) and of the eagle and its high nest (v. 4) is intended to illustrate the Edomites' presumed remoteness and security, which will avail them nothing, as verse 6 indicates.

Verse 6 introduces the use of Esau in Obadiah's prophecy: "How are the things of Esau searched out! how are his hidden things sought up!" The name Esau is used here and seven more times in Obadiah as an alternate designation for Edom. Biblical tradition depicts Edom as the home of Esau, who was Isaac's son, and Jacob's brother, and it depicts Esau's descendants as Edomites (e.g., Genesis 33:16; 36:1, 6–9; Deuteronomy 2:12). Obadiah's use of Esau presumably evoked in the minds of his Israelite hearers and readers the struggles between Jacob and Esau recounted in Genesis 25 and 27, struggles that began in

Rebekah's womb (25:22–24), even though Genesis 33:1–16 and 35:29 suggest some reconciliation in their later years.[13] Note the familial connection emphasized by the use of the phrases "thy brother Jacob" (v. 10) and "thy brother" (v. 12). Historically, the united kingdom of Israel and then the kingdom of Judah were rivals with the Edomites, often contesting control of lucrative trade routes in the Negev region (e.g., 1 Kings 11:14–16; 2 Kings 8:20–22). The Bible does not view this tension-filled relationship as a struggle just between two political entities, but between kin. Thus, Obadiah's use of the name Esau in conjunction with Edom draws on biblical traditions about family connections as well as historical experiences to create an image of Edom, Judah's relative and enemy and the target of YHWH's judgment.

Verse 7 continues the judgment on Edom, indicating that it has been or will be "deceived" and "prevailed against" by its former allies. Verses 8–9 couple the prophesied destruction of both the "wise men" of Edom, a designation for political and military advisers in this context, and its "mighty men," or warriors, thus leaving Edom easy prey for its destruction in spite of the fact that it has "wise" and "mighty men." Teman was an important city in Edom. Here Teman functions as a synecdoche, a figure of speech in which a part (Teman, v. 8) is employed to represent the whole (Edom, v. 7).

YHWH's pronouncement of judgment on Edom concludes in verse 10. But, in reverse of the order that might be expected, verse 10 also transitions into the charge or indictment against Edom (in verses 10–14), the *reason for* the judgment just announced. As indicated previously, the particular historical backdrop for Obadiah's prophecy is best understood as the Babylonian destruction of Jerusalem and Judah, and Edom's ancillary but consensual role in those events: Edom is charged with participating in "violence against thy brother Jacob" (v. 10). The Babylonians were "the [primary] strangers [who] carried away captive his [Judah's] forces, and foreigners entered into his gates" (v. 11). But YHWH charges that the Edomites participated as well: "Even thou wast as one of them" (v 11). Specific charges continue through verse 14, including Edom's rejoicing over Judah's destruction (v. 12); entering into Jerusalem, "the gate of my people," to participate in looting (v. 13); and apprehending those Judahites fleeing the area and those remaining as survivors (v. 14). This assessment finds support from Psalm 137:7: "Remember, O LORD, the children of Edom in the day of Jerusalem; who said, Rase it, rase it, even to the foundation thereof" (cf. Joel 3:19 [Heb. 4:19]).

Verses 15–21

As with verses 1–14, there are various subunits in this second major block of text in Obadiah's prophecy. Conceptually, verse 15 marks a distinct shift in the text, introducing the concept of "the day of the LORD," a concept not fully explained in Obadiah. As depicted in the greater Old Testament, this "day" is fear-filled, dark, and destructive, a time when YHWH unleashes his power against the pride and wickedness of the world, against the enemies of faithful Israelites (e.g., Isaiah 13:6–9; Zephaniah 2:1–5), and against Israelites who have been faithless (e.g., Amos 5:18–20; Ezekiel 7:1–27, especially 19; Joel 1:1–2:11). Although these biblical depictions are generally accepted as eschatological in orientation (the end of the fallen world as we know it), there are occasional applications of this concept to past historical destructions (e.g., Amos 5:18–20; Lamentations 2:2, in reference to the Babylonian destruction of Jerusalem; and Alma 45:14).[14]

Obadiah's use of the Hebrew word *yōm*, "day," as a theme word is readily apparent in verses 11–14, where it occurs ten times. In that context, the "day" was the time of the Babylonian destruction of Jerusalem and Judah, the "day" in which the Edomites participated in despoiling and exploiting the Judahites. That was the "day" in which Judahites suffered, due to the widespread wickedness in their own society (e.g., Jeremiah 2; 7; 1 Nephi 1:4, 18–20).

However, verse 15 pivots to highlight a new and different day, the future "day of the LORD." In harmony with the law of retribution, the wicked—specifically Edom in this prophecy—will be destroyed in that "near" (a relative term[15]) future day, since they themselves had previously been destructive: "Thy reward shall return upon thine own head" (v. 15). This accords with the biblical *lex talionis*, the law of equivalent reciprocation, a "life for life, eye for eye, tooth for tooth, hand for hand, foot for foot, burning for burning, wound for wound, stripe for stripe" (Exodus 21:23–25). Historically, the kingdom of Edom was destroyed by the Babylonians in 553.[16] However, the complete destruction of Edom *and* the subsequent rise of the Israelites and Jerusalem never happened in antiquity as prophesied in Obadiah.

Verse 15 also introduces an additional dimension. Obadiah prophesies that not just Edom will be destroyed, but rather that YHWH's power will impact "all the heathen," the non-Israelite "nations" (Heb. *gôyîm*), *including* the Edomites. This theme continues into verse 16, but with a challenge. The second-person pronouns in verse 15 are singular, and the "you" is Edom/Esau collectively. However, the second-person pronoun in verse 16 is plural: "For as ye [pl.] have drunk on my holy mountain, so shall all the heathen drink continually." One approach assumes the "you/ye" in verse 16 is the Edomites or the Babylonians or both, and it contrasts their celebratory drinking after destroying Jerusalem and the temple, "upon my [YHWH's] holy mountain," with the future "heathen" or nations (*gôyîm*) drinking the cup of YHWH's judgment and being destroyed: "They shall be as though they had not been." But the approach more generally accepted takes the plural "you/ye" in verse 16 as referencing the Judahites. Just as they had drunk from the cup of YHWH's judgment in the recent past, resulting in destruction and exile at the hands of the Babylonians and other tag-alongs like the Edomites, so shall the nations drink "continually" or fully in the future until they are themselves destroyed. Either way, this theme of drinking down the wrath and judgments of YHWH is a powerful metaphor that occurs here and elsewhere in the Old Testament (e.g., Isaiah 51:17–23; Jeremiah 25:15–29; Psalm 75:8 [Heb. 9]).[17]

Based on the universalizing perspective in this portion of Obadiah's prophecy, Edom is part of but also comes to symbolically represent all nations. This function is also evident in Isaiah 34:1–6 (where the KJV inexplicably uses the later Greek form Idumea to render the Hebrew *ʾĕdōm*, "Edom"), with YHWH's pronouncements against the "nations" (*gôyîm*) juxtaposed with pronouncements against Edom. It further plays out with the Greek form of the name, Idumea, in various later texts, including this Restoration passage: "And also the Lord . . . shall come down in judgment upon Idumea, or the world" (D&C 1:36).

By contrast, Obadiah 1:17–18 promises "deliverance" and "holiness" for the righteous on mount Zion, which is the equivalent of "my holy mountain" in verse 16. "Mount Zion" in Obadiah most readily represents Jerusalem, especially the Temple Mount (compare Joel 3:17–20 [Heb. 4:17–20]; Psalm 78:68; 97:8; 135:21; Isaiah 2:3; 10:12; 24:23). In Old Testament prophetic texts, this phrase often designates the future righteous status of Zion or Jerusalem after the Israelites have been cleansed and restored to their lands by YHWH and the powers of the world have been defeated (e.g., Isaiah 4:5; 24:23; Joel 2:32 [Heb. 3:5]; Micah 4:7). Thus, the future holy city of Jerusalem will be populated by then-holy people worshipping and ruled by the Holy One of Israel.

Using the term "house" (descendants) and family names (Jacob and Esau) instead of just political designations, Obadiah indicates the "house of Jacob," all Israelites (not just Judah), will repossess their land and will help turn "the house of Esau" into "stubble"; there will "not be any remaining," or there will be no survivor (*śārîd*). This portion of the prophecy concludes with another expression of divine affirmation, "for the Lord hath spoken it" (v. 18).

Verses 19–20 further emphasize the reversal of the then-current historical situation, in that Israelites will possess the land of the Edomites and will repossess Israelite regions in all directions (see, somewhat similarly, Isaiah 11:14). The Hebrew *yāraš*, "to possess, to dispossess," is a key word here, emphasizing this reversal. This prophesied restoration of Israel is all made possible, of course, by "the day of the Lord," introduced in verse 15, with the destruction of the wicked.

Focusing on Obadiah 1:21

The last verse of Obadiah neatly draws several thematic threads together to conclude this prophecy. Those future faithful Israelites gathered together in mount Zion will "judge" those in mount Esau, representing here the Edomites as well as all the nations of the earth. The Hebrew verb *šāpaṭ*, "to judge," denotes passing judgment in legal decisions but also having authority over, governing. It functions with this latter sense in Obadiah 1:21 and elsewhere (e.g., Judges 10:2; 16:31; 1 Samuel 7:15; compare Isaiah 2:3, "for out of Zion shall go forth the law, and the word of the Lord from Jerusalem"). Of course, YHWH is the ultimate judge and ruler in the Hebrew scriptures (e.g., Judges 11:27; Psalm 7:8). The content of Obadiah 1:21, depicting Israelites on mount Zion governing mount Esau, must be reconciled with that of verse 18—"the house of Esau" being turned into "stubble. . . . There shall not be any remaining." Most likely, the kingdom of Edom is more particularly intended in verse 18, while verse 21 construes mount Esau more broadly as the nations of the world.

The final phrase is the capstone of Obadiah's prophecy: "The kingdom [*mĕlūkâ*] shall be the Lord's." The Hebrew word *mĕlūkâ* can be translated as "kingship" or "dominion" as well as "kingdom" (compare, for example, 1 Kings 21:7 and Psalm 22:29 in the KJV and NRSV). Obadiah 1:21 presents YHWH, exercising his kingship, as the ultimate ruler over all.[18] The hope for this eventuality is also expressed in Psalm 10:16: "The Lord is King for ever and ever: the heathen are perished out of his land" (see also, for example, Zechariah 14:8–9; Psalm 47:2–3; 7–8; 145:10–13).

Significantly, verse 21, with its focus on an ideal time period yet to be realized, contains an important interpretive challenge. Those who will "come up on mount Zion to judge [or govern] the mount of Esau" are described in the traditional Hebrew Bible, known as the Masoretic Text, as *mōšiʿîm*, "deliverers" or "saviors," as translated in the KJV. However, the consonants of this Hebrew term, *m(w)šʿym* (from the lexical root *y-š-ʿ*, "to help, save"), can also be vocalized *mūšāʿîm*, a passive form meaning "those who have been saved." The Jews who produced the early Greek translation of the Hebrew scriptures known as the Septuagint so understood this word, rendering Obadiah 1:21 as "the men who are rescued [or delivered] from Mount Sion shall go up to punish Mount Esau, and the kingdom shall be the Lord's."[19] This passive reading of the word *m(w)šʿym* also occurs in the Syriac translation, is preferred by some modern commentators, and is found in some modern English translations, such as the NRSV and the NET Bible.[20]

Two factors help explain this difference in interpretation and translation. One is textual. Since the written Hebrew text of the Bible consisted only of consonants until the mid-first millennium AD, when the Masoretes added a vocalization system to preserve their traditional reading of the text, it is impossible to determine based on the text alone whether the earliest sense of *m(w)šʿym* was active or passive. As noted above, the Septuagint and the Syriac text traditions support the passive reading, while the Masoretic Text tradition supports the active reading.[21] The *w* in *m(w)šʿym* was often employed to help readers know to pronounce an *o* or *u* sound, so its presence does not solve this problem.

The second reason for differences in how *m(w)šʿym* is interpreted is thematic. Obadiah 1:17 begins with the phrase translated in the KJV as "But upon mount Zion shall be deliverance [*pĕlēyṭâ*]" (compare Joel 2:32). The word *pĕlēyṭâ* can also indicate a "survivor," one who has escaped or been delivered (so translated in NRSV, NET). Thus, the notion of those who escaped the destruction mentioned in verse 17 is carried, by some interpreters, into verse 21: "Those who have been saved shall go up to Mount Zion" (NRSV).[22]

Despite these factors, many commentators and some modern translations (e.g., NIV, NASB, ESV) prefer to follow the Hebrew Masoretic vocalization and read *mōšiʿîm* in verse 21 as, "deliverers" or "saviours," the way the KJV renders it. The singular form of this participle occurs several times in reference to humans in the Hebrew Bible, including Judges 3:9, "The LORD raised up a deliverer [*mōšîaʿ*] to the children of Israel, who delivered them" (see also, Judges 3:15; 2 Kings 13:5), and in reference to YHWH, who declared, "For I am the LORD thy God, the Holy One of Israel, thy Saviour [*mōšîaʿ*]" (Isaiah 43:3). The plural form *mōšiʿîm* occurs only in Obadiah 1:21 and in Nehemiah 9:27, which reads, "According to thy manifold mercies thou gavest them saviours [*mōšîʿîm*], who saved them [*yōšîʿûm*] out of the hand of their enemies." This verse is part of a public prayer in Nehemiah 9:6–37 that reviews Israelite history, including this reference to judges who are recounted in the book of Judges, who were essentially chieftains moved upon by YHWH's spirit to militarily deliver the Israelites from their neighboring enemies.

Given the emphasis in the Hebrew MT on "saviours" (v. 21); on "the day of the LORD" (v. 15), with its divine judgment and doom, and on the Israelites acting as "fire" and "flame" that would "devour" their enemies (v. 18; cf. Malachi 4:1) and who would repossess their own territories formerly controlled by their enemies (vv. 19–20), commentators often suggest a parallel between the military-oriented language in Judges (and elsewhere in the Bible) and with the final verses of Obadiah.[23] The saviors in Obadiah 1:21 are thus often viewed as Israelites who, moved upon by YHWH's spirit and power, deliver their people from their enemies and then judge or govern "mount Esau" under the supreme kingship of YHWH. Thus, the determination to translate *m(w)šʿym* with an active or passive sense is based on interpretive considerations, not on unambiguous textual evidence.

The conclusion to Obadiah's prophecy has two further challenges. They both involve the question of how prophecy is interpreted, what one thinks prophets knew about the future, and how prophets knew it. The first challenge is knowing whether this military-sounding imagery of deliverers (following the Hebrew MT) is intended as literal, as symbolic of spiritual struggles, or both.[24] Obadiah is not clear on this issue, but as reviewed in the previous paragraph, the concepts and terminology in verses 15–21 sound more physically and militarily oriented (see likewise Jeremiah 10:10: "But the LORD is . . . an everlasting king: at his wrath the earth shall tremble, and the nations shall not be able to abide his indignation"). There is nothing explicit in these verses about personal righteousness or spirituality, although the prophesied destructive outcome could conceivably be understood as arising from an absence of that among the Edomites or nations. How this first challenge is dealt with depends, at least in part, on one's answer to the second challenge, which is deciding what "the day of the LORD" and "saviours on mount Zion" represent in Obadiah.

This second challenge lies at the heart of what this prophecy "means." Having just reviewed the contents of Obadiah, it is clear that the words in this biblical book take readers only so far. As Jensen has observed, "The brevity and ambiguity of the verse [21] provides the opportunity for very different interpretations."[25] What readers bring to the text—by way of perspectives, beliefs, and expectations—has a large impact on what meaning they perceive in Obadiah's words, including whether, for example, they even consider the book to be a divinely inspired prophecy. This issue highlights the tension between exegesis, or what is read out of the text in its context (i.e., what a close reading of the text leads one to understand), and eisegesis, what is read into the text (i.e., what one brings to, applies to, and expects to find in the text). Furthermore, it exemplifies the understandable desire to make greater sense of passages that seem less than complete and explicit on their own.

Various commentators have expressed a range of interpretive preferences on the latter portion of Obadiah. For example, Paul R. Raabe points out that commentators are divided on whether "the day of the LORD" was meant eschatologically (the end of "regular" human time) or not, partly because of differing views on how to interpret the modifying clause "is near" (v. 15; see also Joel 1:15). Raabe himself states that as different as the prophesied time period will be, Obadiah "remains congruent with the historical and geographical realities of his own time; . . . he has not moved into the realm of apocalyptic."[26] Similarly, John Barton claims that the latter portion of Obadiah was "conceived as a genuine and specific hope, not as kind of 'utopian' dream" and depicts a "wholly concrete, this-worldly, political Israel that would govern the surrounding areas."[27]

Alternatively, Douglas Stuart finds the prophecy depicting a somewhat vaguely defined "new age," where "pure acknowledgement of Yahweh as God alone will prevail (cf. Isaiah 49:26; 54:10)." He further claims Obadiah, like other Old Testament prophecies about "the new age, has a Christian implication," in that this is not *just* a prophecy about events in the historical world but also about the "ultimate victory of God's people" throughout all the kingdoms of the earth.[28] And Block understands Obadiah as foreseeing a time when Zion "will become a place of everlasting joy," when Obadiah's prophecy is fulfilled in Christ.[29] Whether Daniel I. Block means through an outpouring of God's spirit or the personal presence of Christ is not clear.

Neither Stuart nor Block specifically mention Jesus's Second Coming (a doctrine that many Christians no longer literally believe), thus differentiating themselves from other commentators who, taking a Christian canonical perspective (i.e., reading the whole Bible together from a Christian perspective), see Obadiah 1:15–21—with its references to "the day of the LORD" and to "mount Zion," when "the kingdom shall be the LORD's"—as a prophecy about Jesus's Second Coming in power and glory and the establishment of his millennial kingdom on earth. The current academic trend is to read the Old Testament as a pre-Christian and usually a non-Christian anthology, so this Christ connection is no longer typically addressed by commentators. One obvious reason for this is that neither Obadiah nor any other Old Testament prophet explicitly mention the Second Coming of YHWH/Jehovah/Jesus, although several prophets do emphasize a dramatically different ideal future, including a Davidic, messianic ruler (e.g., Ezekiel 34:23–24; 37:24–25) and wonderfully productive changes in the earth (Amos 9:11–15; Joel 3:18). Obadiah's prophecy, however, lacks these features. Nonetheless, some earlier Christian commentators did connect Obadiah's prophecy with Jesus's Second Coming, such as Carl F. Keil, who wrote, "The fulfillment of [Obadiah] vers. 17–21 can only belong to the Messianic times . . . at the second coming of our Lord."[30] Many commentators would label this conviction an example of *sensus plenior*, the idea that there is a fuller meaning to a text that was intended by God, whether or not the earlier prophet understood the concept.

Surveying Obadiah 1:15–21 in the context of other eschatologically oriented prophecies in the Old Testament, my reading of the latter verses of Obadiah resonates with Keil's perspective, in accepting that Obadiah was a prophet of God, that he prophesied something that has not yet fully come to pass (Israel prevailing over all its enemies, mount Zion being holy, and YHWH's kingdom being established on earth), and that what he prophesied will only fully occur with Jesus's Second Coming and the advent of the Millennium. But I also recognize that this is not specifically in Obadiah. I have brought a set of perspectives to the content of verses 15–21 that go beyond what this prophecy explicitly says.

This analysis of the book of Obadiah, with its emphasis on verse 21, sets the stage for examining how Latter-day Saints have used this verse, with its phrase "saviours . . . on mount Zion."

Reading Obadiah 21 with Latter-day Saints

As noted at the beginning of this paper, Latter-day Saints have regularly used the phrase "saviors on mount Zion" in connection with proxy temple work for the dead in this latter-day dispensation. The notion of humans participating as "saviors" in someone else's spiritual progression is an interesting concept.

There are no passages in the Bible (excluding Obadiah 1:21) or the Book of Mormon that refer to someone other than YHWH/Jehovah/Jesus as "savior" in a *theological* sense, but there are two of them in the Doctrine and Covenants. The first is in D&C 86:11—part of a revelation given to Joseph Smith in Kirtland, Ohio, dated 6 December 1832—and is an expansion on Jesus's parable of the wheat and the tares (Matthew 13:24–32). This passage clearly suggests Latter-day Saint priesthood holders can collectively function as a "savior" to "my people Israel." The phrase "my people" is consistently employed in the Old Testament and other scriptures to refer to covenant Israelites and seems to do so here as well.[31] So D&C 86:11 does not mention other peoples being saved by this collective "savior."

The second reference to someone other than YHWH/Jesus as a savior in uniquely Latter-day Saint scripture occurs in D&C 103:9–10, part of a revelation given to Joseph Smith in Kirtland, Ohio, dated 24 February 1834. This passage expands on Jesus's commission to his disciples in Matthew 5:14 to be "the light of the world" and is spoken to and about "my people." Here, it does appear that covenant Church members in general can function as "saviors" representing Jesus and his gospel to the rest of the world. Obviously, this notion of some people participating as "saviors" to others extends, but does not replace, the great saving power of Jesus's atoning sacrifice.

Set beside this early Restoration theological use of "saviors" plural, the phrase "mount Zion" occurs five times in the book of Psalms, seven times in Isaiah, twice in Obadiah, and once each in Joel and Micah. It also occurs three times in 2 Nephi, in chapters that quote Isaiah. And the form "mount Sion" occurs in the KJV of Hebrews 12:22 and Revelation 14:1. Thus, Joseph Smith encountered this phrase multiple times in his Book of Mormon translation and JST efforts.

The phrase "mount Zion" also occurs in D&C 133:18 and 56 in a revelation given through Joseph Smith on 3 November 1831.[32] The context of these two occurrences in D&C 133 is clearly Jesus's Second Coming. This phrase again occurs in D&C 76:66, in the vision given to Joseph Smith and Sidney Rigdon on 16 February 1832, which draws upon the language of Hebrews 12:22 and which occurs in the description of those inheriting a celestial glory. And the phrase "mount Zion" occurs at least sporadically in subsequent remarks from Joseph Smith.[33]

These two threads—"saviors" and "mount Zion"—come together in a sermon by Joseph Smith on 16 May 1841: "The election of the promised seed still continues, and in the last days, they shall have the priesthood restored unto them, and they shall be the 'Saviors on mount Zion' [Obadiah 1:21] the 'ministers of our God' [Isaiah 61:6], if it were not for the remnant which was left, then might we be as Sodom and as Gomorrah [paraphrasing Isaiah 1:9]."[34] Although Joseph Smith did not mention Obadiah or Isaiah by name in this statement, he clearly quoted a phrase from each prophetic book. Neither did he explicitly connect either of these passages to temple ordinances, although he did several months later. The report of a discourse on 3 October 1841 describes, "President Joseph Smith, by request of some of the Twelve, gave instructions on the doctrine of Baptism for the Dead; which was listened to with intense interest by the large assembly. The speaker presented 'Baptism for the Dead' as the only way that men can appear as saviors on mount Zion."[35]

The phrase "saviors on mount Zion" and the temple ordinances come most fully together in the 15 April 1842 edition of the *Times and Seasons*, in which Joseph Smith taught the following:

> And now as the great purposes of God are hastening to their accomplishment and the things spoken of in the prophets are fulfilling, as the kingdom of God is established on the earth, and the ancient order of things restored, the Lord has

> manifested to us this duty and privilege, and we are commanded to be baptized for our dead thus fulfilling the words of Obadiah when speaking of the glory of the Latter Day. "And saviours shall come up upon mount Zion to judge the remnant of Esau; and the kingdom shall be the Lords." A view of these things reconciles the scriptures of truth, justifies the ways of God to man; places the human family upon an equal footing, and harmonizes with every principle of righteousness, justice, and truth.[36]

Here, Joseph Smith specifically cited Obadiah 1:21 and connected the phrase "saviours . . . on mount Zion" with Latter-day Saints who perform proxy temple baptisms for their ancestors. He reiterated this concept on 21 January 1844, asking, "But how are they [the Saints] to become Saviors on Mount Zion? By building their temples" and performing all the requisite temple ordinances for their ancestors.[37] Thus, it appears that the more Joseph Smith learned and taught about proxy temple ordinances, the more focused his use of "saviors on mount Zion" became.

A number of subsequent latter-day prophets and apostles have reiterated this connection in general conference addresses and elsewhere. Due to space limitations, only a few examples are provided here for illustration. On 31 July 1859, Brigham Young is reported to have preached the following in Salt Lake City:

> It is recorded in the Bible that in the last days the God of heaven will set up a kingdom [Daniel 2:44]. . . . It will save every person that will and can be saved. The doctrines of the Saviour reveal and place the believers in possession of principles whereby saviours will come upon Mount Zion to save the house of Esau, which is the Gentile nations, from sin and death. . . . Men and women will enter into the temples of God, . . . and officiate year after year for those who have slept thousands of years.[38]

Although Brigham Young did not specifically mention Obadiah, he clearly drew upon Obadiah 1:21. And he transformed Obadiah's "saviours . . . to judge the mount Esau" to "saviours . . . to save the house of Esau," identifying this "house of Esau" as "the Gentile nations" of the earth, thereby specifically linking Obadiah 1:21 with missionary and temple work.

In the April 1943 general conference, Elder John A. Widtsoe taught, "The Lord came upon earth and, in our behalf, in behalf of the whole race of God's children, did work which will bring us eternal life and joy and blessings. So, in a humbler manner may we, each one of us, do work for the dead that will bless them eternally, if they accept our service. We, also, may become saviors —'saviors on Mount Zion' (Obad. 1:21). That is a glorious thought."[39] President Gordon B. Hinckley taught at the October 2004 general conference that we can

> go to the house of the Lord and there serve in a vicarious relationship in behalf of those who are beyond the veil of death. . . . We literally become saviors on Mount Zion [Obadiah 1:21]. What does this mean? Just as our Redeemer gave His life as a vicarious sacrifice for all men, and in so doing became our Savior, even so we, in a small measure, when we engage in proxy work in the temple, become as saviors to those on the other side who have no means of advancing unless something is done in their behalf by those on earth.[40]

And in April 2016, Quentin L. Cook similarly taught this principle, citing Obadiah 1:21.[41]

Furthermore, Church-produced materials and commentators have generally followed suit, connecting Obadiah 1:21 with vicarious temple work. For example, the 2014 *Old Testament Seminary Teacher Manual* encourages a discussion of temple work in relation to Obadiah 1:17–21.[42]

The beauty of this connection—"saviours . . . on mount Zion" and vicarious temple ordinances—first expressed by Joseph Smith, is immediately evident. This Restoration-based view aligns with the Lord's statement in D&C 103:9–10, that his people can function as "saviors" under his direction and power. This spiritually oriented understanding of the contents of Obadiah 1:21 emphasizes "saviors" who represent the Lord in extending ordinance opportunities to those in need of such assistance. This view seems to also draw on verse 17—"But upon mount Zion shall be deliverance, and there shall be holiness"—to suggest a temple-based connection for these saviors. Understood this way, it is obvious that the active rendition of *mōšiʿîm* in Obadiah 1:21 in the traditional Hebrew Bible and in the KJV (as opposed to the passive reading, "those who are saved") has had a significant impact on how Latter-day Saints have utilized the language of that verse.[43]

However, reading Obadiah 1:15–21 with a text-based and contextualized interpretive approach yields a different outcome and raises questions about connecting Obadiah 1:21 with temple ordinances. For example, neither the temple nor its ordinances—for the dead or the living—are specifically mentioned in the book of Obadiah, although, as indicated above, "mount Zion" can reference the temple mount as well as the city of Jerusalem (and Latter-day Saints sometimes use "mount Zion" to designate the American New Jerusalem; see, for example, D&C 84:2–3; 133:56). Also, living in the Mosaic dispensation, the ancient Israelites did not perform vicarious ordinances for the dead, a practice that began only after Jesus's resurrection, about six hundred years after Obadiah.[44] There is no evidence that Obadiah's audience understood such a concept, even if one were to assume that Obadiah, as a prophet, was aware of the future prospects of "work for the dead."

Furthermore, it is not entirely clear in verse 21 how the "saviours . . . on mount Zion" who are to "judge" or govern "mount Esau" equate with Latter-day Saints performing temple ordinances for the dead,[45] especially given the more military and administrative depiction in Obadiah 1:15–21, with the implicit connections to past Israelite judges.[46] And although contrasted with "mount Esau," "mount Zion" in verse 21 seems intended, in context, to reference Jerusalem or just its temple mount, not multiple latter-day temples. Finally, in the quotations included above, Joseph Smith and Brigham Young both applied Obadiah 1:21 to the temple activity of Latter-day Saints in *this* time period, not to a future time following "the day of the Lord." This is especially true if that is understood as the destruction of the wicked prior to the initiation of a new era at Christ's return (D&C 43:17–29 and 45:39 use the phrase "the great day of the Lord" in reference to Jesus's Second Coming).

So the question arises: Was Obadiah *primarily* prophesying about "saviors on Mount Zion" in connection with issues that would arise through the course of centuries, just in our latter-day dispensation, or in the Millennium? This is a classic illustration of how interpretive decisions are influenced by the preconceptions and beliefs that one brings to the text when interpreting a passage of scripture. As outlined previously, multiple interpretations have been given of what is intended by Obadiah 1:21 and its context, including the following:

- A hopeful but primarily "this-worldy" historical perspective
- A vague future fulfillment when Israelites will triumph over their enemies and live God's law
- A more general Christian reading of some future day of greater spirituality and righteousness brought about by Christ
- The specific view of many members of The Church of Jesus Christ of Latter-day Saints about performing temple ordinances for the dead in any dedicated latter-day temple
- A specific Christian reading of Jesus's Second Coming and the early Millennium

Given the content and tone of Obadiah 1:15–21, and in the context of other scriptural passages, I think the latter option is more likely (allowing that this prophecy can mean various things to various people), and so do a few other Latter-day Saint commentators. For example, Victor Ludlow has connected Obadiah's "holy mountain of Zion ([Obadiah] verses 16, 17, 21)" with "John's new Jerusalem . . . (Rev. 21:7, 27)," and Obadiah 1:21 with Revelation 11:15, passages that are regularly understood as millennial by Latter-day Saints.[47] In this millennial context, we may see YHWH's appointed "saviors" governing those who survived the destructive "day of the Lord" but who are not yet fully part of his kingdom, politically or spiritually. In this setting, they may help administer saving ordinances for the living and the dead.[48]

As a Latter-day Saint, there appear to me to be two possible approaches to understanding the commonly expressed Latter-day Saint perspective on this verse. One is that Obadiah 1:21 was intended to primarily portray the Church's premillennial vicarious temple work and related activities, that it took the Restoration and latter-day prophets to reveal and make this clear, and that The Church of Jesus Christ of Latter-day Saints is the kingdom of God mentioned by Obadiah.[49] This may be the assumption, thought through or not, of many Latter-day Saints.

The more likely option, in my opinion, is that Obadiah prophesied something that made sense to his contemporary audience in the sixth century BC, something about the Lord helping them regain their land in an undefined but different future and, in a reversal of their then-current fortunes, something about their ruling over the peoples around them with the aid of and under the ultimate kingship of YHWH. Promises of future deliverance, restoration, and righteousness no doubt provided hope to sixth-century Israelites, even if Obadiah's prophecy of the future was fairly vague as to specifics. It thus could have been intended to convey an eschatological message, something yet to be fulfilled, which for many Christians connects with the Second Coming of Jesus Christ. So whether one assumes Obadiah himself understood future vicarious temple ordinances, he does not appear to have been teaching his contemporaries about them.

If one takes this second approach (as I do), then it follows that Joseph Smith and those who succeeded him were *applying* Restoration knowledge to Obadiah's ancient prophecy rather than announcing the interpretation of the prophecy *per se* in its biblical context. In this particular case, Joseph Smith appears to me to have done with Obadiah 1:21 what Peter did with Joel 2:28–32, as recounted in Acts 2:17–21, only weeks after Jesus's resurrection. Referring to events at Pentecost, with its multiple manifestations of the Holy Spirit, Peter declared that "this is that which was spoken by the prophet Joel" (v. 16), who, among other things, prophesied that YHWH would "pour out my Spirit upon all flesh." However, about 1,800 years later, Moroni told Joseph Smith that this same prophecy of Joel "was not yet fulfilled, but was soon to be" (JS—H 1:41). Thus, Peter *applied* an Old Testament prophecy to events in his day because of certain connections and overlaps that were evident to him, even though the primary focus of the prophecy was really something still in his future (as is readily evident from Joel 2:30–31; Acts 2:19–20). This models what Joseph Smith and other Latter-day Saints have done with Obadiah 1:21, because of its powerful and pliable imagery, by applying to our latter-day dispensation a prophecy that seems to focus primarily on the Second Coming of Jesus and his early millennial reign on earth ("the kingdom will be the LORD's").

This process of application is different from a prophet giving a definitive interpretation of all aspects of a prophecy in its context. The value in recognizing and appreciating both approaches for what they are—an interpretation of a passage in its literary, historical, and canonical context, *and* a particular application of a passage that does not necessarily employ or conform to its scriptural context—is important to ensuring that one option does not come to obscure the other. There is real value in understanding Obadiah 1:21 in its own context, just as there is value in understanding how latter-day prophets have employed the evocative language of verse 21 to teach relevant truths in this dispensation. Thus, just as we can appreciate what Peter was doing with Joel's prophecy in Acts, so we can also appreciate what latter-day Church leaders have done, in my opinion, with Obadiah 1:21, without claiming their use is the only or final way to interpret that verse.

Understanding this situation is important in part because Latter-day Saints have made other applications of the phrase "saviors on mount Zion" that extend the vision of this phrase to additional activities in this latter-day time period besides temple work but which again are not likely the primary fulfillment of the phrase as found in its context in Obadiah. For example, Gary Gillum, after sharing stories of family abuse, observed that "in likening the scriptures to ourselves, Latter-day Saints can be saviors on Mount Zion not only for the dead but also for the living . . . by helping the world overcome and eliminate the barbarisms of abuse, war, torture, force, genocide, poverty, ignorance, exclusion, bigotry, and hatred."[50] Elders Matthias Cowley, Charles Penrose, and Mark E. Petersen applied this phrase to teaching family members the restored gospel.[51] Henry Moyle applied the phrase to missionary work in general.[52] And Elder Jeffrey R. Holland applied this phrase to the nurturing love and service rendered to children by their mothers.[53] All of these illustrate the power of employing beautiful poetic language to express important concepts. They also illustrate the practice of applying a scriptural phrase to various situations that are different from the one primarily represented by the particular phrase's context itself.

Concluding Thoughts

This study has discussed how one phrase from Obadiah 1:21 fits within the context of the verse in which it occurs and within that verse's greater context, especially verses 15–21, as well as how Latter-day Saints have applied this phrase to temple work and other gospel-related activities. Wrestling with the text of prophetic statements, old or new, in their contexts, often proves to be quite challenging. However, it can be very fruitful as well, by demonstrating what a text says in its own right and in its own context and by delineating what subsequent uses and applications have been made of that text so that each can be appreciated and utilized for what it is. Whether or not one agrees with the perspective I have presented here, Obadiah's teaching about the "day of the Lord" and the establishment of his kingdom that will follow the destruction of the wicked is a significant doctrinal concept, as is the vicarious temple work that Latter-day Saints perform for the dead.

Notes

1. I thank my student assistant Austin Metcalf for helping with some of the research for this paper. I also thank my wife, Jane Allis-Pike, my colleague Kent P. Jackson, and two unnamed peer reviewers for their helpful feedback.

   The Bible translations cited in this study are known by the following abbreviations: KJV, King James Version (1611/1769); NRSV, New Revised Standard Version (1989); NASB, New American Standard Bible (1971/1995); NET, New English Translation (2005); ESV, English Standard Version (2001/2011); and NIV, New International Version (1978/2011).
2. There is only one chapter in Obadiah. Some publications simply omit a chapter designation, e.g., Obadiah 21, while others include a chapter designation, e.g., Obadiah 1:21. I follow this latter practice, since it represents the style generally used by the LDS Church.
3. See my paper on Ecclesiastes 12:7 and a forthcoming paper on the breath of life for other illustrations of this practice of Latter-day Saints *applying* meaning to a biblical passage. Dana M. Pike, "The 'Spirit' That Returns to God in Ecclesiastes 12:7," in *Let Us Reason Together: Reflections on Study*

and Faith, Essays in Honor of Robert L. Millet, ed. J. Spencer Fluhman and Brent L. Top (Provo, UT: Religious Studies Center; Salt Lake City: Deseret Book, 2016), 189–204.

4. A number of non-LDS and LDS commentaries have been produced on the book of Obadiah. For convenience, I cite here some of the more recent ones, which may be consulted for further discussion of Obadiah than is possible in this paper.

   Recent non-LDS commentaries: Daniel I. Block, *Obadiah: The Kingship Belongs to YHWH* (Grand Rapids, MI: Zondervan, 2013); Philip Peter Jensen, *Obadiah, Jonah, Micah: A Theological Commentary* (New York: T & T Clark International, 2008); Johan Renkema, *Obadiah* (HCOT; Leuven: Peeters, 2003); John Barton, *Joel and Obadiah* (OTL; Louisville, KY: Westminster John Knox, 2003); Ehud Ben Zvi, *A Historical-Critical Study of the Book of Obadiah* (BZAW 242; New York: de Gruyter, 1996); Paul R. Raabe, *Obadiah, A New Translation with Introduction and Commentary* (ABD24; New York: Doubleday, 1996). Although somewhat dated in parts, see also Diana Vikander Edelman, ed., *You Shall Not Abhor an Edomite for He is Your Brother: Edom and Seir in History and Tradition* (Atlanta: Scholars Press, 1995).

   LDS publications generally provide fewer comments on Obadiah. They include D. Kelly Ogden and Andrew C. Skinner, *Verse by Verse, The Old Testament*, vol. 2, *1 Kings through Malachi* (Salt Lake City: Deseret Book, 2013), 338–40; Darrell L. Matthews, "The Book of Obadiah," in *1 Kings to Malachi*, ed. Kent P. Jackson, vol. 4 of *Studies in Scripture* (Salt Lake City: Deseret Book, 1993), 264–66; Ellis T. Rasmussen, *A Latter-day Saint Commentary on the Old Testament* (Salt Lake City: Deseret Book, 1993), 651–52; Monte S. Nyman and Farres H. Nyman, *The Words of the Twelve Prophets: Messages to the Latter-day Saints* (Salt Lake City: Deseret Book, 1990), 61–69; and Sidney B. Sperry, *The Voice of Israel's Prophets* (Salt Lake City: Deseret Book, 1965), 317–25.

5. See portions of Isaiah 34, Jeremiah 49, and Ezekiel 25 and 35. For a recent examination of these and related passages, see Else K. Holt, Hyun Chul

Paul Kim, and Andrew Mein, eds., *Concerning the Nations: Essays on the Oracles Against the Nations in Isaiah, Jeremiah and Ezekiel* (New York: Bloomsbury, 2015).

6. For an overview of pertinent issues, such as whether the Book of the Twelve was intentionally arranged and redacted based on specific literary and theological factors, see for example, the pros and cons cited in Ehud Ben Zvi and James D. Nogalski, *Two Sides of a Coin: Juxtaposing Views on Interpreting the Book of the Twelve / the Twelve Prophetic Books* (Piscataway, NJ: Gorgias, 2009). See also the discussion in Jensen, *Obadiah, Jonah, Micah*, 7.
7. For further discussion, see Dana M. Pike, "The Name and Titles of God in the Old Testament," *Religious Educator* 11, no. 1 (2010): 17–31, especially 19–21; and Dana M. Pike, "Biblical Hebrew Words You Already Know, and Why They Are Important," *Religious Educator* 7, no. 3 (2006): 97–114, especially 106–9.
8. Obadiah / *ʿbdyh*, elsewhere alternatively written as *ʿbdyhw*, is a common form of personal names in Israel and the rest of the ancient Near East, consisting of a title compounded with a divine name. Compare, for example, the Israelite name *ʿbdʾl* / Abdiel, "servant of El/God," and the Phoenician name *ʿbdbʿl*, "servant of Baal." For further discussion of such theophoric personal names, see Dana M. Pike, "Names, Theophoric," in *Anchor Bible Dictionary*, ed. David N. Freedman (New York: Doubleday, 1992), 4:1018–19.
9. For a summary overview of positions on dating Obadiah, see Block, *Obadiah*, 23–24.
10. See, for example, Block, *Obadiah*, 23, 27; and Ehud Ben Zvi, "Obadiah," in *The Oxford Encyclopedia of the Books of the Bible*, vol. 2., ed. Michael D. Coogan (New York: Oxford, 2011), 124.
11. On the interesting form "Lord God," with "God" in small caps, see Pike, "The Name and Titles of God in the Old Testament," 25, available at https://rsc.byu.edu/archived/name-and-titles-god-old-testament.
12. The Septuagint is the early Greek translation of Hebrew scriptures produced by Jews living in Egypt in the third through second centuries BC.

See, for example, *A New English Translation of the Septuagint,* ed. Albert Pietersma and Benjamin G. Wright (New York: Oxford, 2009).

13. It is worth noting that Genesis 36 relates many of Esau's descendants. And Edom may be the setting for Job and his experiences; see Job 1:1–3 and Lamentations 4:21. For a recent analysis of biblical passages dealing with Esau and Edomites, see Elie Assis, *Identity in Conflict: The Struggle Between Esau and Jacob, Edom and Israel* (Winona Lake, IN: Eisenbrauns, 2016).
14. See, for example, the helpful overview by Richard H. Hiers, "Day of the Lord," in the *Anchor Bible Dictionary,* ed. David Noel Freedman (New York: Doubleday, 1992), 2:82–83.
15. Compare Nephi's use of "the time cometh speedily" and "must shortly come" in reference to the last days and Millennium; 1 Nephi 22:15, 18.
16. The evidence for this claim, during year three of the reign of Nabonidus, is fragmentary but fairly certain; see Mordechai Cogan, *The Raging Torrent: Historical Inscriptions from Assyria and Babylonia Relating to Ancient Israel* (Jerusalem: Carta, 2008), 214.
17. See the extended excursus on this biblical motif by Raabe, *Obadiah,* 206–42.
18. A number of biblical passages, such as 1 Samuel 12:12, Psalm 98:6, Isaiah 6:5, and Jeremiah 51:57, refer to YHWH as "king."
19. So translated by George E. Hubbard in *A New English Translation of the Septuagint,* 804. Darrell Matthews, "The Book of Obadiah," 266n3, is the only LDS commentator I am aware of who even cites the Septuagint reading when discussing Obadiah 1:21.
20. For commentators who favor this passive reading, see Barton, *Joel and Obadiah,* 154; Douglas Stuart, *Hosea-Jonah* (WBC 31; Waco, Texas: Word, 1987), 413; and citations in Renkema, *Obadiah,* 216n393–94.
21. Based on the Septuagint reading, some scholars have posited seeing Hebrew *mūšāʿîm,* a form that does not otherwise occur in the Masoretic Text, as a corrupted form of the passive *nōšāʿîm,* "the ones who were helped" (compare the singular form in Isaiah 45:17: "Israel shall be saved [*nōšaʿ*] in the Lord"), but this seems unlikely.

22. For further discussion of the active versus the passive interpretation of *m(w)š'ym*, see Raabe, *Obadiah*, 268–69; and Renkema, *Obadiah*, 215–17.
23. See Raabe, *Obadiah*, 269, 272; Block, *Obadiah*, 102–3; and Renkema, *Obadiah*, 216–17.
24. See also the language in an eschatological context in Zechariah 10, in which future Judahites are referred to as a "goodly horse in the battle" (v. 3) and "as mighty men, which tread down their enemies in the mire of the streets in the battle: and they shall fight, because the Lord is with them" (v. 5).
25. Jensen, *Obadiah, Jonah, Micah*, 26.
26. Raabe, *Obadiah*, 272, and see the comments on 192.
27. Barton, *Joel and Obadiah*, 157.
28. Stuart, *Hoshea–Jonah*, 421–22.
29. Block, *Obadiah*, 108.
30. Carl Friedrich Keil, *The Twelve Minor Prophets*, vol. 1 in C. F. Keil and F. Delitzsch, *Biblical Commentary on the Old Testament*, trans. James Martin (Grand Rapids, MI: Eerdmans, 1949; originally pub. 1878), 378. See also, to some extent, John A. Thompson, "The Book of Obadiah," in *The Interpreter's Bible* (New York: Abingdon, 1956), 6:867. Victor L. Ludlow, *Unlocking the Old Testament* (Salt Lake City: Deseret Book, 1981), 211, is the only LDS commentator I am aware of who emphasizes this view of Obadiah 15–21.
31. There are multiple examples of this expression in the Old Testament as part of a covenant formula. See, for example, Exodus 6:7, Jeremiah 24:7, and for further citations and discussion, Rolf Rendtorff, *The Covenant Formula, an Exegetical and Theological Investigation*, trans. Margaret Khol (Edinburgh: T&T Clark, 1998).
32. "Revelations printed in *The Evening and the Morning Star*, June 1832–June 1833," [1], http://www.josephsmithpapers.org/paper-summary/revelations-printed-in-the-evening-and-the-morning-star-june-1832-june-1833/19.
33. See a 7 July 1834 proclamation in which Joseph Smith reportedly referenced Joel 2:32, in History, 1838–1856, volume A-1 [23 December 1805–30 August 1834], 517, The Joseph Smith Papers, http://www.josephsmith

papers.org/paper-summary/history-1838-1856-volume-a-1-23-december-1805-30-august-1834/523.

34. Discourse, 16 May 1841, as Reported by *Times and Seasons*, 430, The Joseph Smith Papers, http://www.josephsmithpapers.org/paper-summary/discourse-16-may-1841-as-reported-by-times-and-seasons/2.
35. Discourse, 3 October 1841, as Reported by *Times and Seasons*, 577, The Joseph Smith Papers, http://www.josephsmithpapers.org/paper-summary/discourse-3-october-1841-as-reported-by-times-and-seasons/1.
36. *Times and Seasons*, 15 April 1842, 761, The Joseph Smith Papers, http://www.josephsmithpapers.org/paper-summary/times-and-seasons-15-april-1842/11. This editorial is signed "Ed.," which is presumably Joseph Smith, since he functioned as the editor of *Times and Seasons* at this time.
37. History, 1838–1856, volume E-1 [1 July 1843–30 April 1844], 1866, The Joseph Smith Papers, http://www.josephsmithpapers.org/paper-summary/history-1838-1856-volume-e-1-1-july-1843-30-april-1844/238.
38. Journal of Discourses (London: Latter-day Saints' Book Depot, 1859), 6:344, http://contentdm.lib.byu.edu/cdm/ref/collection/JournalOfDiscourses3/id/9602. There are challenges in utilizing the sermons in the *Journal of Discourses* as a source for specific wording, since they are based on shorthand transcriptions of what was verbally presented over the pulpit. See, more fully, Gerrit Dirkmaat and LaJean Purcell Carruth, "The Prophets Have Spoken, but What Did They Say? Examining the Differences between George D. Watt's Original Shorthand Notes and the Sermons Published in the *Journal of Discourses*," in *BYU Studies Quarterly* 54, no. 4 (2015): 25–118.
39. John A. Widtsoe, "The Way of Salvation," in Conference Report, April 1943, 37–39.
40. Gordon B. Hinckley, *Ensign*, November 2004, 105.
41. Quentin L. Cook, "See Yourself in the Temple," *Ensign*, May 2016, 98.
42. *Old Testament Seminary Teacher Manual*, https://www.lds.org/manual/old-testament-seminary-teacher-manual/introduction-to-the-book-of-obadiah/lesson-151-obadiah?lang=eng. See also, for example, Daniel H. Ludlow, *A Companion to Your Study of the Old Testament* (Salt Lake City: Deseret Book,

1981), 373–74; and Ogden and Skinner, *Verse by Verse, The Old Testament,* vol. 2, *1 Kings through Malachi,* 339–40.

43. So also, presumably, has the KJV translation of Hebrew *mōšiʿîm* as "saviours," as opposed to the less theologically oriented "deliverers," which is also a legitimate rendition.

44. Furthermore, D&C 84:25–27 and Joseph Smith Translation, Exodus 34:1–2 indicate to Latter-day Saints that Israelites living in the land of Canaan before Christ's mortal ministry did not generally have access to Melchizedek Priesthood–based ordinances but only Aaronic Priesthood ones. Therefore, ancient Israelites as a group did not experience a full temple endowment themselves (if they had *any* endowment experience), making it difficult for them to understand Obadiah's prophecy if what he was specifically referring to was latter-day temple ordinances.

45. Victor Ludlow's explanation (*Unlocking the Old Testament,* 211) that "Latter-day Saints can easily associate 'saviors on Mount Zion' (verse 21) with such record keeping and righteousness (as demonstrated through books of remembrance and temple work)" is not self-evident in Obadiah 1:21, and neither is Sperry's claim (*The Voice of Israel's Prophets,* 325) that "those who hold the [priesthood] keys of this work shall judge the wicked world represented by the 'Mount of Esau.'"

46. D&C 64:37–38 does mention the restored Church as a "judge," but it goes on to indicate that the "inhabitants of Zion shall judge all things pertaining to Zion," thus contextualizing the judging as related to Church members (borne out further in verses 39–40), not the judging of Edom or the world.

47. Ludlow, *Unlocking the Old Testament,* 210–11. See also Ogden and Skinner, *Verse by Verse, The Old Testament,* vol. 2, *I Kings through Malachi,* 339, who sound like they favor a millennial interpretation of Obadiah 1:15–21, even though they do not use that word: "The prophet makes a sudden transition [in verse 15] from the immediate to ultimate things. . . . In contrast to those who choose to remain outside the kingdom of God (the 'heathen'), those within it will inherit the earth after it is cleansed by fire. Certain helpers, saviors, will 'come up on mount Zion' in the day of the Lord."

48. For a brief discussion of these matters, see Robert L. Millet, "Millennium," in *LDS Beliefs: A Doctrinal Reference*, ed. Robert L. Millet, Camille Fronk Olson, Andrew C. Skinner, and Brent L. Top (Salt Lake City: Deseret Book, 2011), 425–31, especially 428–30.
49. See "Kingdom of God or Kingdom of Heaven," in *The Guide to the Scriptures*, https://www.lds.org/scriptures/gs/kingdom-of-god-or-kingdom-of-heaven?lang=eng.
50. Gary P. Gillum, "Obadiah's Vision of Saviors on Mount Zion," in *Voices of Old Testament Prophets*, 26th Annual Sidney B. Sperry Symposium (Salt Lake City: Deseret Book, 1997), 129–30.
51. Matthias Cowley, in Conference Report, October 1903, 55; Charles W. Penrose, in Conference Report, April 1918, 22; and Mark E. Petersen, "Going Steady," in Conference Report, October 1959, 14.
52. Henry D. Moyle, "The Saints in Europe," in Conference Report, October 1958, 34.
53. Jeffrey R. Holland, "Behold Thy Mother," *Ensign*, November 2015, 50.

4

"Precept upon Precept, Line upon Line"

An Approach to Understanding Isaiah 28:7–13

Terry B. Ball

Terry B. Ball is a professor of ancient scripture at Brigham Young University.

Isaiah 28:7–13 is one of the more controversial and enigmatic passages of the eighth-century prophet's text, with verses 10 and 13 of the pericope perhaps being the most difficult to translate and interpret. To illustrate, compare the following English renditions of verse 10:

> For precept *must be* upon precept, precept upon precept; line upon line, line upon line; here a little, *and* there a little:
>
> King James Version

> For it is: Do this, do that, a rule for this, a rule for that; a little here, a little there.
>
> New International Version

> He tells us everything over and over—one line at a time, one line at a time, a little here, and a little there!
>
> New Living Translation

> "For He says, 'Order on order, order on order, Line on line, line on line, A little here, a little there.'"
>
> New American Standard Bible

> That same mutter upon mutter, murmur upon murmur. Now here, now there! For it is precept by precept, precept by precept, line by line, line by line; here a little, there a little.
>
> Jewish Publication Society of America Version

> You don't even listen—all you hear is senseless sound after senseless sound.
>
> Contemporary English Version

> They speak utter nonsense.
>
> GOD'S WORD Translation

> Indeed, they will hear meaningless gibberish, senseless babbling, a syllable here, a syllable there.
>
> NET Bible[1]

The discrepancies in translation and understanding of this verse appear to arise primarily from two issues: (1) the difficulty in translating the obscure Hebrew phrase *saw lāsāw saw lāsāw qaw lāqāw qaw lāqāw* found in verses 10 and 13, and (2) the difficulty in identifying the voice that is speaking in verses 9 through 13 of the pericope.

This study will review several of the commonly proposed approaches to translating this difficult passage and then discuss an approach that perhaps resolves some of the difficulties in understanding the text by interpreting it in the context of entrapment rhetoric. It will further discuss how, in the context of entrapment rhetoric, language from the King James Version (KJV) of the text may relate to the use of similar language found in Restoration scripture.[2]

The Meaning of *saw lāsāw saw lāsāw qaw lāqāw qaw lāqāw*

The meaning and correct translation of the Hebrew phrase *saw lāsāw saw lāsāw qaw lāqāw qaw lāqāw*, translated as "precept upon precept; line upon line" in the KJV (Isaiah 28:10, 13), is widely debated among scholars. For example, by giving a different vocalization to the Hebrew letters of the text than does the KJV, Kennett suggests that the words are actually a parody of a schoolteacher giving a simple spelling lesson to little children. He sees the teacher explaining to the children that *sadeh* (צ) and *waw* (ו) spell *saw* (צו), repeating it twice, and that *qoph* (ק) and *waw* (ו) spell *qaw* (קו), again repeating it twice.[3]

Hallo, on the other hand, finds evidence in Ugaritic abecedaries[4] indicating to him that the original names of the Hebrew letters *sadeh* and *qoph* may have simply been *saw* and *qaw*. Rather than a spelling lesson, Hallo appears to see the phrase as an attempt to mimic a schoolmaster trying to teach children the successive letters of the Hebrew alphabet, *sadeh* and *qoph*, using their original names, *saw* and *qaw*. Thus, he renders verse 10, "For it is *saw* for *saw*, *saw* for *saw*, *qaw* for *qaw*, *qaw* for *qaw*."[5] Watts points out how incoherent such a lesson would be when taught by a drunken teacher.[6]

Driver agrees that *saw* and *qaw* could indeed be the original monosyllabic names for the Hebrew letters *sadeh* (צ) and *qoph* (ק), for which the vocalization *sadeh* and *qoph* where later substituted, but he feels no direct evidence has yet been found to support the idea. He further wonders why, if this is a lesson in the alphabet, the teacher would begin in the middle of the alphabet rather than the beginning, and even why a teacher would be trying to teach the alphabet to just weaned infants. He rather understands *saw* and *qaw* to be nothing more than the senseless cries and shouts of the drunken priests and prophets asking for more drink, perhaps chosen to echo the Hebrew words *qî* meaning "vomit" and *sōʾāh* meaning "filth" or "excrement" in verse 8. He translates verses 9 and 10, "To whom is the prophet giving instruction, Whom will he make to understand what they hear—babes newly weaned, just taken from the breast? [internal quotation marks omitted]. He then explains, "No, but it is 'Ho!' answering to 'Ho!', 'Hey!' to 'Hey!' and 'another drop here, another drop there!"[7]

Rogers, too, suggests an intentional connection between the *sōʾāh* and *qîʾ* of verse 8 with the similar-sounding *saw* and *qaw* in verse 10. He concludes that *saw* is actually a parody of a small child trying to say *sōʾāh* and that *qaw is* a similar infantile attempt to say *qîʾ*. Accordingly, he translates verse 10 with childish English equivalents for excrement and vomit rendering the verse, "Doo-doo to doo-doo, doo-doo to doo-doo, Yuk-yuk to yuk-yuk, yuk-yuk to yuk-yuk, A little here, a little there." [8]

Van der Toorn puts an entirely different twist on the interpretation. He sees the prophecy as a polemic against necromancy. He argues that *saw lāsāw saw lāsāw qaw lāqāw qaw lāqāw* is an attempt to mock the bird-like uttering of necromancers, pretending to communicate with the dead that leaders had been seeking counsel from rather than God.[9] Equally as ingenious is van Selms's hypothesis that *saw lāsāw saw lāsāw qaw lāqāw qaw lāqāw* is not Hebrew at all, but rather Assyrian language which should be translated as, "Go out! Let him go out! Go out! Let him go out! Wait! Let him wait! Wait! Let him wait!"[10]

Other possible interpretations of the phrase include an attempt to imitate the meaningless babble of babies, a mocking summary of Isaiah's teachings spoken through the slurred and drunken lips of Isaiah's adversaries, or even an attempt to imitate a postulated speech impediment that Isaiah suffered.[11] Hays and Irvine combine approaches by concluding that the phrase is intended to show how God's words to the drunken priest and prophets "will be like childish gibberish but will be taught by the Assyrians."[12] Some avoid the issue in verse 10 by leaving the phrase entirely untranslated.[13]

These examples of how *saw lāsāw saw lāsāw qaw lāqāw qaw lāqāw* has been translated and interpreted over the years are intended to be illustrative rather than exhaustive. Still, they demonstrate that this obscure passage has attracted a considerable amount of attention and generated a wide range of ideas.

The Question of Voice in Verses 9–13

Identifying the voice throughout the passage has been equally problematic. Verses 9–13 are couched in a confrontation that Isaiah is apparently having with the political and religious leaders of the kingdoms of Israel (Isaiah 28:1–8) and Judah (Isaiah 28:14–22) in regards to the Assyrian crisis.[14] It seems clear in verses 7 and 8 of the passage that Isaiah is rebuking the priests and prophets of Israel who have either literally or figuratively so intoxicated themselves that, as they wallow in their own vomit and filth, have lost both the proper vision and the clear judgment needed to deal with the Assyrian threat. "But they also have erred through wine, and through strong drink are out of the way; the priest and the prophet have erred through strong drink, they are swallowed up of wine, they are out of the way through strong drink; they err in vision, they stumble in judgment. For all tables are full of vomit and filthiness, so that there is no place clean" (Isaiah 28:7–8). However, in the following verses, 9 and 10, it is unclear whether Isaiah continues to speak or if the words in these verses are the response of the drunken priests and prophets to Isaiah's scolding. "Whom shall he teach knowledge? and whom shall he make to understand doctrine? them that are weaned from the milk, and drawn from the breasts. For precept must be upon precept, precept upon precept; line upon line, line upon line; here a little, and there a little" (Isaiah 28:9–10). Brevard Childs illustrates the difficulty in identifying the voice in the passage when he concludes that verses 7–13 must be a redactor's collection of several "independent units from different periods" assembled into a "kerygmatic unity," leaving one with little information to help sort out the various speakers involved in the verbal exchange.[15]

The Voice of Isaiah

If one understands the voice in verses 9 and 10 to be Isaiah, then a common way to understand the KJV text is to interpret it as the prophet's further attempts to explain to the drunken priests and prophets, at least those who have been weaned from their mother's milk (Isaiah 28:9), that God gives knowledge and doctrinal understanding to individuals "precept upon precept, . . . line upon line, . . . here a little and there a little" (Isaiah 28:10). [16] The KJV translates "precept," from the Hebrew *saw,* apparently considering the word a derivative of the primal root *swh,* meaning *to command, appoint, order,* etc. It translates "line" from the Hebrew *qaw* apparently considering the word a derivative of the primal root *qwh* meaning *to tie or bind,* hence a line or chord used for measuring.[17] This interpretation continues with the warning that those who "would not hear" will not enjoy God's rest but would find God speaking with "stammering lips and another tongue" and ultimately "fall backward, and be broken, and snared, and taken" (Isaiah 28:11–13). While this interpretation is common and popular, many do not find it tenable. For example, Driver notes that while "precept" is a formally possible translation of *saw,* it is not found anywhere else in the Old Testament. Moreover, he does not find translating "upon" from the Hebrew preposition *lamed* (ל) in *lāsāw* and *lāqāw* justifiable in this context.[18]

Hays and Irvine, who identify Isaiah as the voice in verses 9–10, but, who, like Driver, find the KJV translation untenable, understand the prophet to be using the phrase *saw lāsāw saw lāsāw qaw lāqāw qaw lāqāw* to illustrate to the irresponsible leaders how infantile or nonsensical the Lord's word will sound to them as a consequence of their drunken state.[19] In contrast, Watts suggests that Isaiah is using the phrase to liken the incompetence of the leaders to that of drunken teachers trying to teach little children.[20]

While the identity of the voice in verses 9–10 is much debated, most scholars agree that the voice of verses 11–13 is Isaiah's, and the verses themselves are understood to be a warning that because of their rejection of Isaiah's words, the rebellious leaders would come to be taught and chastised through the "stammering lips" of "another tongue," likely an allusion to the language of the Assyrian invaders (Isaiah 28:11). Further, because they would not hear the "rest" and "refreshing" that God offered (Isaiah 28:12), his words would continue to sound like the babyish or nonsensical *saw lāsāw saw lāsāw qaw lāqāw qaw lāqāw* to them, resulting in their fall and capture (Isaiah 28:13).[21]

The Voice of Israel's Priests and Prophets

The preponderance of commentators prefer to identify the voice in verses 9 and 10 to be not that of Isaiah, but rather that of the inebriated priests and prophets he scolded in verses 7 and 8 of the passage. From this perspective, verse 9 can be understood as the drunkards taking exception to the way Isaiah has spoken to them, indignantly questioning, "Who does Isaiah think he is trying to teach? Little children just weaned?" The priests and prophet's resentful questions of verse 9 are then followed in verse 10 by their attempt to mockingly mimic Isaiah's words to them, complaining that they sound like *saw lāsāw saw lāsāw qaw lāqāw qaw lāqāw.* If this phrase is, indeed, an attempt by the offended leaders to mock the way Isaiah has tried to scold them, then whether one translates it as a childish school lesson, the slurring of drunkards, a cry for more wine, the chirping of a necromancer, the language of the Assyrians, or some form of baby talk, the message is the same. The leaders deem Isaiah's words as too infantile, unintelligible, insignificant, or uninteresting to be worthy of their consideration. In response to their mocking rejection of his words, Isaiah then issues the warning of verses 11–13, typically interpreted as discussed above.

Another Approach: Entrapment Rhetoric

Most interpretations reasonably assume that the phrase *saw lāsāw saw lāsāw qaw lāqāw qaw lāqāw* should have essentially the same meaning in both verses 10 and 13. Wildberger, however, concludes that in verse 13, Isaiah intentionally uses the same mocking phrase spoken by his opponents in verse 10 to give them a new meaning.[22] While Wildberger does not indicate what that new meaning might be, Watts presents an intriguing suggestion. In his translation, he leaves the phrase *saw lāsāw saw lāsāw qaw lāqāw qaw lāqāw* untranslated in verse 10, but in verse 13, much like the KJV, he translates it "Precept for precept. Precept for precept. Line for line. Line for line."[23] He suggests that as the mocking words of the drunkards are spoken by Jehovah through his prophet in verse 13, they are turned "into an authentic word to Israel." Thus, as Isaiah speaks the phrase, he does so in such a way that *saw* is indeed understood as precept or command and *qaw* is indeed understood as line. Watts concludes, "What began in v[erse] 10 as mumbling incompetence is turned by the Lord in v[erse] 13 to be an instrument of judgment leading to their [the drunken leaders'] destruction."[24]

Watts's translation makes excellent sense if the passage is interpreted in the context of an entrapment episode. Kangas defines entrapment as a rhetorical device wherein one frames their message "in such a way that the real meaning is not revealed until the listener has engaged themselves fully. The listener is forced to render judgement on themselves when the curtain is pulled back and the subject of judgment is shown to be the hearer." [25]

Entrapment rhetoric is common in the Old Testament. One of the earliest uses of the device can be found in the parable of the ewe lamb that the prophet Nathan used to lure David into pronouncing his own condemnation (1 Samuel 12:1–14). Other examples include the smitten prophet who used entrapment to lead Ahab into pronouncing his own death sentence (1 Kings 20:35–42), Elisha's entrapment of Joash to warn of his future limited success in combating Syria (2 Kings 13:14–19), and Tamar's desperate entrapment of her father-in-law, Judah (Genesis 38:1–26). O'Connell sees entrapment as a major rhetorical strategy throughout the Book of Judges as it makes the case for a monarchy,[26] and others see it employed in the opening chapters of Amos to lure Israel and Judah into their condemnation.[27] Isaiah himself uses a form of entrapment to foretell the Babylonian captivity to the perhaps overly-hospitable Hezekiah (Isaiah 39), and, in the song of the vineyard, to warn of the punishment awaiting the apostate covenant people as he invites them to ponder, "What could have been done more to my vineyard?" (Isaiah 5:1–7). In each of these examples, a trap is set by creating a situation that leads the hearer to pronounce or think of a condemnation or judgment, only to learn that in doing so they have incriminated themselves.

Interpreting Isaiah 28:7–13 in the context of entrapment rhetoric can be an insightful approach. In verses 7–8 the prophet sets the trap as he tells drunken prophets and priests that they "have erred through wine, and through strong drink are out of the way; the priest and the prophet have erred through strong drink, they are swallowed up of wine, they are out of the way through strong drink; they err in vision, they stumble in judgment. For all tables are full of vomit and filthiness, so that there is no place clean" (Isaiah 28:7–8). The priests and prophets "take the bait" when they indignantly respond to the rebuke by taking exception to the condescending manner in which Isaiah has spoken to them asking, "Who does Isaiah think he is talking to, little children just weaned?" (Isaiah 28:9). They then attempt to mock and mimic Isaiah's teachings in some fashion with the words "*saw lāsāw saw lāsāw qaw lāqāw qaw lāqāw*" (Isaiah 28:10), thereby springing the trap. Isaiah then responds by explaining to them how they have pronounced their own condemnation. He declares that they will indeed be confronted by those speaking with stammering lips and in another tongue (Isaiah 28:11), even the Assyrians.[28] Moreover, their refusal to hear his warning has caused them to forfeit the opportunity to enjoy the "rest" God offered them (Isaiah 28:12). Then, as Watts suggests, Isaiah takes the very phrase they used to mock him, *saw lāsāw saw lāsāw qaw lāqāw qaw lāqāw*, and turns it deadly serious by changing the tone and context, perhaps using a play on the words, to give it the exact meaning that the KJV translators understood—a description of how God has tried to teach them, "precept upon precept; line upon line . . . here a little and there a little," the rejection of which will cause them to "fall backward" and "be broken and snared, and taken" (Isaiah 28:13).

Isaiah 28:7–13 and Restoration Scripture

Interpreting Isaiah 28:7–13 in the context of entrapment rhetoric may help Latter-day Saints better understand the occurrence and relationship of similar language to that of the KJV found in Restoration scripture. The similar phrase "line upon line, precept upon precept" occurs three times in Restoration scripture. In each case, it appears to be explaining the way God reveals truth to his children on earth. In the Book of Mormon, the prophet Nephi declares, "For behold, thus saith the Lord God: I will give unto the children of men line upon line, precept upon precept, here a little and there a little; and blessed are those who hearken unto my precepts, and lend an ear unto my counsel, for they shall learn wisdom; for unto him that receiveth I will give more; and from them that shall say, We have enough, from them shall be taken away even that which they have" (2 Nephi 28:30). Similarly, in August of 1833, Joseph Smith declared in prophetic fashion to the Latter-day Saints who had suffered physically and lost property to persecutors in Missouri, "I give unto you a commandment, that ye shall forsake all evil and cleave unto all good, that ye shall live by every word which proceedeth forth out of the mouth of God. For he will give unto the faithful line upon line, precept upon precept" (D&C 98:12). Nine years later, in a letter written to Church members, Joseph Smith reviewed events and revelations that were part of his prophetic experience and explained that they were given "line upon line, precept upon precept; here a little, and there a little; giving us consolation by holding forth that which is to come, confirming our hope" (D&C 128:21).

Because the phrase "line upon line, precept upon precept" is clearly being used to explain how God reveals truth to his children in these passages, one might question what the relationship is between the language in these Restoration scriptures and the similar KJV phrase "precept upon precept" in Isaiah 28, which, by most interpretations, has an entirely different meaning. Several possible explanations for the occurrence of the similar language exist.

Some may conclude that because the meaning of the language appears to be very different as used in Restoration scripture and Isaiah 28, the similar language must be coincidental and unrelated. This explanation is not very convincing. Nephi declared that his soul delighted in Isaiah's words and he quoted from them often, admonishing his people to liken them to their own situation (1 Nephi 15:20; 19:23; 2 Nephi 6:4–5; 11:2, 8; 12–25). It is hard to imagine that he was not thinking of Isaiah when he explained "For behold, thus saith the Lord God: I will give unto the children of men line upon line, precept upon precept, here a little and there a little" (2 Nephi 28:30). Bokovoy sees Nephi's inversion of the KJV phrase in the Book of Mormon from "precept upon precept; line upon line," to "line upon line, precept upon precept" as an example of Seidel's Law, wherein one intentionally inverts a phrase to alert the listener that he is quoting from a familiar source.[29] Not only in Nephi's writing, but also throughout the English translation of the Book of Mormon, the text consistently uses KJV language wherever Isaiah is quoted (e.g., Mosiah 14; 3 Nephi 22), thereby affirming the close relationship between the texts. Likewise, KJV Isaiah is found throughout the Doctrine and Covenants. Nearly one third of the revelations recorded in the Doctrine and Covenants share some characteristic language, phrases, or terms with prophecies recorded in Isaiah. While some of the shared language in the Doctrine and Covenants occurs in the form of extended passages taken from Isaiah's writings, the preponderance of the language found in the two texts is in the form of short phrases and terminology.

Moreover, the Doctrine and Covenants draws language and phrases from more than half of the chapters of Isaiah, yet surprisingly, nearly 80 percent of the shared language or phrases are used three times or less in the entire Doctrine and Covenants text. Thus, the Doctrine and Covenants draws both broadly and abundantly from the words of Isaiah.[30] Again, given this ubiquitous use of Isaianic language in the Doctrine and Covenants, it would be difficult to argue that the occurrence of "line upon line, precept upon precept" (D&C 98:12; 128:21) in the text is coincidental and unrelated to Isaiah 28.

Some may conclude that Nephi and Joseph Smith simply misunderstood what the KJV "precept upon precept, line upon line" really meant, and so, in their ignorance, misused the similar language in Restoration scripture to describe how God reveals truth. Ascribing ignorance to prophets is not a satisfying or convincing resolution for most. Others may conclude that Nephi and Joseph Smith understood well what the KJV "precept upon precept, line upon line" really meant, but as God spoke to them he repurposed the language and meaning to teach how he reveals truth. This seems a more tenable resolution.

Some may conclude that because the Restoration scriptures use the phrase "line upon line, precept upon precept" to explain how God reveals truth, only the KJV has the translation of Isaiah 28: 7–13 correct and it must be understood to have the same meaning in all texts. This conclusion is likewise not entirely convincing. The reasoning and evidences presented for many of the various other interpretations as discussed above are typically logical, well founded, convincing and, for the most part, not easily dismissed. However, in light of the controversy among scholars over how to understand the passage, those who accept Restoration scriptures as part of their canon should feel free to reasonably argue that the affinity of those texts for Isaiah and their clear support for the KJV interpretation of the passage should also be allowed to inform the discussion.

Perhaps the most reasonable explanation for the similar language in Restoration scripture and Isaiah 28:7–13 can be found if the Isaiah passage is interpreted in the context of entrapment rhetoric. As an entrapment episode, Isaiah is allowed to cleverly change the meaning of the drunkards mocking phrase in verse 10 to teach God's paradigm of revelation in verse 13. Thus, the verse 13 language would be the very inspiration and meaning for the similar language's use in Restoration scripture. If one prefers this explanation for the relationship between the texts, then it seems wiser to reference verse 13 rather than verse 10 of Isaiah 28 when cross-referencing the Restoration scripture language with Isaiah.

The debate over the proper interpretation of Isaiah 28:7–13 and its relationship to Restoration scripture will likely persist in the years to come. This study has endeavored to illustrate that there are many tenable approaches and answers.

Notes

1. Interestingly, the Septuagint, perhaps in line with the first copy of Isaiah in the Dead Sea corpus, renders the verse with words that, when translated into English, read "take for your selves tribulation upon tribulation hope upon hope, yet a little, yet a little." For a discussion, see Hans Wildberger, *Isaiah 28–39*, trans. Thomas H. Trapp (Minneapolis: Fortress Press, 2002), 16.
2. I use the term "Restoration scripture" to refer collectively to the Book of Mormon, the Doctrine and Covenants, and the Pearl of Great Price.
3. R. H. Kennett, *Ancient Hebrew Social Life and Custom as Indicated in Law, Narrative and Metaphor* (London: Oxford University Press, 1933), 12.
4. An alphabet table.
5. William W. Hallo, "Isaiah 28:9–13 and the Ugaritic Abecedaries," *Journal of Biblical Literature*, 77, no. 4 (December 1958): 324–38.
6. John D. W. Watts, *Isaiah 1–33*, vol. 24 in *Word Biblical Commentary* (Waco, TX: Word Books, 1985), 363.
7. G. R. Driver, "Another Little Drink," *Words and Meanings: Essays Presented to David Winton Thomas* (Cambridge: Cambridge University Press, 1968), 54–56, 62.
8. J. J. M. Rogers, *First Isaiah: A Commentary*, vol. 29 in *Hermeneia—A Critical and Historical Commentary on the Bible* (Minneapolis: Fortress Press, 2015), 348, 351.
9. K. van der Toorn, "Echoes of Judean Necromancy in Isaiah 28, 7–22," *Zeitschrift für die alttestamentliche Wissenschaft* 100, no. 2 (1988): 199–217.
10. A. van Selms, "Isaiah 28:9–13: An Attempt to Give a New Interpretation," *Zeitschrift für die alttestamentliche Wissenschaft* 85, no. 3 (1973): 332–39.
11. Wildberger, *Isaiah 28–39*, 23. For a review and bibliography of these and other such interpretations, see K. van der Toorn, "Echoes of Judean Necromancy in Isaiah 28, 7–22," *Zeitschrift für die alttestamentliche Wissenschaft* 100:2 (1988): 199–217.
12. John H. Hayes and Stuart A. Irvine, *Isaiah the Eighth-Century Prophet: His Times & His Teachings* (Nashville: Abingdon Press, 1987), 325.
13. For an example, see Wildberger, *Isaiah 28–39*, 14.

14. In the eight century BC, Assyria was building its empire by conquering neighboring nations and making them vassal states.
15. Brevard S. Childs, "Isaiah and the Assyrian Crisis," *Studies in Biblical Theology*, Second Series 3 (London: SCM Press, 1967), 27–28. For another discussion of the issue of voice, see A. van Selms, "Isaiah 28:9–13: An attempt to give a New Interpretation," *Zeitschrift für die alttestamentliche Wissenschaft* 85, no. 3 (1973): 332–39.
16. See for example *The Interpreter's Bible*, 12 vols. (New York: Abingdon Press, 1956), 5:316; Matthew Henry, *An Exposition of the Old and New Testament* (New York: Robert Carter & Brothers, 1853), 126–27.
17. Watts, *Isaiah 1–33*, 361.
18. Driver, *Words and Meanings*, 54.
19. Hayes and Irvine, *Isaiah the Eighth-Century Prophet*, 325. The Contemporary English Version and NET Bible translations presented above appear to follow the Hays and Irvine interpretation.
20. Watts, *Isaiah 1–33*, 363. The GOD'S WORD Translation presented above appears to follow Watts's interpretation.
21. For examples of this interpretation, see Rogers, *First Isaiah*,351; van Selms, "Isaiah 28:9–13," 332–39; Joseph Jensen, *Isaiah 1–39* (Wilmington, Delaware: Michael Glazier, Inc., 1984), 217.
22. Wildberger, *Isaiah 28–39*, 25.
23. Watts, *Isaiah 1–33*, 359.
24. Watts, *Isaiah 1–33*, 364.
25. Billy Kangas, "Entrapment: The Biblical Art of Cloak and Dagger Rhetoric," *Patheos*, http://www.patheos.com/blogs/billykangas/2012/02/entrapment-the-biblical-art-of-cloak-and-dagger-rhetoric.html.
26. Robert H. O'Connell, *The Rhetoric of the Book of Judges* (New York: E. J. Brill, 1996), 6, 268–304.
27. "Amos," *Bible.org*, https://bible.org/seriespage/3-amos.
28. It is also tenable that verse 11 is still the voice of the drunkards, in which case they appear to be accusing Isaiah of speaking to them with stammering lips and in another tongue.

29. David Bokovoy, "Inverted Quotations in the Book of Mormon," *Insights* 139 (2000): 2.
30. Terry B. Ball and Spencer Snyder, "Isaiah in the Doctrine and Covenants," in *You Shall Have My Word: Exploring the Text of the Doctrine and Covenants*, ed. Scott C. Esplin, Richard O. Cowan, and Rachel Cope (Provo, UT: Religious Studies Center; Salt Lake City: Deseret Book, 2012), 108–33.

5

From King Ahaz's Sign to Christ Jesus

The "Fulfillment" of Isaiah 7:14

Jason R. Combs

Jason R. Combs is a visiting assistant professor of ancient scripture at Brigham Young University.

Most Latter-day Saints are familiar with a particular image of Isaiah.[1] A bearded, gray-haired Isaiah writes with his quill, hunched over a large stone table. Two witnesses, perhaps Uriah and Zechariah (Isaiah 8:2), peer over his shoulders, watching him work. His scroll lies open, flowing over the edge of the stone slab. No words appear on the scroll. Yet the message he writes is made clear by strokes of light that sweep upward from the point where his quill touches the parchment. They draw the viewer's attention upward, across the green valley in the background and into the light blue sky, where an image takes shape. There, Mary and Joseph, framed by two young lambs, gaze lovingly upon their newborn son, cradled in a pillow of hay. Commissioned by the Church and painted by Harry Anderson in the late 1960s, this painting conveys important Church doctrines: for instance, prophets testify of Christ, and Christ's coming was part of a foreordained divine plan.[2]

Nevertheless, as a depiction of a particular account from the Bible, the painting better represents Matthew's interpretation of Isaiah than the words of Isaiah alone.[3] At the beginning of his Gospel, Matthew interrupts the narrative of Jesus's birth with this declaration: "Now all this was done, that it might be fulfilled which was spoken of the Lord by the prophet, saying, Behold, a virgin shall be with child, and shall bring forth a son, and they shall call his name Emmanuel, which being interpreted is, God with us" (Matthew 1:22–23).[4] Ever since Matthew wrote these words, Christians have read Isaiah 7:14 predominantly, if not solely, as a description of Jesus's birth. This is reflected in Anderson's painting. Yet Isaiah never claims to have witnessed the birth of Jesus in a vision.[5] What's more, in the larger literary and historical context of Isaiah 7, the Immanuel prophecy seems to refer directly to events that occurred in Isaiah's own lifetime.

This is a study of the relationship between Isaiah's Immanuel prophecy and its "fulfillment" in the Gospel of Matthew. Rather than read Isaiah through the lens of Matthew's Gospel, we will begin by studying Isaiah in Isaiah's own historical context.[6] This includes the study of the political situation that lies behind Isaiah 7, Isaiah's use of symbolism, and the possible identity of Immanuel in the time of Isaiah. Then I will show how Matthew uses this prophecy, which was fulfilled in the time of Isaiah, in order to teach his readers about the divine mission of Jesus Christ.

Isaiah 7 in its Historical Context

Isaiah was a prophet in Jerusalem during turbulent times.[7] Almost two hundred years before Isaiah, just after the death of King Solomon, the united kingdom of Israel fractured (c. 930 BC).[8] The ten tribes to the north seceded and became the new "Kingdom of Israel"—sometimes called the Kingdom of Ephraim. The remaining tribes to the south, which continued to be ruled from the city of Jerusalem, became the Kingdom of Judah. Tensions and frequent outbreaks of violence between the Northern Kingdom of Israel and the Southern Kingdom of Judah persisted to the time of Isaiah. Sometimes Judah would form an alliance with a neighboring kingdom and wage war against Israel, other times Israel was the aggressor (for instance, see 1 Kings 15). Both Israel and Judah also faced threats beyond their internecine disputes—the neighboring kingdoms were not always allies.[9]

By the time of Isaiah, the menace of regional politics paled in comparison to the looming threat posed by the increasingly powerful Assyrian force. Tiglath-pileser III, king of Assyria (c. 747–727 BC), sometimes called Pul (see 2 Kings 15:19), made incursions into the land and began to collect tribute from Israel and Judah as well as from neighboring kingdoms, such as Syria to the north of Israel (2 Kings 15:19–20). During the reign of Pekah, king of Israel (c. 735–732 BC), Assyria took captive the people of "Galilee, all the land of Naphtali," and several major cities in Israel (2 Kings 15:29). A fragmentary Assyrian record from the period corroborates the biblical account. In that record, Tiglath-pileser boasts of the tribute that he received from Ahaz of Judah (identified by his full name, Jehoahaz):

> In all the countries which . . . [I received] the tribute of Kushtashpi of Commagene, Urik of Qu'e, Sibitti-be'l of Byblos, . . . Enil of Hamath, Panammu of Sam'al, Tarhulara of Gumgum, Sulumal of Militene, . . . Uassurme of Tabal, Ushhitti of Tuna, Urballa of Tuhana, Tuhamme of Ishtunda, . . . [Ma]tan-be'l of Arvad, Sanipu of Bit-Ammon, Salamanu of Moab, . . . Mitinti of Ashkelon, Jehoahaz of Judah, Kaush-malaku of Edom, Muzr[i . . .], Hanno of Gaza, (consisting of) gold, silver, tin, iron, antimony, linen garments with multicolored trimmings, garments of their native (industries) (being made of) dark purple wool . . . all kinds of

> costly objects be they products of the sea or of the continent, the (choice) products of their regions, the treasures of (their) kings, horses, mules (trained for) the yoke.[10]

As is clear from this record, Judah's neighbors suffered similar losses. In an effort to staunch the rising tide of Assyrian aggression or to expand their own territorial control, Rezin, king of Syria, attempted to form a coalition of those kingdoms that had been subjugated by Assyria; this included both the Kingdom of Israel and the Kingdom of Judah.[11] Israel, under the rule of Pekah, joined with Rezin, but Judah would not. This was the political situation when the twenty-year-old Ahaz son of Jotham became king of Judah.

Ahaz is characterized by the author of 2 Kings as a wicked man who "walked in the way of the kings of Israel" (16:3). Despite his affinity for the idolatrous ways of Israel, he would not join the alliance. So Pekah and Rezin responded with force. In an effort to depose Ahaz and replace him with a king who would be more sympathetic to their cause—the otherwise unknown "son of Tabeal" mentioned in Isaiah 7:6—Pekah and Rezin laid siege to Jerusalem (2 Kings 16:5).[12] This attack against Judah is known as the Syro-Ephraimite War (c. 734 BC), so named because of the alliance between the kingdom of Syria and Ephraim, the northern Kingdom of Israel. Ahaz responded to this attack by appealing to Assyria for help: "So Ahaz sent messengers to Tiglath-pileser king of Assyria, saying, I am thy servant and thy son: come up, and save me out of the hand of the king of Syria, and out of the hand of the king of Israel, which rise up against me. And Ahaz took the silver and gold that was found in the house of the Lord, and in the treasures of the king's house, and sent it for a present to the king of Assyria" (2 Kings 16:7–8). According to 2 Kings, Assyria's response was swift and decisive. Tiglath-pileser III captured Damascus the capital of Syria, killed Rezin, and took his people captive (2 Kings 16:9).

This is the historical context of Isaiah 7. Both 2 Kings and Isaiah describe the siege of Jerusalem laid by the armies of Pekah and Rezin, but only Isaiah includes an account of prophetic intervention.

> And it came to pass in the days of Ahaz the son of Jotham, the son of Uzziah, king of Judah, that Rezin the king of Syria, and Pekah the son of Remaliah, king of Israel, went up toward Jerusalem to war against it, but could not prevail against it. And it was told the house of David, saying, Syria is confederate with Ephraim. . . . Then said the Lord unto Isaiah, Go forth now to meet Ahaz, thou, and Shear-jashub thy son, at the end of the conduit of the upper pool in the highway of the fuller's field; And say unto him, Take heed, and be quiet; fear not, neither be fainthearted for the two tails of these smoking firebrands, for the fierce anger of Rezin with Syria, and of [Pekah] the son of Remaliah. (Isaiah 7:1–4; compare 2 Kings 16:5)[13]

Isaiah's message is one of faith and patience. Ahaz should not fear the kingdoms of Syria and Israel because the Lord is aware of their plans (see Isaiah 7:5–6) and will not allow them to succeed: "Thus saith the Lord God, It shall not stand, neither shall it come to pass" (Isaiah 7:7). Isaiah promises Ahaz not only that this immediate attack would fail but also that Ahaz's enemies would soon cease to be a threat: "Within threescore and five years [that is, sixty-five years] shall Ephraim be broken, that it be not a people" (Isaiah 7:8).[14] In a time when a twenty-year reign was impressive, the promise of a sign sixty-five years in the future may have been too distant for Ahaz to accept. It is clear that Ahaz was not convinced since Isaiah next asks Ahaz to choose another sign that would convince him: "Moreover the Lord spake again unto Ahaz, saying, Ask thee a sign of the Lord thy God; ask it either in the depth, or in the height above" (Isaiah 7:10–11). When Ahaz refuses to ask for a sign, Isaiah provides one anyway:

> Therefore the Lord himself shall give you a sign; Behold, a virgin shall conceive, and bear a son, and shall call his name Immanuel. Butter and honey shall he eat, that he may know to refuse the evil, and choose the good. For before the child shall know to refuse the evil, and choose the good, the land that thou abhorrest shall be forsaken of both her kings. The LORD shall bring upon thee, and upon thy people, and upon thy father's house, days that have not come, from the day that Ephraim departed from Judah; even the king of Assyria. (Isaiah 7:14–17)

For Ahaz, this prophecy was about his immediate concern: the threat posed by Ephraim and Syria—what Isaiah calls, "the land that thou abhorrest." With this understanding of the historical and political context of Isaiah's prophecy, we can now turn to the prophecy itself.

Isaiah's Prophetic Symbolism

In order to fully understand Isaiah's message to King Ahaz, it is necessary to understand the symbolism he employs. In antiquity, prophets often conveyed their messages through symbolic proclamations and gestures (for example, Ezekiel 4–5 or Hosea 1:6, 9).[15] In Isaiah's prophecies to Ahaz about the various threats facing Judah, three children and their unique names function as symbolic representations or confirmations of Isaiah's messages (see Isaiah 8:18). When Isaiah first approaches Ahaz, he brings his son Shear-jashub (Isaiah 7:3). The Hebrew name Shear-jashub means "a remnant shall return."[16] Isaiah prophesies that Israel, the northern kingdom, will be destroyed and will no longer be a threat to Judah if Ahaz will have faith (Isaiah 7:4–9). Isaiah does not explain the connection between this son's name and his prophecy. Since Isaiah's promises are often conditional, "a remnant shall return" may refer either to Israel, since a mere remnant of Israel would not be a threat to Ahaz (see Isaiah 10:20–23), or it may refer to Judah, since Ahaz is warned of impending disaster if he is not faithful (Isaiah 7:9).[17] Next, Isaiah promises Ahaz that a child would be born who would be called "Immanuel" (Isaiah 7:14). This name means "God is with us," and it supports Isaiah's message that the fate of the kingdom of Judah was ultimately in the hands of God (Isaiah 7:14–25).[18] Finally, Isaiah and "the prophetess" have another child, whom he is commanded to name "Maher-shalal-hash-baz," which means "the spoil speeds, the prey hastens" (Isaiah 8:1–3).[19] This name coincides with Isaiah's prophecy that "the riches of Damascus [the capital of Syria] and the spoil of Samaria [the capital of Israel] shall be taken away before the king of Assyria" (Isaiah 8:4).[20] The names of each of these children function as prophetic signs (Isaiah 8:18), second witnesses to each of Isaiah's prophetic messages.

In the cases of both Immanuel and Maher-shalal-hash-baz, their ages also serve as prophetic signs. Regarding Immanuel, Ahaz is promised, "Before the child shall know to refuse the evil, and choose the good, the land that thou abhorrest shall be forsaken of both her kings" (Isaiah 7:16). Likewise, the Lord reveals through Isaiah that before Maher-shalal-hash-baz "shall have knowledge to cry, My father, and my mother, the riches of Damascus and the spoil of Samaria shall be taken away" (Isaiah 8:4). In both instances, the ages of these children become chronological markers on the Lord's timetable. Through these children, Ahaz could count down the years before his enemies would fall. The lives of these children attest to the imminent end of Ahaz's troubles.

The Identity of Immanuel in Isaiah's Lifetime

Two of the three prophetic children, Shear-jashub and Maher-shalal-hash-baz, are clearly identified as Isaiah's sons (see Isaiah 7:3 and 8:3). The identities of Immanuel and his parents, however, are not so clear. Immanuel's mother is described only as *'almâ* (עַלְמָה) in the original Hebrew and *parthenos* (παρθένος) in an ancient Greek translation of Isaiah.[21] Although *'almâ* is most commonly translated as "young woman" and *parthenos* as "virgin," neither of those English words perfectly captures the meaning of the Hebrew or Greek words.[22] Regarding the translation of the Hebrew *'almâ,* John Watts explains, "It is difficult to find a word in English that is capable of the same range of meaning. 'Virgin' is too narrow, while 'young woman' is too broad."[23] Likewise, regarding the translation of the Greek *parthenos,* Ronald Troxel has shown that this term can sometimes be used to connote "young woman" even though its basic meaning is "virgin."[24] This means that Isaiah's prophecy did not originally emphasize the sexual inexperience of Immanuel's mother or present her pregnancy as miraculous.[25] As we have seen, the miraculous sign Isaiah provided to Ahaz was not about Immanuel's mother or her pregnancy.[26] Rather, the prophecy foretold how changing political circumstances would correspond with Immanuel's age: "Before the child shall know to refuse the evil, and choose the good, the land that thou abhorrest shall be forsaken of both her kings" (Isaiah 7:16). The sign was Immanuel's maturation, not his birth.

So who was Immanuel's mother in the time of Isaiah and Ahaz? It was likely someone present at the time of Isaiah's prophecy. In the King James Version, Isaiah 7:14 reads, "A virgin shall conceive," as if the young woman was unknown. Yet both the original Hebrew and the ancient Greek translation of this verse include a definite article—not "*a* virgin" but "*the* virgin"—suggesting that Isaiah referred to a specific, known "young woman."[27] The identity of this specific young woman is still debated today.[28] In antiquity, however, she was sometimes identified as the wife of King Ahaz.

There are good reasons to think that Immanuel referred to a particular son of King Ahaz, the future king, Hezekiah. First, the prophecy is directed to King Ahaz; the sign is specifically for him: "The Lord spake again unto Ahaz, saying, Ask thee a sign of the Lord thy God" (Isaiah 7:10–11). And Isaiah implies that the sign is relevant not only for Ahaz himself but also for his royal house:

"Hear ye now, O house of David" (Isaiah 7:13). This suggests that the child called Immanuel, or "God is with us," likely belonged to the house of David. The name is appropriate since the house of David is often described in terms of its special relationship with God—God is "with" David's house (see 2 Samuel 7:9; 2 Samuel 23:5; 1 Kings 1:37, 11:38; and Psalms 89:22, 25).[29] For instance, the author of 2 Kings praises Hezekiah, King Ahaz's son, when he ascends to the throne by writing that "the Lord was with him" (18:7).[30] So Immanuel was a fitting title for a future Davidic king.

Perhaps the most compelling evidence that Isaiah's Immanuel prophecy points to the reign of King Hezekiah is the lesser-known reference to Immanuel in Isaiah 8, a prophecy with parallels to Isaiah 7.[31] In Isaiah 7, King Ahaz is warned that the Lord would bring Assyria into his land: "The Lord shall bring upon thee, and upon thy people, and upon thy father's house, days that have not come, from the day that Ephraim departed from Judah; even the king of Assyria" (7:17). In Isaiah 8, Immanuel is given the same warning, that the Lord would bring Assyria into his land: "And he [the king of Assyria] shall pass through Judah; he shall overflow and go over, he shall reach even to the neck; and the stretching out of his wings shall fill the breadth of thy land, O Immanuel" (8:8). This parallel between the prophecies addressed to King Ahaz and to Immanuel suggests that Immanuel was likewise a Davidic king. In fact, Isaiah 8:8 states explicitly that the Kingdom of Judah belongs to Immanuel.[32] And under the reign of King Ahaz's son Hezekiah, the land of Judah was indeed invaded by Assyria (see Isaiah 36–37, 2 Kings 18–19, and 2 Chronicles 32). In an Assyrian record from c. 701 BC, Sennacherib, the Assyrian ruler at the time of Hezekiah, boasts of this invasion:

> As for Hezekiah, the Judean, I besieged 46 of his fortified walled cities and surrounding smaller towns, which were without number. Using packed-down ramps and applying battering rams, infantry attack by mines, breeches, and siege

> machines, I conquered them. I took out 200,150 people, young and old, male and female, horses, mules, donkeys, camels, cattle, and sheep, without number, and counted them as spoil. He himself I locked up within Jerusalem, his royal city, like a bird in a cage.[33]

The reference to Immanuel in Isaiah 8:8 and its parallel in Isaiah 7:17, therefore, seem to confirm that Isaiah's prophecy is fulfilled through the life of Hezekiah.

It is clear that Isaiah's reference to Immanuel applied to someone born in the time of King Ahaz and that Immanuel's mother was someone present or known at the time of Isaiah's prophecy. Yet some scholars have argued that the Immanuel prophecy was not fulfilled by Hezekiah.[34] Admittedly, if Hezekiah was the prophesied Immanuel, then there is a problem with the chronology of 2 Kings and 2 Chronicles.[35] According to 2 Kings 16:2 and 18:2, Hezekiah assumed the throne when he was twenty-five years old, after his father Ahaz had ruled for sixteen years.[36] If this chronology is correct, then Hezekiah was born almost a decade before Ahaz was king, long before Isaiah pointed to that young woman in King Ahaz's court and prophesied about her son, Immanuel. There is reason to believe that the dates and years provided by Kings and Chronicles are not precise.[37] Yet the problem with the date of Hezekiah's birth has led some to suggest that Immanuel was not Ahaz's son Hezekiah but Isaiah's son Maher-shalal-hash-baz.[38] This interpretation has the advantage of identifying all three symbolic children from Isaiah 7–8 as Isaiah's sons (see Isaiah 8:18), but it also presents a chronological problem. When Isaiah prophesies of the young woman (*'almâ*) who would bear a son, he is accompanied by his son Shear-jashub (Isaiah 7:3). This makes it improbable that Isaiah's wife could be described as a young woman of marriageable age (*'almâ*). As Raymond Brown explains, "The proposal that the *'almâ* was Isaiah's own wife, 'the prophetess' mentioned in 8:3, is most unlikely; for the fact that she had already borne Isaiah a son old enough to walk with him (7:3) makes such a designation for her implausible."[39] What's more, the earliest evidence that anyone interpreted Immanuel to be Isaiah's son rather than Hezekiah does not appear until the Middle Ages, approximately 1,800 years after Isaiah.[40] By contrast, the earliest evidence that people interpreted Immanuel to be Ahaz's son, Hezekiah, appears not long after the Gospel of Matthew was written.[41]

Ultimately, no definitive conclusion can be reached regarding the precise identity of Immanuel in the time of Isaiah. Nevertheless, at least four facts seem clear from the text of Isaiah 7–8: (1) this child, Immanuel, was to be born during Ahaz's lifetime; (2) Immanuel's mother was someone present or known to Ahaz at the time of Isaiah's prophecy; (3) the prophecy was for Ahaz and assumed that he would observe the boy, Immanuel, as he grew; and (4) the land of Judah could be described as belonging to Immanuel, which makes it likely that he was a Davidic heir.

Isaiah 7:14 in the Gospel of Matthew

Since Isaiah's prophecy was directed to King Ahaz and focused on events that would occur in Ahaz's future, why does Matthew say that Jesus fulfilled this prophecy? Was Matthew unfamiliar with the historical and literary context of Isaiah 7? How do we make sense of Matthew's quotation of Isaiah and his declaration that Isaiah's words were fulfilled in Jesus's conception and birth? In order to make sense of this passage, one must understand first what Matthew means by the word *fulfill* and second how Matthew reads scripture.

A Fuller Understanding of Fulfillment

To understand Matthew's quotation of Isaiah 7:14, we have to understand what Matthew means when he talks about fulfillment. Isaiah 7:14 appears in the Gospel of Matthew as the first in a series of "fulfillment passages." In Matthew, unlike the Gospels of Mark or Luke, the narrative of Jesus's life is frequently interrupted by Old Testament quotations that follow statements such as "Now all this was done, that it might be fulfilled which was spoken of the Lord by the prophet" (Matthew 1:22). Similar statements appear fourteen times in the Gospel of Matthew.[42]

In the New Testament, the word *fulfill* can have different meanings. In an important study on "fulfillment words," C. F. D. Moule demonstrated that there are at least three potential meanings: fulfillment can describe (1) the actualization of an event foretold precisely as it would occur; (2) the "completion" of something that began in the past; and (3) the "consummation" of a covenant-promise.[43] In other words, it is possible that Matthew saw in Isaiah's Immanuel prophecy a specific revelation pointing solely to Jesus's birth.[44] Yet Matthew's fulfillment passage might show how Jesus in some way completes a prophecy which was satisfied in part by events in the past.[45] Additionally, a fulfillment passage might reveal how a scripture that describes God's covenant relationship with his people in the past finds its consummation (its fullness or *ful*fillment) in the life of Jesus—after all, Jesus came not only to prove individual prophecies but also to fulfill all the law and the prophets (see Matthew 5:17–18).

These three potential meanings of the word *fulfillment* could also be understood in terms of models of interpretation. David L. Turner, in his commentary on the Gospel of Matthew, proposes three types of interpretation that can be mapped broadly onto Moule's meanings of fulfillment: Turner categorizes these models as (1) "predictive," (2) "multiple fulfillment," and (3) "typological."[46] When applied to Matthew's Gospel, the "predictive interpretation" model presumes that Isaiah prophesied directly about Jesus and only about Jesus. The "multiple-fulfillment interpretation" model, on the other hand, suggests that a single prophecy of Isaiah could be fulfilled by two or more distinct events—for instance, one in the time of Ahaz and another in the time of Jesus.[47] Given Matthew's historical context, it is possible he believed that Isaiah prophesied directly or secondarily about events in his (Matthew's) own time. The Dead Sea Scrolls, written in the century before Matthew, demonstrate a similar conviction—that the prophets foretold events precisely as experienced especially by the founder of the community behind the Dead Sea Scrolls.[48] This historical parallel, however, does not explain why Matthew would have seen Isaiah 7:14 in particular as a messianic prophecy fulfilled by Jesus's birth. Recall that in Isaiah 7 the sign is not the birth but the maturation of Immanuel: "For before the child shall know to refuse the evil, and choose the good, the land that thou abhorrest shall be forsaken of both her kings" (Isaiah 7:16). If Matthew read Isaiah 7:14 as no more than a prediction about Jesus, it would seem that either Matthew was not aware of the full literary context of Isaiah 7 or he rejected parts of that prophecy.[49] Yet, as I will argue hereafter, there is evidence to suggest that Matthew was keenly aware of the broader literary context of Isaiah.

Turner's "typological" model of interpretation, as the name implies, suggests that Matthew understood the prophecy of events that occurred in the time of Ahaz as a "type" for the events that occurred in the early life of Jesus.[50] This is closest to Moule's notion of the consummation of a covenant-promise.[51] This model has the advantage of leaving Isaiah's prophecy fully intact rather than dissecting it into some parts that refer only to Ahaz's Immanuel and others that refer only or secondarily to Jesus. In this model, the entire prophecy is directed to Ahaz and speaks to events that would come to pass in his lifetime. At the same time, it also allows for those events to foreshadow or reveal truths about Jesus's life and divine purpose as Matthew understood them. As Turner describes it, "Thus Isa. 7:14 is viewed as a sign to Ahaz that was fulfilled during his days, and Matthew sees in the passage a historical pattern that comes to climatic fulfillment with Jesus."[52]

How Matthew Reads Scripture

Matthew does not specify what he means by the word *fulfillment* when he says, "All this was done, that it might be fulfilled which was spoken of the Lord by the prophet" (Matthew 1:22). Matthew may not have distinguished between these models of interpretation in the way that scholars do today. In order to understand what Matthew means by including this prophecy, we have to understand how Matthew reads scripture.

Matthew's quotations of Old Testament passages have led some to believe that Matthew was not a careful reader.[53] For instance, Matthew says that Hosea 11:1 was fulfilled when Mary, Joseph, and Jesus returned from their refuge in Egypt: "And [they stayed] there until the death of Herod: that it might be fulfilled which was spoken of the Lord by the prophet [Hosea], saying, Out of Egypt have I called my son" (Matthew 2:15). Yet Hosea identified the son as the people of Israel and was clearly speaking about the exodus: "When Israel was a child, then I loved him, and called my son out of Egypt. . . . They sacrificed unto Baalim, and burned incense to graven images" (Hosea 11:1–2). This apparent discrepancy between what Matthew says a passage means and what the passage meant has led some to suggest that Matthew was working from a list of proof-texts removed from their original literary context.[54] This argument, however, does not do justice to the literary complexity of Matthew's Gospel.

Matthew alludes to the story of Israel's exodus from Egypt multiple times before he quotes that passage from Hosea. Through his emphasis on a dreamer named Joseph (Matthew 1:20; 2:12–13, 19, 22; compare to Genesis 37:5, 8–10, 19–20; 42:9), on a ruler who kills infants (Matthew 2:16; compare to Exodus 1:22), and on a return from Egypt to the promised land (Matthew 2:21; compare to Exodus 3:7–10), Matthew has woven into the narrative of Jesus's life the story of God's deliverance of Israel.[55] For Matthew, Jesus does not simply *fulfill* a prediction from Hosea; rather, he *fills out* the divine message that Hosea had conveyed about Israel's deliverance. Richard Hays explains:

> Matthew's use of the quotation depends upon the reader's recognition of its original sense: if Hosea's words were severed from their reference to the original exodus story, the literary and theological effect of Matthew's reading would be stifled. . . . The effect of the juxtaposition [between Jesus's flight and Israel's exodus] is to hint that Jesus now will carry the destiny of the people Israel and that the outcome will be the rescue and vindication of Israel, as foreshadowed in the exodus story and brought to fulfillment in the resurrection of Jesus.[56]

Matthew's quotation of Hosea was not a misguided use of a proof-text but the continuation of a theme already established in his narrative of Jesus's life: the salvation-history of Israel is bound up in the story of Jesus.

The same careful use of intertextual allusions can also be seen in Matthew's employment of Isaiah 7:14.[57] The beginning of the Gospel of Matthew is all about Davidic kings. The very first sentence introduces Jesus as the Davidic Messiah, or Christ: "The book of the generation of Jesus *Christ*, the *son of David*" (Matthew 1:1; emphasis added). The genealogy traces the origins and history of the Davidic family line, which includes Ahaz and Hezekiah (Matthew 1:2–16).[58] Although many of the men named in the genealogy are kings, only one is explicitly identified as such: "And Jesse begat David *the king*; and David *the king* begat Solomon" (Matthew 1:6; emphasis added). When Matthew summarizes the genealogy in periods of fourteen generations, the only people he names again, besides Abraham, are King David and Christ (Matthew 1:16–17).[59] In the story of Jesus's birth, Joseph is addressed by an angel as "Joseph, thou son of David" (Matthew 1:20). At this point, Matthew inserts Isaiah 7:14 and proclaims its fulfillment (Matthew 1:22–23). Then, after describing Jesus's birth, Matthew adds the account of the arrival of "wise men from the east" who ask, "Where is he that is born *King* of the Jews?"

(Matthew 2:2; emphasis added). With this emphasis on Davidic kingship, surely Matthew was aware of the context of Isaiah 7:14 and included it here with the hope that his readers would understand its message about Davidic kingship.

The reign of the Davidic king Ahaz was threatened by the alliance of Rezin, the king of Syria, and Pekah, the king of Israel (Ephraim). As Isaiah explained to King Ahaz: "Syria, Ephraim, and the son of Remaliah, have taken evil counsel against thee, saying, Let us go up against Judah, and vex it, and let us make a breach therein for us, and set a king in the midst of it, even the son of Tabeal" (Isaiah 7:5–6). The threat that Ahaz would be replaced by a foreign king was not a threat to Ahaz alone. God had promised King David through the prophet Nathan, "Thine house and thy kingdom shall be established for ever before thee: thy throne shall be established for ever" (2 Samuel 7:16). The overthrow of Ahaz could mean the end of Davidic rule and the failure of God's covenant promise. Yet, through Isaiah, the Lord reassures Ahaz—in fact, the Lord reassures the entire house of David (Isaiah 7:13)—that this threat to Davidic rule would not succeed: "For before the child [Immanuel] shall know to refuse the evil, and choose the good, the land that thou abhorrest shall be forsaken of both her kings" (Isaiah 7:16). Isaiah's prophecy was fulfilled. Rezin and Pekah failed and their land was "forsaken of both her kings." The house of David continued, and God was with them (see Isaiah 8:10 and 2 Kings 18:7).

By the time of Matthew, however, there was no king on David's throne—Herod the Great was not from the House of David.[60] Notice that, in Matthew's genealogy, the exile of the Jews to Babylon is mentioned, but the return from Babylon is not (see Matthew 1:11–12). This is most likely intentional to emphasize the continued "exile" of Davidic rule. Matthew and his audience would have known that Babylonian exile brought an end to Davidic rule. After Jews returned from Babylonian exile, Zerubbabel (spelled Zorobabel in the KJV of Matthew 1:12–13) functioned as the Persian governor of Jerusalem.[61] Despite being the Davidic heir, neither Zerubabbel nor any his descendants were ever crowned as king.[62] Matthew's summary of the genealogy reiterates this problem—the loss of Davidic rule—and presents Christ as the solution, part of a divinely-timed plan: "So all the generations from Abraham to David are fourteen generations; and from David until the carrying away into Babylon are fourteen generations; and from the carrying away into Babylon unto Christ are fourteen generations" (Matthew 1:17). W. D. Davies and Dale Allison summarize Matthew's message here as follows: "That the second major break point in Matthew's genealogy is the Babylonian captivity gives us a clue to the evangelist's [theology]. . . . Is not the reader to infer that the kingdom that was inaugurated with David and lost at the captivity is restored with the coming of Jesus, the Davidic Messiah?"[63] The implied answer is yes! Matthew presents Jesus as the new Davidic king.

For Ahaz, Immanuel was a sign of God's promise that he (Ahaz) would not be overthrown and that Davidic rule would not end with him. For Matthew, Immanuel is the sign of a new Davidic rule, one that more fully satisfies God's promise to Ahaz and to King David. When Matthew quotes Isaiah 7:14, he draws attention to the name Immanuel by providing its interpretation: "They shall call his name Emmanuel, which being interpreted is, God with us" (1:23).[64] For Matthew, Jesus is not just another Davidic king who will rule until he is conquered or dies. He is *the* Davidic king. And, as "God with us," the only one who could fully satisfy the promise made to David: "Thine house and thy kingdom shall be established for ever before thee: thy throne shall be established for ever" (2 Samuel 7:16). Matthew demonstrates the eternality of Jesus's Davidic reign by concluding his Gospel the same way he began it. The first fulfillment passage in Matthew's Gospel declares that Jesus, at his birth, is "God with us" (Matthew 1:23).[65] In the final words of Matthew's Gospel,

Jesus himself, now resurrected, reiterates that promise: "I am with you alway, even unto the end of the world. Amen" (Matthew 28:20).[66]

Conclusion

Certainly Matthew chose to include Isaiah 7:14 because of details within that passage that paralleled his account of Jesus's life. Could there be a better description of Jesus's miraculous birth than "a virgin shall be with child" (from the Greek translation of Isaiah)? And a child "conceived . . . of the Holy Ghost" (Matthew 1:20) is aptly described by the title "God is with us." Yet given what we have seen about the context of Isaiah 7:14, its history of interpretation, and the range of meanings in the word *fulfill,* Matthew likely had other reasons for including this scripture. Unlike certain Book of Mormon authors, Matthew never claims that he is writing for our day.[67] Matthew was writing for his day. He was writing to a particular audience, one whom he expected to be familiar with Isaiah but not necessarily with all the details of Jesus's life.[68] So Matthew relies on familiar stories and prophecies from the Old Testament in order to teach about Jesus's divine purpose.

I have suggested that the relationship between Isaiah's Immanuel prophecy and its fulfillment in the Gospel of Matthew is not as straightforward as is sometimes assumed. Rather than read Isaiah 7:14 as a prediction that refers directly and only to Jesus's birth, I have argued that the prophecy was originally understood to refer to a Davidic heir in Isaiah's time, perhaps Hezekiah. I have shown that Matthew was likely familiar with the larger literary context of Isaiah 7:14 and its emphasis on Davidic kingship. Matthew, who elsewhere writes that Jesus is the fulfillment of all the law and the prophets (Matthew 5:17), adopts this important prophecy from Isaiah to show that something greater than the past Davidic kings is here (see Matthew 12:42). Isaiah's promise to Ahaz originally referred to a child born in the king's court whose maturation would be a sign of both the end of Ahaz's political troubles and the perpetuation of King David's house. Yet, as Matthew testifies, Jesus fulfills the prophecy of Isaiah 7:14 because he is *the* Davidic King and the fullness of "God with us."

Notes

1. Harry Anderson, *Isaiah Writes of Christ's Birth (The Prophet Isaiah Foretells Christ's Birth)*, https://www.lds.org/media-library/images/prophet-isaiah-foretells-christs-birth-39469.
2. For more on the Harry Anderson paintings commissioned by the LDS Church, see Robert T. Barrett and Susan Easton Black, "Setting a Standard in LDS Art: Four Illustrators of the Mid-Twentieth Century," *BYU Studies* 44, no. 2 (2005): 42–57.
3. I will refer to the author of the Gospel of Matthew as Matthew for convenience. The Gospel of Matthew is formally anonymous, and questions remain about the author and his or her audience; see note 68 of this chapter.
4. All quotations of the Bible are from the Latter-day Saint edition of the King James Version unless otherwise indicated.
5. Nephi says that Isaiah saw the "Redeemer, even as [he had] seen him" (2 Nephi 11:2). Yet that does not mean that Isaiah had the same experience that Nephi describes in 1 Nephi 11:13–22. In fact, Isaiah describes his vision of "the Lord" (Yahweh or Jehovah) in Isaiah 6 (compare 2 Nephi 16).
6. In doing so, we heed the counsel of Nephi that Isaiah's words are easier to understand with knowledge of his own cultural, religious, and geographical contexts (2 Nephi 25:5–7). If we begin with Matthew, we might assume that everything in Isaiah is a direct prophecy about the life of Jesus. This can make it difficult to understand Isaiah's message. For a discussion of this challenge, see Joseph M. Spencer, *The Vision of All: Twenty-five Lectures on Isaiah in Nephi's Record* (Salt Lake City: Greg Kofford Books, 2016), 33–34.
7. Not much is known about the life of Isaiah. It is clear that he had direct access to members of the royal court, so it is likely that he was a member

of Jerusalem's upper class. On the life of Isaiah, see Robert R. Wilson, *Prophecy and Society in Ancient Israel* (Philadelphia: Fortress Press, 1980), 271. For an LDS discussion of Isaiah's life, see Victor L. Ludlow, *Isaiah: Prophet, Seer, and Poet* (Salt Lake City: Deseret Book, 1982), 1–3.

8. According to 1 Kings 11–12, the division resulted from the stubbornness of Rehoboam, Solomon's son, who would not concede to the needs of the oppressed northern tribes.
9. On the history of the divided kingdom, see Siegfried H. Horn and P. Kyle McCarter Jr., "The Divided Monarchy: The Kingdoms of Judah and Israel" in *Ancient Israel: From Abraham to the Roman Destruction of the Temple*, ed. Hershel Shanks, 3rd ed. (Washington, DC: Biblical Archaeology Society, 2011), 129–207.
10. Translation from James B. Pritchard, ed., *The Ancient Near East: An Anthology of Texts and Pictures* (Princeton: Princeton University Press, 2011), 264; adapted, transliterations excluded.
11. As Horn and McCarter have noted, "Most historians came to agree that Damascus and Israel launched the Syro-Ephraimite war . . . to intimidate Ahaz, so that he would renounce his policy of neutrality and join the anti-Assyrian cause. Nevertheless, there is now wide agreement that the initial motivation of Rezin and Pekah was probably more commercial than conspiratorial" (Horn and McCarter, "The Divided Monarchy," 172).
12. They may have attacked surrounding cities as well (see 2 Chronicles 28:5–7). See also note 10 above.
13. For an alternate account, see 2 Chronicles 28.
14. It is not clear whether Isaiah's statement about "sixty-five years" was intended to refer to a specific event. Blenkinsopp says, "['Sixty-five years'] gives us a date (669) long after the collapse of the Northern Kingdom (722). It coincides with the death of Esarhaddon and the accession of Ashurbanipal, who may have carried out further deportations subsequent to rebellion in the western provinces (Ezra 4:2, 9–10)." Joseph Blenkinsopp, *Isaiah 1–39: A New Translation with Introduction and Commentary*, Anchor Bible Commentary 19 (New York: Doubleday, 2000), 229, note g.

15. See David E. Aune, *Prophecy in Early Christianity and the Ancient Mediterranean World* (Grand Rapids, MI: Eerdmans, 1983), 100–101. For an introduction to this subject that was written for a popular LDS audience, see Donald W. Parry, "Symbolic Action as Prophecy in the Old Testament" in *Sperry Symposium Classics: The Old Testament*, ed. Paul Y. Hoskisson (Provo, UT: Religious Studies Center; Salt Lake City: Deseret Book, 2005), 337–55.
16. Blenkinsopp, *Isaiah 1–39*, 231; see also LDS edition Isaiah 7:3, footnote a.
17. See Blenkinsopp, *Isaiah 1–39*, 231; J. J. M. Roberts, *First Isaiah: A Commentary*, Hermeneia (Minneapolis: Fortress Press, 2015), 109–10.
18. See Blenkinsopp, *Isaiah 1–39*, 232–34; see also LDS edition Isaiah 7:14, footnote e. On the significance of the name in context, see also Roberts, *First Isaiah*, 119–20, 134.
19. See Blenkinsopp, *Isaiah 1–39*, 238, and Roberts, *First Isaiah*, 129. See also LDS edition Isaiah 8:1, footnote d.
20. Blenkinsopp, *Isaiah 1–39*, 237–38; Roberts, *First Isaiah*, 129–30.
21. For an introduction to the Septuagint, the ancient Greek translation of the Old Testament, that addresses its origin as well as its importance for the New Testament authors, see Timothy Michael Law, *When God Spoke Greek: The Septuagint and the Making of the Christian Bible* (Oxford: Oxford University Press, 2013).
22. The most common Hebrew word for *virgin* is *betûlâ* (בְּתוּלָה), not *ʿalmâ* (עַלְמָה).
23. John D. W. Watts, *Isaiah 1–33*, Word Biblical Commentary 24 (Waco, TX: Word Books, 1985), 99.
24. Ronald L. Troxel, "Isaiah 7,14–16 through the Eyes of the Septuagint," *Ephemerides Theologicae Lovanienses* 79 (2003): 14–16; for example, in the Greek version of Isaiah 23:4, "young women" (παρθένους) appears in a poetic parallel structure with "young men" (νεανίσκους).
25. This may sound strange to anyone who is more familiar with Matthew's Gospel than with the book of Isaiah. Yet it need not detract from Matthew's testimony about the miraculous nature of Jesus's birth from the virgin (*parthenos*), Mary. It does, however, suggest that the birth of the Immanuel

in Isaiah's time was not miraculous. See the section of this chapter that discusses Matthew. For direct prophecy about Mary, see 1 Nephi 11:13–23 and Mosiah 3:8.

26. The complete sign encompasses Isaiah 7:13–17 (perhaps 7:13–25), but Immanuel's mother and his birth are mentioned in only half a sentence in 7:14. Likewise, regarding the ancient Greek translation, Troxel notes: "It is clear that the translator's concern was not with the character of the child's mother, but with that of the child." Troxel, "Isaiah 7,14–16," 22.
27. Although the KJV renders the Hebrew *hʿalmâ* as "*a* virgin," omitting the definite article (compare 2 Nephi 17:14), a number of important modern translations (for example, NRSV, NIV, JPS) include the article: "*the* virgin." For more on this, see Raymond E. Brown, *The Birth of the Messiah: A Commentary on the Infancy Narratives in Matthew and Luke*, 2nd ed. (Garden City, NY: Doubleday, 1993), 147–48.
28. As Blenkinsopp notes, "Scholarly debate on the designation of the woman and the name of the child practically defies documentation." *Isaiah 1–39*, 233.
29. See Watts, *Isaiah 1–33*, 101–2.
30. For more on this, see Blenkinsopp, *Isaiah 1–39*, 234.
31. Some have argued that the parallels between Isaiah 7 and 8 suggest that the child in Isaiah 7 is that same child mentioned in Isaiah 8—that is, Isaiah's son; see note 38 of this chapter.
32. Blenkinsopp refers to Isaiah 8:8, 10 as "a fairly transparent allusion to Hezekiah"; see Blenkinsopp, *Isaiah 1–39*, 234.
33. Assyrian Sennacherib Prism (Taylor Prism), trans. M. Cogan, in *The Raging Torrent: Historical Inscriptions from Assyria and Babylonia Relating to Ancient Israel* (Jerusalem: Carta, 2008), 112–15, as adapted by Michael D. Coogan, in *The Old Testament: A Historical and Literary Introduction to the Hebrew Scriptures*, 3rd ed. (New York: Oxford University Press, 2014), 340.
34. See references in note 38 of this chapter.
35. The author of 2 Chronicles used 2 Kings as a source for his writing; see Coogan, *The Old Testament*, 445.
36. See 2 Chronicles 28:1 and 29:1.

37. For instance, if the passages cited (2 Kings 16:2 and 18:2) are correct, then Ahaz fathered Hezekiah when he was only ten years old. For more on chronological problems with the reign of King Ahaz, including discrepancies between the Biblical accounts and the Assyrian record, see Watts, *Isaiah 1–33*, 86; and T. R. Hobbs, *2 Kings*, Word Biblical Commentary 13 (Waco, TX: Word Books, 1985), 204–5, 212. Ultimately, as Joseph Blenkinsopp has argued, "[A] conclusion cannot be reached on chronological grounds alone either permitting or excluding identification of Immanuel with Hezekiah." Blenkinsopp, *Isaiah 1–39*, 234.
38. This interpretation began in the Middle Ages with Rabbi Ibn Ezra and Rashi; see Blenkinsopp, *Isaiah 1–39*, 233. It has been accepted by some modern scholars; for example, Coogan, *The Old Testament*, 339; and Roberts, *First Isaiah*, 119–20. Some evangelical scholars have argued for Immanuel as Isaiah's son in order to suggest that the prophecy was only partially fulfilled in Isaiah's time. For instance, John Oswalt argues, "One significance of this equation [Immanuel with Isaiah's son] is that it clearly means that if the ultimate meaning of the Immanuel sign is that God will be with us in and through a son of David . . . , then the fulfillment in Ahaz' own time was not the ultimate one [since Isaiah's son was not a son of David]." John N. Oswalt, *The Holy One of Israel: Studies in the Book of Isaiah* (Cambridge: James Clarke, 2014), 131. Many LDS authors have also suggested that Immanuel referred in part to Isaiah's son: see Ludlow, *Isaiah*, 143; Keith A. Meservy, "God Is with Us (Isaiah 1–17)," in *Studies in Scripture*, vol. 4: *1 Kings to Malachi*, ed. Kent P. Jackson (Salt Lake City: Deseret Book, 1993), 95–98; Donald W. Parry, Jay A. Parry, and Tina M. Peterson, *Understanding Isaiah* (Salt Lake City: Deseret Book, 1998), 73; Elder Jeffrey R. Holland, "'More Fully Persuaded': Isaiah's Witness of Christ's Ministry," in *Isaiah in the Book of Mormon*, ed. Donald W. Parry and John W. Welch (Provo, UT: FARMS, 1998), 6; and Kent P. Jackson, "Foretelling the Coming of Jesus" in *The Life and Teachings of Jesus Christ*, vol. 1: *From Bethlehem through the Sermon on the Mount*, eds. Richard Neitzel Holzapfel and Thomas A. Wayment (Salt Lake City: Deseret Book, 2005), 13–14.

39. Brown, *Birth of the Messiah,* 148. Roberts has to argue that Shear-jashub is no older than three or four in order to suggest that "Isaiah's wife could still have been in her teens" and therefore technically still a "young woman" (*'almâ*); see Roberts, *First Isaiah,* 119.
40. See note 38 in this chapter.
41. Justin Martyr, a Christian writing c. AD 147, quotes his Jewish interlocutor, Trypho, refuting his (Justin's) interpretation of Isaiah 7:14, saying: "The quotation is not, *Behold a virgin shall conceive and bear a son,* but *Behold a young woman shall conceive and bear a son,* and so forth, as you quoted it. Furthermore, the prophecy as a whole refers to Hezekiah, and it can be shown that the events described in the prophecy were fulfilled in him." Justin Martyr, *Dialogue with Trypho,* 67.1, see also 43.8, in *St. Justin Martyr: Dialogue with Trypho,* trans. Thomas B. Falls (Washington, DC: Catholic University of America Press, 2003). That this was a common Jewish interpretation seems to be corroborated by *Midrash Exodus Rabbah* 18.5 and *Midrash Numbers Rabbah* 14.2.
42. Fulfillment passages include Matthew 1:22–23; 2:5–6, 15, 17–18, 23; 3:3; 4:14–16; 8:17; 12:17–21; 13:14–15, 35; 21:4–5; 26:56; 27:9–10; see also 26:54.
43. C. F. D. Moule, "Fulfilment-Words in the New Testament: Use and Abuse," *New Testament Studies* 14, no. 3 (April 1968): 293–320; here 293–94, 297–99. The word translated as "fulfilled," the Greek *plēroō* (πληρόω), has other meanings. You can get a sense of the range of meanings by looking at how this word is translated in other contexts. It can mean "to fill (something)," for instance, a net can be full (*plēroō*) of fish (Matthew 13:48), a sound or a scent can fill (*plēroō*) a space (John 12:3, Acts 2:2), or a person can be full (*plēroō*) of joy (John 3:29, 15:11, 16:24). It can also mean "to finish" or "to accomplish" something, such as Jesus "ended [*plēroō*] all his sayings" (Luke 7:1), heavenly messengers speak about what Jesus will "accomplish [*plēroō*] at Jerusalem" (Luke 9:31). See also Matthew 5:17; the opposite of "destroy" is to "finish" or "complete."
44. One LDS scholar, Monte S. Nyman, has interpreted Isaiah 7:14 in this way based on two general conference talks, one by Hugh B. Brown

(Conference Report, October 1960, 93) and one by Mark E. Petersen (Conference Report, October 1965, 60); see Monte S. Nyman, *Great Are the Words of Isaiah: An Understandable Guide to Isaiah's Monumental Message* (Salt Lake City: Bookcraft, 1980), 56–57. For other LDS interpretations, see note 38 of this chapter.

45. On Isaiah 7:14 as a dual prophecy, see LDS authors cited in note 38 of this chapter. For a discussion of the problems with a dual-prophecy or multiple-fulfillment interpretation, see notes 47 and 49 of this chapter.
46. David L. Turner, *Matthew*, Baker Exegetical Commentary on the New Testament (Grand Rapids, MI: Baker Academic, 2008), 70–71. Turner argues that Matthew's interpretation is most likely typological.
47. The concept of multiple fulfillment is sometimes described as dual prophecy. The term *dual prophecy* seems to imply that the divine source of a revelation intended that the single prophecy would apply to two different historical situations. Since divine intent is beyond the reach of the historian's methodologies, scholars more often speak of "multiple fulfillment." Multiple fulfillment suggests that, with the perspective of hindsight, an author or reader might interpret a prophecy as fulfilled through two or more distinct historical events, regardless of original intent.
48. These writings that apply prophetic texts to their own community—called *pesharim* because they are often introduced with the Hebrew word for "interpretation" (*pesher*)—feature quotations and commentary on multiple passages from Isaiah and other prophetic texts. For a basic introduction to *pesharim*, see James VanderKam and Peter Flint, *The Meaning of the Dead Sea Scrolls: Their Significance for Understanding the Bible, Judaism, Jesus, and Christianity* (New York: HarperCollins, 2002), 303–6.
49. Arguments for multiple fulfillment do not solve this problem. As Turner notes, "The multiple-fulfillment view introduces an unwarranted distinction between what the prophet predicted and what God intended to reveal by the text. . . . Instead of this view, which posits an enigmatic double entendre and subsequent divine inspiration to recognize it, one does much better to assert a typological connection in which the biblical historical

events contain theological motifs that anticipate the Christ event when seen with Christian hindsight." Turner, *Matthew*, 71. Furthermore, the notion of multiple fulfillment or dual prophecy implies an equivalency between fulfillments, which Matthew would likely reject. For Matthew, the fulfillment in the time of Ahaz is not the same as the fulfillment in Jesus because Jesus is the fullness of God's word made manifest.

50. For Turner, the typological model is the most compelling; see Turner, *Matthew*, 70–71. Latter-day Saints sometimes refer to this kind of interpretation as "likening," based on the injunction in 1 Nephi 19:23–24 that we "liken all scriptures unto us, that it might be for our profit and learning."
51. Moule, "Fulfilment-Words in the New Testament," 298–99.
52. Turner, *Matthew*, 70.
53. For instance, Brigham Young University professor Kent Jackson says, "In some instances, the New Testament writers or speakers stated that the Old Testament words were fulfilled in New Testament events, even when a connection may not seem apparent, or even possible, to modern readers." Jackson, "Foretelling the Coming of Jesus," 12–13. Jackson's first example is Isaiah 7:14.
54. For example, see S. Vernon McCasland, "Matthew Twists the Scriptures," *Journal of Biblical Literature* 80, no.2 (June 1961): 143–48. For a summary and rebuttal of such arguments, see Richard B. Hays, *Echoes of Scripture in the Gospels* (Waco, TX: Baylor University Press, 2016), 108.
55. See Hays, *Echoes of Scripture in the Gospels*, 109–39; Brown, *Birth of the Messiah*, 111–16.
56. Hays, *Echoes of Scripture in the Gospels*, 113–14.
57. On intertextuality, see Nicholas Frederick's chapter in this volume.
58. In the KJV of Matthew, their names are written as Achaz and Ezekias (Matthew 1:9).
59. The emphasis on the number fourteen may itself refer to King David. See the discussion on gematria in W. D. Davies and Dale C. Allison Jr., *A Critical and Exegetical Commentary on The Gospel According to Saint Matthew: Introduction and Commentary on Matthew I–VII* (Edinburgh: T&T Clark, 1988), 163–65.

60. For a discussion of Herod's genealogy, see Peter Richardson, "Herod (Family)," in *Eerdmans Dictionary of the Bible*, ed. David Noel Freedman (Grand Rapids, MI: Eerdmans, 2000), 579–80. In Matthew 2:1–3, notice how "Herod the king" and "all Jerusalem" respond to the wise men when they ask, "Where is he that is born *King* of the Jews?" (emphasis added): "He was troubled, and all Jerusalem with him."
61. See Ezra 2–5; Haggai 1–2; Zechariah 4; and Josephus, *Antiquities of the Jews*, 11.33–78.
62. This was contrary to the hopes of Haggai 2:23 and Zechariah 4:6–10.
63. Davies and Allison, *The Gospel According to Saint Matthew*, 180.
64. David D. Kupp argues, "The added editorial explanation . . . in 1.23 brings into even sharper focus the quotation's anticipation that Jesus will be called 'God with us.'" David D. Kupp, *Matthew's Emmanuel: Divine Presence and God's People in the First Gospel* (Cambridge: Cambridge University Press, 2005), 163. By contrast, notice that Matthew does not provide an interpretation of "Jesus," but assumes that his audience understands its significance: "For he shall save his people from their sins" (Matthew 1:21). The name Jesus (a transliteration from Greek) and its equivalent Joshua (transliterated from Hebrew) means "Yahweh [or Jehovah] is Salvation"; see Davies and Allison, *The Gospel According to Matthew*, 210.
65. It is not clear from this passage alone, how Matthew would have understood the title "God with us" in regard to Jesus's nature (his humanity or divinity or both). Hays understands the title as a declaration of Jesus as "the one in whom God will be palpably present to his people"; see Hays, *Echoes of Scripture in the Gospels*, 163. Yet there are other possible interpretations; see Kupp, *Matthew's Emmanuel*, 169–75; and Davies and Allison, *The Gospel According to Matthew*, 217–18.
66. Kupp argues that this motif appears at significant points throughout the Gospel: "This motif in 1.21–3 opens a major inclusio of Emmanuel presence which will close, but not end, with Jesus' final promise in 28.20, and will arise in the story at crucial points (e.g., 8.23–7; 10.41–2; 12.6; 14.22–33; 17.17; 18.20; 25.31–46; 26.29)." Kupp, *Matthew's Emmanuel*, 175.

67. On Book of Mormon authors writing for our day, see Mormon 8:34–35. For a study on the Book of Mormon narrators' sense of audience, see Grant Hardy, *Understanding the Book of Mormon: A Reader's Guide* (Oxford: Oxford University Press, 2010).
68. For more on the anonymous author of the Gospel of Matthew and his or her intended audience, see Brown, *Birth of the Messiah*, 45–48. For a more detailed analysis of authorship and audience, see Davies and Allison, *The Gospel According to Matthew*, 7–58, 138–47.

6

The Use of the Old Testament in the New Testament Gospels

Nicholas J. Frederick

Nicholas J. Frederick is an assistant professor of ancient scripture at Brigham Young University.

The study of the relationship between different texts is commonly referred to as *intertextuality*. The concept behind intertextuality is that texts can communicate meaning through the adoption and adaption by one text of words, images, and phrases that refer explicitly or implicitly to another text. Thus intertextuality can be viewed as "the literal presence (more or less literal, whether integral or not) of one text within another."[1] French theorist Julia Kristeva famously stated that every text is a "mosaic of quotations," whether that text is nonfiction, fantasy, or, in the case of the Bible, scripture.[2] Biblical scholar James A. Sanders, building on Kristeva's ideas, provides a useful definition of intertextuality that has a more direct bearing on biblical studies. According to Sanders, intertextuality is the "recognition that all literature is made up of previous literature and reflects the earlier, through citation, allusion, use of phrases and paraphrases of older literature to create newer references to earlier literary episodes, even echoes of earlier familiar literature in the construction of the later." Sanders adds that "recognition that the reader is also a text and that reading is in essence an encounter between texts. The reader is a bundle of hermeneutics, as it were, engaging a text that is itself a bundle of hermeneutics."[3]

Biblical scholars have long been aware of the textual connections between the Old and the New Testament.[4] Early Christian writers living during the first century AD relied upon the language and stories of the Old Testament as they began to conceptualize the radical changes made to their religious conceptions by Jesus, in particular, the paradoxical nature of Jesus's death.[5] Could true salvation, they asked, really spring from the crucifixion?[6] Sorting through this question and others like it forced writers like Matthew, Mark, Luke, and John to search Israel's textual history and traditions for answers. As one scholar has written, "Christian faith has its beginnings in an experience of profound contradictoriness, an experience which so questioned the religious categories of its time that the resulting reorganization of religious language was a centuries-long task."[7] The result of this "reorganization of religious language" was a tendency toward what Richard B. Hays has termed "retrospective reinterpretation," meaning that the Gospel writers essentially began to read their scripture "backwards" through the lens of "new revelatory events."[8] The writings produced were more than just history; they represented God's close interaction with and the inspiration he delivered to his covenant people. The authors of Christian texts saw themselves as part of God's ongoing interaction with humanity, and thus found contemporary application in the archaic works of the Hebrew prophets and scribes. As a result of this, as New Testament writers composed their texts, they often integrated quotations and allusions to the Old Testament throughout their own writings, linking God's work in the present with his work in the past. The recent decades have seen a bourgeoning of attention paid to exploring these intertextual links more closely, due primarily to the work of Hays and Gregory K. Beale, among others.[9]

The purpose of this chapter is to provide for Latter-day Saints a brief examination of some of the ways that the New Testament, specifically the four Gospels, appropriated the language of the Hebrew Bible.[10] This paper will proceed as follows. Each of the four Gospels will be examined individually, first looking briefly at how each evangelist generally integrates the Old Testament into his own text, followed by a closer examination of three specific passages. A summary statement of what can be said about each Gospel writer's approach to the Old Testament based upon those three readings will then follow. The paper will then conclude with a few general observations. It is hoped that by the end of the paper the reader will have a basic understanding of how each Gospel writer has adopted and adapted the text of the Old Testament into the New Testament.[11]

Matthew

Of all the Gospel writers, Matthew's use of the Hebrew Bible is the most extensive. His Gospel contains approximately 124 quotations and allusions, the highest total among the Evangelists.[12] This heavy reliance upon Old Testament language informs readers that one of Matthew's primary interests is "the kingdom as the fulfillment of the OT (Old Testament) expectation."[13] This "OT expectation" can be seen quite early on in the Gospel. In his first two chapters, Matthew includes a series of vignettes describing the birth and early years of Jesus's mortal life, centered upon five quotations from the Old Testament that Matthew feels are explicitly fulfilled in the birth of the Messiah, even if the original authors had different ideas.[14] Matthew continues to return to this theme of prophetic fulfillment throughout Jesus's ministry.[15] This section will briefly examine three of Matthew's fulfillment prophecies, and then conclude with a short discussion of how readers might make sense of Matthew's interpretative moves.

Isaiah 7:14–16/Matthew 1:22–23

When Gabriel appears to Joseph, he tells Joseph that he is to name his son Jesus, "for he shall save his people from their sins" (Matthew 1:21). Matthew then tells his readers that this was done so that

> It might be fulfilled which was spoken of the Lord by the prophet, saying, Behold, a virgin shall be with child, and shall bring forth a son, and they shall call his name Emmanuel, which being interpreted is, God with us. (Matthew 1:22–23)

Gabriel is here quoting from Isaiah 7:14:

> Therefore the Lord himself shall give you a sign; Behold, a virgin shall conceive, and bear a son, And shall call his name Immanuel. (Isaiah 7:14)

The contemporary context of Isaiah's prophecy was the reign of Ahaz, king of Judah, and the Syro-Ephraimite war (734 BC). Two enemy kings in particular, Rezin of Syria and Pekah of Israel, troubled the kingdom of Judah. Both kings wanted Ahaz to join their coalition against Assyria. Isaiah had approached Ahaz, king of Judah, and asked him to ask the Lord for a sign affirming that Jehovah will destroy the enemies of Ahaz, thus confirming the instruction not to join their coalition. Ahaz declined to ask for a sign, but Isaiah gives him one anyway:

> Behold, a virgin shall conceive, and bear a son, and shall call his name Immanuel. Butter and honey shall he eat, that he may know to refuse the evil, and choose the good. For

> before the child shall know to refuse the evil, and choose the good, the land that thou abhorrest shall be forsaken of both her kings. (Isaiah 7:14–16)

Based upon the events of the next chapter (Isaiah 8), the "son" Isaiah is referring to is perhaps his own son, Maher-Shalal-Hash-Baz, and Isaiah's wife, the "prophetess," is the "virgin." On the other hand, perhaps the birth of Hezekiah fulfilled this prophecy.[16] The immediate fulfillment of this prophecy remains a riddle. The primary purpose of the prophecy, however, was to inform Ahaz that by the time this "son" has learned to choose between good and evil, both Rezin and Pekah will be dead the and the present crisis no longer relevant.[17]

Hosea 11:1/Matthew 2:15

A second, similar "prophecy" involves the flight of Joseph, Mary, and the young Jesus to Egypt in order to escape Herod's sword. When Joseph and Mary eventually return from Egypt with Jesus, Matthew interprets this return as the fulfillment of Old Testament prophecy:

> And was there until the death of Herod: that it might be fulfilled which was spoken of the Lord by the prophet, saying, Out of Egypt have I called my son. (Matthew 2:15)

The prophecy in question is Hosea 11:1:

> When Israel was a child, then I loved him, and called my son out of Egypt. (Hosea 11:1)

The immediate context of Hosea 11:1 is the relationship between Jehovah and Israel.

Jehovah, as Father, is reminding Israel, his "Son," that he has always loved them, and proof of this love can be found in the origins of Israel, the divine exodus of Israel from Egypt.[18] Unfortunately, as the next verse indicates, Israel rebelled and abandoned Jehovah in favor of idols. However, the important difference between this passage and the Isaiah passage discussed above is that where Isaiah was delivering a prophecy about the *future*, Hosea was referring to an event in Israel's distant *past*.[19] Hosea's explicit connections with Israel's past, however, does not preclude him from speaking prophetically and implicitly foreshadowing the future flight of Jesus to Egypt.[20] Nor does it preclude Matthew from using Hosea's words to speak about Jesus.

Zechariah 9:9/Matthew 21:5

Matthew 21:5 presents readers with one of Matthew's more enigmatic Old Testament quotations. Here Jesus, in preparation for the triumphal entry into Jerusalem, instructs his disciples to "go into the village over against you, and straightway ye shall find an ass tied, and a colt with her: loose them, and bring them unto me" (Matthew 21:2).[21] Matthew writes that the acquisition of the animals fulfills the prophecy given by Zechariah: "Rejoice greatly, O daughter of Zion; shout, O daughter of Jerusalem: behold, thy King cometh unto thee: he is just, and having salvation; lowly, and riding upon an ass, and upon a colt the foal of an ass" (Zechariah 9:9). The original context of the Zechariah passage is the eschatological arrival of a triumphant king, one who finds favor with Jehovah and one whose humility is underscored by the mode of his arrival. A triumphant king may be expected to arrive on the back of a stallion, but this one arrives riding upon a donkey. What is noteworthy here is that Jesus is the one who initiates the fulfillment of the prophecy. He is the one who requests that the animals be brought, and he is the one who willingly rides into Jerusalem in a deliberate manner.[22] To those awaiting his arrival, the implications of Jesus's provocative actions were clear: their King, the triumphant Son of David, has arrived, but in a fashion that would give pause to those viewing his entry into Jerusalem as the first movement toward an insurrection.[23]

For modern readers, it can be difficult to understand how to interpret Matthew's use of Old Testament prophecy.[24] The prophecy from Zechariah 9:9 is perhaps the easiest to unfold, as it appears to serve partially as *predictive* prophecy, a mode of prophecy that anticipates an event occurring in the future, in this case Jesus's arrival in Jerusalem, without a fulfillment contemporary to the actual pronouncement. But what of Isaiah 7:14, which explicitly refers to events in the life of Isaiah, or Hosea 11:1, which speaks of a past event rather than a future one? How can Jesus be the "fulfillment" of these passages? In the Isaiah passage, readers could interpret Matthew's interpretive move as an example of *multiple fulfillment* prophecy, meaning that one prophecy can have a partial fulfillment in the time in which it is given, and a further fulfillment at a later time. The future fulfillment, however, should not be taken as more "correct" or important than the original. As for the Hosea passage, Matthew's interpretation can be seen as an example of *typological* prophecy, meaning that Matthew sees in the life of Jesus "the fullest expression of a significant pattern of events" that occur and reoccur throughout the biblical narrative.[25] Understood typologically, Matthew understands Jesus retracing "in his own life the foundational experience of Israel in being called by God out of Egypt."[26] The presence of fulfillment prophecies in Matthew's Gospel reveal an author who is a careful reader of Israel's scripture and one who sees Jesus's life and ministry as a, if not *the*, crucial focal point of Old Testament prophecy and the culmination of Israel's history.

Mark

The use of the Old Testament in Mark's Gospel differs from Matthew in two significant ways. First, Mark contains only approximately seventy quotations and allusions, as opposed to Matthew's 124 (although Mark's Gospel is admittedly shorter).[27] Second, as discussed above,

Matthew used the Old Testament to frame his messsage that Jesus's ministry represented the fulfillment of prophecy—Jesus's life, ministry, and death represented the culmination of Israel's history. Mark, however, does not use Old Testament quotations to further his narrative. With the exception of one quotation that we will examine below (Mark 1:2–3), every Old Testament quotation in Mark's gospel comes from words spoken by Jesus. Mark seems much less interested in interpreting Jesus's ministry in light of scripture or prophetic fulfillment. Rather, one of his primary concerns is to employ Old Testament scripture in a way that demonstrates clearly that Jesus is the divine son of God.[28]

Mark 1:2–3/Isaiah 40:3; Malachi 3:1; Exodus 23:20

Mark 1:2–3 is notable for two important reasons. First, as mentioned above, Mark 1:2-3 represents the only place in Mark's Gospel where Mark quotes from the Old Testament in a narrative fashion rather than having the quotation spoken by Jesus. Second, although Mark claims that he is quoting from Isaiah, Mark 1:2-3 is actually a composite quotation drawn from three separate texts.[29]

Here is Mark's quotation:

> As it is written in the prophets, <u>Behold, I send my messenger before thy face</u>, *which shall prepare thy way before thee.* **The voice of one crying in the wilderness, Prepare ye the way of the Lord, make his paths straight.** (Mark 1:2–3)

Now compare Mark's words to these verses:[30]

> <u>Behold, I send an Angel</u> <u>before thee</u>, to keep thee in the way, and to bring thee into the place which I have prepared. (Exodus 23:20)
>
> Behold, I will send my messenger, and he *shall prepare the way before me*: and the Lord, whom ye seek, shall suddenly come to his temple, even the messenger of the covenant,

Terminology here is key. "Christ" is the English rendering of the Hebrew/Aramaic title "Messiah," or "anointed one," a title that generally referred to prophets, priests, and kings but by the time of Jesus had become associated by some Jews with a national liberator.[36] The first "Lord" is the Hebrew title Jehovah (Yahweh), and the second "Lord" is the Hebrew term *Adonai*. Both are rendered in the Greek of Psalm 110:1 and Mark's Gospel as *Kyrios*. In the original context of Psalm 110, the setting was likely a coronation, where the "LORD" (God) inducts the "Lord" (King) as his co-ruler and invites him to sit as his right hand.[37] By the time of Jesus, however, the Psalm appears to have taken on a different meaning, where "LORD" still refers to Jehovah but "Lord" now refers to the Messiah. Jesus's question thus goes something like this: "David said that Jehovah (the Lord) spoke to the Messiah (my Lord) and said 'Sit at my right hand.' How can the Messiah then be both David's Lord (as Psalm 110:1 claims) and also David's son (as his audience has come to believe)?" Because it would be silly to refer to a son as a Lord, the answer is simple: He cannot be both. While not rejecting the David lineage of the Messiah, Jesus appears to be suggesting that a re-evaluation of the connections between David and the Messiah is needed, and that the Messiah is better understood not as "Son of David" but as "Son of God."

Daniel 7:13–14/Mark 13:26

This re-evaluation of Jesus's divine identity reaches a further stage of development in Mark 13, the scene of Jesus's climactic eschatological discourse about the Temple. Midway through the discourse, Jesus describes a future time when "the sun will be darkened, and the moon will not give its light." Jesus relays that those alive during this time will

> see the Son of man coming in the clouds with great power and glory. And then shall he send his angels, and shall gather

> together his elect from the four winds, from the uttermost part of the earth to the uttermost part of heaven. (Mark 13:26–27)

Jesus's words are an allusion to Daniel 7:13:

> I saw in the night visions, and, behold, *one* like the Son of man came with the clouds of heaven, and came to the Ancient of days, and they brought him near before him. And there was given him dominion, and glory, and a kingdom, that all people, nations, and languages, should serve him: his dominion *is* an everlasting dominion, which shall not pass away, and his kingdom *that* which shall not be destroyed. (Daniel 7:13–14)

What is notable here is the title "Son of Man," which Jesus has applied to himself through the Gospel of Mark and has become his "distinctive self-designation."[38] Overall, the title Son of Man appears fourteen times in the Gospel of Mark.[39] Earlier in Mark, Jesus stated that the Son of Man "must undergo great suffering, and be rejected by the elders, the chief priests, and the scribes, and be killed, and after three days rise again" (Mark 8:31). Now, in Mark 13, this same "Son of Man" figure comes "with great power and glory."

The title "Son of Man" itself appears several times in the Old Testament, where it seems to be a literal translation of the Aramaic phrase *bar nasha.*' In Ezekiel, where it appears ninety-three times, the title seems to simply be another way of saying that someone is a "human being." Additionally, "Son of Man" may even have functioned as a circumlocution for "I."[40] Daniel's use of the title seems to refer possibly to a divine being who will arrive on Earth at a future point and establish an everlasting kingdom, or possibly to a ceremony where Jehovah, surrounded by his angels, enthrones the Son of Man as ruler over the Earth. The exact nature of Daniel's use of the title remains unclear to biblical scholars,[41] but it is likely that

Jesus adopted it for a specific reason and with a specific meaning in mind. Jesus's use, especially in Mark 13, leaves "no doubt that in his interpretation of Daniel's vision it is he himself who is to receive that ultimate authority."[42] The title Son of Man then becomes the perfect designation for one who is both conquered (put to death) and conqueror (overcame death).[43]

As we saw above, an important element of Matthew's use of Old Testament scripture, particularly writings from the prophets, was directed toward demonstrating Jesus's life and ministry as the fulfillment of prophecy. The scriptures and the events they described found a realization, if not *the* realization, in Jesus. An important element of Mark's use of the Old Testament is to demonstrate that Jesus Christ is more than a human prophet. Jesus is the representative of Jehovah, whose path must be prepared. He is more than the Son of David, a nationalistic figure who will lead to political liberation. He is the divine Son of Man whose majestic arrival will signal a new age in Israel's history. He is ultimately the Son of God.

Luke

Luke stands second to Matthew among the Gospel writers in his use of Old Testament quotations and allusions (109 vs. 124).[44] In contrast to Matthew, who saw Jesus and his ministry as the *culmination* or *climax* of the Old Testament period, Luke sees Jesus and his ministry as the *continuation* of the Old Testament period. In other words, Luke does not see the life and ministry of Jesus Christ strictly as the fulfillment of prophecy or as a new, separate age, but as the continuation of a story that has been unfolding since the creation and has as its central motif the ability and power of God to *save*. As one scholar writes, "Luke sees the Scripture fulfilled . . . in terms of the reintroduction and fulfillment of OT (Old Testament) patterns that point to the presence of God's saving work."[45] Not surprisingly, one of the major points of emphasis, in particular toward the beginning of Luke's Gospel, is God's extension of salvation to Israel through the Abrahamic covenant. While Luke explicitly mentions Abraham in Luke 1:55 and 73,[46] Lucan scholar Joel B. Green has noted that the infancy stories of Mary, Elisabeth, and Zacharias in Luke 1–2 contain about twenty-five allusions to the story of Abraham and Sarah in Genesis 11–21, including the barrenness of a woman (Genesis 11:30/Luke 1:7), a miraculous conception (Genesis 21:2/Luke 1:24), and God's favor being with the child (Genesis 21:20/Luke 2:40).[47] These allusions indicate that Luke "regards his opening chapters as though they were the continuation of the story rooted in the Abrahamic covenant," a theme that will continue throughout the Gospel.[48] This extension of a means of salvation beyond Judaism would have particularly resonated with Luke's (presumably) Gentile audience, who realize that the New Israel will include both Jews and Gentiles, the primary conditions for membership being faith in Jesus Christ and repentance for sins. With this in mind, this section will look at three Old Testament usages by Luke that bring the Abrahamic covenant and the continuation of Israel's story into focus.

Malachi 4:5–6/Luke 1:17

Luke 1:16–17 represents Gabriel's words to Zacharias while the latter was ministering in the Temple. Gabriel informs Zacharias that the mission of his son will involve the redemption of God's people:

> And many of the children of Israel shall he turn to the Lord their God. And he shall go before him in the spirit and power of Elias, to turn the hearts of the fathers to the children, and the disobedient to the wisdom of the just; to make ready a people prepared for the Lord. (Luke 1:16–17)

This statement is an allusion to Malachi:

> Behold, I will send you Elijah the prophet before the coming of the great and dreadful day of the Lord:
>
> And he shall turn the heart of the fathers to the children, and the heart of the children to their fathers, lest I come and smite the earth with a curse. (Malachi 4:5–6)

The context of Malachi 4:5–6 is an eventual eschatological reconciliation between God and his people, with Elijah, who performed a similar unification during the time of Ahab and Jezebel, leading the way. Malachi's prophecy ends ominously, with a warning predicting "the annihilation of the land of Judah with its people. . . . unless the Lord sends his messenger to change the hearts of his people."[49]

Gabriel's allusion to the Malachi prophecy contains a few noteworthy shifts. Many, but not all, of Israel will respond to Elijah's eschatological call. Gabriel also omits the phrase "And he shall turn the heart of the fathers to the children," from Malachi, but that may have simply been a way to accommodate the inclusion of the second phrase, "and the disobedient to the wisdom of the just."[50] Finally, Gabriel's declaration ends on a much happier note: the purpose of this eschatological call is to ready the righteous for God's imminent kingdom. Gabriel's point is that Zacharias's son, John the Baptist, will play the role of Elijah in preparing Israel for the new age.[51]

The key phrase here is one that is well known to Latter-day Saints, "And he shall turn the heart of the fathers to the children." Jesus quoted this verse when he visits the Nephites (3 Nephi 25), and Moroni quoted it (with a few changes) to Joseph Smith in 1823 (cf. D&C 2). Malachi's language hints specifically to the reconciliation and restoration of family relationships: "fathers and sons are reconciled to one another and neighbours to one another, and so together they seek God."[52] The ultimate expression of this "reconciliation" may be that of God the Father to his wayward children. Green argues: "God himself is presented as the Father who cares for his children and acts redemptively on their behalf, and human fathers can be characterized along similar lines."[53] What John the Baptist introduces, then, is a "renewal of family harmony," a reconciliation that may extend to all God's children, not only the Jews.[54] Based upon the abundance of Abrahamic material in the opening chapters of Luke (even Zacharias's subsequent response to Gabriel in the next verse echoes that of Abraham), Luke appears to have viewed the Christian era not as a "new" period of time but as the "next" period of time, one where the Gentiles receive their invitation into God's covenant, joining with those Jews who also respond to him to form his people "Israel."

Luke 20:17/Psalm 118:22

In Luke 20, Jesus delivers the "parable of the vineyard," in which the servants, or husbandmen, hired by the owner of a vineyard, reject all the messengers sent by the owner to check on their progress, even rejecting the son of the owner himself, whom they cast out and kill. The result of these actions, Jesus explains, is that the owner of the vineyard "shall come and destroy these husbandmen, and shall give the vineyard to others" (Luke 20:16). His audience, likely reacting in horror to such a violent end, cry out "God forbid." In order to help his audience understand the message behind the parable, Jesus makes the following statement:

> And he beheld them, and said, What is this then that is written, The stone which the builders rejected, the same is become the head of the corner? (Luke 20:17).

Jesus's answer contains a quotation from Psalm 118:22:

> The stone which the builders refused is become the head stone of the corner. (Psalm 118:22)

In context, Psalm 118 is a "thanksgiving liturgy related to entrance to the sanctuary," one that commemorates Jehovah's devotion and favor toward Israel.[55] The verse quoted by Jesus may have been a proverb expressing "transition from humiliation to honor, in which a generally discarded stone became the foundation stone stabilizing two adjacent walls."[56] The "stone" mentioned in 118:22 could then refer to a king or to Israel herself—she has long been rejected by the other nations of the world, but when God's plan of redemption is made apparent, the world will see that Israel plays a key role, the cornerstone of God's kingdom.[57]

Jesus takes this verse from Psalm 118 and its application to the parable of the vineyard and makes two key interpretive moves. First, He re-orients the original meaning of the cornerstone so that it now refers to him (cf. Luke 20:19): *he* is the son of the vineyard owner who has been "refused" by the Jews, and actions of the husbandmen in the parable serve, then, to foreshadow Jesus's own death at the hands of the Jews. However, in a remarkable reversal, this "discarded stone" will triumph and be vindicated, foreshadowing Jesus's resurrection.[58] Second, when Mark and Matthew give their accounts of the "parable of the vineyard," they include quotations from both Psalm 118:22 and 23:

> The stone which the builders refused is become the head stone of the corner. This is the Lord's doing; it is marvellous in our eyes. (Psalm 118:22–23)

Notably, Luke includes only 118:22 and avoids 118:23. The omission of "it is marvelous in our eyes," a phrase that encapsulates the optimism of this thanksgiving psalm, allows Luke to maintain an emphasis upon the stone:

> Whosoever shall fall upon that stone shall be broken; but on whomsoever it shall fall, it will grind him to powder. (Luke 20:18)

This statement, itself an allusion to Daniel 2:44–45 and Isaiah 8:14–15, serves to reinforce the great importance of the "stone." For Luke, it is Jesus who will be overlooked by the nations of the world, yet it is Jesus who is the cornerstone of God's new kingdom and his suffering and vindication of ultimate importance. Entrance into the new covenant must go through him—there is no other way. His words include a warning—those who wish to align themselves with God must distance themselves from the "tenants," who will soon face their own destruction.

Luke 23:29–30/Hosea 10:8

This warning to those who would reject Jesus and his Kingdom implicit in Luke 20:18 becomes explicit in Luke 23:29–32, a final plea from the lips of Jesus to the inhabitants of Jerusalem. While walking toward Calvary to be crucified, Jesus encounters a group of women who "bewailed and lamented him" (Luke 23:27). Jesus turns to them and says:

> Daughters of Jerusalem, weep not for me, but weep for yourselves, and for your children. For, behold, the days are coming, in the which they shall say, Blessed are the barren, and the wombs that never bare, and the paps which never gave suck. Then shall they begin to *say to the mountains, Fall on us; and to the hills, Cover us*. For if they do these things in a green tree, what shall be done in the dry? (Luke 23:28–31)

Jesus's statement contains an allusion to Hosea 10:8:

> The high places also of Aven, the sin of Israel, shall be destroyed: the thorn and the thistle shall come up on their altars; and *they shall say to the mountains, Cover us; and to the hills, Fall on us.* (Hosea 10:8)

In the context of Hosea, these words "constitute an oracle of judgment sealing the fate of Jerusalem."[59] Hosea prophesies about the fate of those who would substitute idolatrous practices for the worship of Jehovah: once Jehovah has exposed the idols as false, the guilt of Israel will be so great that they will lament for mountains to "cover us."[60] By quoting this passage from Hosea, Jesus informs those witnessing his suffering that, if they do not take this one last opportunity to repent, then they will also stand guilty before God. The covenant and the Kingdom stand open, but only if those listening hear his words and seek repentance. Otherwise, just as the idol-worshippers wished for death, so would those who now stand and watch their Redeemer march to the cross mourn after his crucifixion.[61] The result, Jesus declares, is that the state of affairs in Jerusalem will grow so catastrophic that it will be better for women to not give birth to children and bring them into such a desperate circumstance.[62] In a bitter touch of irony, Jesus hints that the mourners are right in their act of mourning but wrong in their mourning for him—it is they and their children who should be mourned.

Luke's story stresses that salvation, through a recapitulation of the story of Abraham, is available to all those who recognize that in Jesus lies a power to save that represents a continuation of the biblical narrative: "In Luke's telling, God's intent to reveal salvation to all flesh was part of Israel's plotted role from the beginning."[63] Luke's allusion to Malachi 4 demonstrated that harmonious family relationships will provide a central facet of the New Israel. Jesus's interpretation of Psalm 118 brought into sharp relief the necessity of faith in Jesus Christ and the intimation that the vanquished would quickly become the vanquisher. Finally, Jesus's quotation of Hosea 10 provided a stern warning to those who would resist the charge to repent of their sins and align themselves with him. Through his use of the Old Testament, Luke provides a beacon of light and hope to those who eagerly search for salvation, all the while reminding those who reject his covenant message in favor of another path that justice awaits.[64]

John

John's Gospel is a very different text than the Gospels of Matthew, Mark, or Luke. John's Gospel contains no parables, no Sermon on the Mount, and no infancy stories. John even shifts the chronology of such key events as the cleansing of the temple and the day of the crucifixion.[65] It is noteworthy that, compared with Matthew (124), Mark (70), and Luke (109), John contains only twenty-seven quotations and allusions. John does use some of the same Old Testament passages that the synoptic authors used, such as Isaiah 40:3 (John 1:23) and Zechariah 9:9 (John 12:15). However, John also includes several passages from the Old Testament that are not found in the other three gospels. Of the fifteen probable direct quotations in John's gospel drawn from the Old Testament, eleven are unique to John.[66]

One reason for John employing fewer quotations is that he "prefers to focus on the artistically selected instance that repays sustained meditation."[67] Like Matthew, John endeavors to portray Jesus's ministry as the fulfillment of prophecy, but John is not as interested in compiling quotations as evidence or proof. In additional to the few quotations he does include, John "relies upon evoking *images* and *figures* from Israel's Scripture."[68] In this way, he is able to portray Jesus as the premortal Son of God, the *logos* (word) who has existed from "the beginning" and through whom the Father speaks to his children.[69] John describes Jesus using images and symbols that are often drawn from the Old Testament—He is "In the Beginning" (John 1:1; cf. Genesis 1:1),[70] the "Good Shepherd" (John 10:11; cf. Jeremiah 23:1–4; 2 Samuel 5:2), the "Living Water"

(John 4:10; cf. Zechariah 14:8), and the "Bread of Life" (John 6:35; cf. Exodus 16:4). In this section, this paper will look at three uses of the Old Testament in John's Gospel: one that serves as an allusion to the Old Testament, and two quotations spoken by Jesus that highlight elements of his ministry.

John 1:51/Genesis 28:12

At the conclusion of the first chapter of John's Gospel, Jesus encounters a man named Nathanael, whom Jesus identifies as "an Israelite indeed, in whom is no guile" (John 1:47). Nathanael, impressed at Jesus's identification of someone he did not know, declares "Rabbi, thou art the Son of God; thou art the King of Israel" (John 1:49). Jesus, in response, promises Nathanael if he follows Jesus he will see far more impressive events than this:

> Verily, verily, I say unto you, Hereafter ye shall see heaven open, and the angels of God ascending and descending upon the Son of man. (John 1:51)

The noteworthy phrase here is "the angels of God ascending and descending upon the Son of man," an allusion to Genesis 28:12:[71]

> And he dreamed, and behold a ladder set up on the earth, and the top of it reached to heaven: and behold the angels of God ascending and descending on it. (Genesis 28:12)

Jacob has this dream in the midst of traveling to Haran. The purpose of Jacob's vision is largely to allow the Lord to reaffirm the covenant he had made with Abraham and Isaac (Genesis 28:13–15).[72] Jacob appears to view this encounter as occurring upon sacred space. He declares, "this is none other but the house of God, and this is the gate of heaven" (Genesis 28:17) and, fittingly, names the location of the dream "Beth-el" (House of God).[73]

On one level, we can see Jesus's words in John's gospel having a similar intent as they did in Genesis. Jesus is reaffirming that the Abrahamic covenant is still in effect for Abraham's descendants. On another level, this allusion says something fundamental about the nature of Jesus Christ himself. Notice that in Jacob's dream, the angels "ascended and descended" upon the ladder. One way of understanding Jacob's ladder is to view it as representing a link between Heaven and Earth.[74] However, in John's account, the angels are "ascending and descending" upon *Jesus*. He has become the ladder, the link uniting heaven and earth.[75] If any desire to travel to heaven, they can only arrive through the assistance of Jesus. After all, as Jesus states later in John, "I am the door: by me if any man enter in, he shall be saved, and shall go in and out, and find pasture" (John 10:9). Jesus, then, becomes the new Beth-el, the true "gate of heaven."[76]

John 10:34–35/Psalm 82:6

John's Gospel is notable for the many controversies that arise between Jesus and some members of his Jewish audience, often over his claims of divinity.[77] For example, one such encounter occurs when Jesus heals a lame man on the Sabbath, a miracle that almost becomes violent when the Jews "sought the more to kill him" (John 5:18). In John 10, Jesus again risks the wrath of the Jews when he makes the "blasphemous" claim that "I and *my* Father are one" (John 10:30). Once more, the Jews "took up stones again to stone him" (John 10:31). At this point, Jesus asks the Jews to explain for which of his "good works" they want to stone him. The Jews respond that it is not Jesus's good works, but his blasphemous statements that have led them to consider killing him, "because that thou, being a man, maketh thyself God" (John 10:33). In defense of his claims to divinity, Jesus asks:

> Is it not written in your law, I said, Ye are gods? If he called them gods, unto whom the word of God came, and the scripture cannot be broken. (John 10:34–35)

The scripture quoted here by Jesus comes from Psalm 82:6:

> I have said, Ye are gods; and all of you are children of the most High (Psalm 82:6).

In its original context, Psalm 82 is a likely a condemnation of those who rule unjustly in Israel.[78] The Psalm opens in the midst of a council or assembly convened by Jehovah and involving a group identified as "the gods."[79] The purpose of the assembly appears to be Jehovah's address of the unjust actions of those he had earlier appointed as judges. Because the power to rule is seen as belonging strictly to God, those to whom he grants power incur God's wrath when they fail in their commission.[80] The verse in question, Psalm 82:6, appears to be a reference to the moment when Jehovah elevated the "gods" to their position as judges. The subsequent verse records their punishment and condemnation: "But ye shall die like men, And fall like one of the princes" (Psalm 82:7).[81] These unjust rulers are thus not "Gods" in the sense that they are divine beings who are ontologically similar to Jehovah. Rather, they are "gods" in the sense that they are exercising authority granted unto them by God.[82]

This context is important for understanding why Jesus chooses to quote Psalm 82:6 at this point. His logic seems to be this: if the scriptures "cannot be broken," and if the scriptures contain references to beings other than Jehovah as "gods," then how can the Jews condemn him for "making himself God" when their own scriptures apply the title of "god" to beings other than Jehovah? Even more so, Jesus argues that he is simply the "Son of God," the implication being that if he could be justified in calling himself

"God," he is even more justified in calling himself "Son of God."[83] The irony, of course, lost on most of his audience is that Jesus actually is God made flesh, as John's prologue so carefully establishes (cf. John 1:1-3).

John 13:18/Psalm 41:9

The washing of the Apostles' feet provides the setting for the second quotation from the Gospel of John. Following the washing, Jesus encourages the Twelve to follow his example and seek humility. Then he makes the following statement:

> I speak not of you all: I know whom I have chosen: but that the scripture may be fulfilled, He that eateth bread with me hath lifted up his heel against me. (John 13:18)[84]

The quotation comes from Psalm 41:9:

> Yea, mine own familiar friend, in whom I trusted, which did eat of my bread, hath lifted up his heel against me. (Psalm 41:9)

Psalm 41 is a thanksgiving psalm about seeking relief from serious illness. The speaker, presumed to be David, bemoans the betrayal of someone he considered close enough to share his dinner, the betrayal of this hospitality being a particular black mark against the offender.[85] In the rabbinic tradition, the events referred to in this Psalm were believed to be the rebellion of Ahithophel (David's counselor and the grandfather of Bathsheba) and Absalom (David's son) against David, as recounted in 2 Samuel 15.[86]

The Gospel setting is filled with dramatic irony. The identity of the one who has "lifted up his heel against me" comes as no surprise to readers of the Gospel of John, as Judas's betrayal had been foreshadowed earlier in the narrative (cf. John 12:4–8). However, Judas's betrayal remains unknown at this point to the Apostles, who wonder aloud who this treacherous figure could be.

Even Jesus's handing the sop to Judas does not offer a full clarity of the situation to them. Additionally, the situation is clouded by the uncomfortable nature of what Jesus has asked them to do, namely sharing bread with him prior to "lifting up their heels," albeit to be washed by Jesus.[87] Not surprisingly, John's quotation presents readers with a difficult passage to unpack. However, Jesus's subsequent words in John 13:19–20 suggest that Jesus has a specific reason for making this quotation. Whereas in Matthew, where Old Testament quotations were largely employed to provide prophetic evidence of fulfillment to readers, Jesus's quotation of Psalm 41:9 in John appears to have been provided specifically for the benefit of the Apostles; that as they looked back after the events of the next few days, their confusion over Jesus's words and actions would crystalize into clarity and provide them with an additional witness of his divinity as they recognized the deeper meaning behind his words.

Conclusion

The Gospel writers present the life of Jesus as a tapestry. The framework is a singular view of time and history, while Israel's own text and traditions provide threads that are carefully woven together in a way that poignantly evokes the power of Jesus's life and death. The image that emerges over the course of the Gospels is the life and ministry of Jesus, one that is the fulfillment of prophecy (Matthew), the path of the Son of God (Mark), the continuation of Abraham's promises (Luke), and the re-creation of Israel's own story (John). Readers of the Gospels who do not fully recognize or grasp the intertextuality at work between the Old Testament and the New Testament can still be richly rewarded as they work their way through the different narratives of Jesus's ministry. But to truly understand the nuances, the ebbs and flows, and the shades and degrees that each Evangelist carefully invests into his story, readers ought to seek out and commit to study the same texts that provided a context and a frame of reference for the Evangelists, namely the writings of the Old Testament.

Notes

1. Gerard Genette, *The Architext: An Introduction*, trans. Jane E. Lewin (Berkeley: University of California Press, 1992), 81–82.
2. "Word, Dialog and Novel," ed. Toril Moi, *The Kristeva Reader* (New York: Columbia University Press, 1986), 37. It was in Julia Kristeva's groundbreaking work *Semiotike: Recherchés pour une semanalyse* (Collections Tel Quel Paris: Le Seuil, 1969), that notions of "Intertextuality" began to develop. Kristeva argued that all texts share links between them that "intersect and neutralize one another." *Desire in Language: A Semiotic Approach to Literature and Art*, ed. Leon S. Roudiez (New York: Columbia University Press, 1980), 36.
3. James A. Sanders, "Intertextuality and Dialogue: New Approaches to the Scriptural Canon," in *Canon vs. Culture: Reflections on the Current Debate*, ed. Jan Gorak (New York: Garland Publishing, 2001), 180.
4. Old Testament quotations present in the New Testament were first organized by J. Rendel Harris in his two volumes entitled *Testimonies* (Cambridge, 1916–20). For the work of later studies that built upon Harris's work, see C. H. Dodd, *According to Scriptures: The Sub-Structure of New Testament Theology* (London: Nisbet, 1952); E. Earle Ellis, *St. Paul's Use of the Old Testament* (London: Oliver and Body, 1957); Krister Stendahl, *The School of St. Matthew and its Use of the Old Testament* (Philadelphia: Fortress Press, 1968); Barnabas Lindars, *New Testament Apologetic: The Doctrinal Significance of the Old Testament Quotations* (London: SCM Press LTD, 1961); and F. F. Bruce, *New Testament Development of Old Testament Themes* (Grand Rapids, MI: Eerdmans, 1968).

5. I recognize that titles like "Hebrew Bible," "First Testament," or "Sacred Jewish Writings" are perhaps more appropriate, but for the purpose of this paper I will use "Old Testament" as a way of referring to the thirty-nine canonized writings contained in the King James Bible.
6. For example, Luke 24:20–21.
7. Rowan Williams, *The Wound of Knowledge: A Theological History from the New Testament to Luther and St. John of the Cross* (Eugene, OR: Wipf & Stock, 1998), 1.
8. Hays, *Echoes of Scripture in the Gospels*, 4–5. See also the discussion in Hays, *Reading Backwards: Figural Christology and the Fourfold Gospel Witness* (Waco, TX: Baylor University Press, 2014), 1–6.
9. See, for example, Richard B. Hays, *The Conversion of the Imagination: Paul as Interpreter of Israel's Scripture* (Grand Rapids, MI: Eerdmans, 2005); Richard B. Hays, *Echoes of Scripture in the Letters of Paul* (New Haven: Yale University Press, 1989). One subsequent work on this topic acknowledged the debt to Hays, ironically enough, through allusion: Christopher A. Beetham, *Echoes of Scripture in the Letter of Paul to the Colossians* (BIS 96: Leiden: Brill, 2008). See also G. K. Beale and D. A. Carson, *Commentary on the New Testament Use of the Old Testament* (Grand Rapids, MI: Baker Academic Books, 2007).
10. As noted above, the topic of intertextuality has become quite popular in the Academy, and there are a great deal of ongoing discussions and dialogues about topics such as the Evangelists' use of the Old Testament. For the sake of audience, this paper will not be directly engaging those discussions beyond the introduction to the topic presented in this paper. Relevant secondary sources will be cited throughout for those wishing to engage the topic further.
11. A note on terminology: I will use the technical term "quotation" to refer to a passage in the New Testament that has been explicitly cited by the gospel author, meaning that the author specifically states that he is referring to an Old Testament passage. Usually this is done through a formula quotation, such as "As it is written" or "In order that the scripture be fulfilled." I will

use the term "allusion" to refer to a passage in the New Testament that has been implicitly cited by the Gospel author, meaning that the author is likely to have had the Old Testament passage in mind, even though he doesn't explicitly state that he does.

12. I borrow this and subsequent totals of quotations and allusions from Hays, *Echoes of Scripture in the Gospels*, 284. It should be noted that numbers of quotations and allusions are continually debated. Depending upon the criteria one employs in evaluation, this number could increase substantially. For example, D. A. Hagner writes that Matthew contains "well over sixty explicit quotations from the OT (not counting a great number of allusions), more than twice as many as any other Gospel." D. A. Hagner, *Matthew 1–13* (Dallas: Word Books, 1998), liv. However, R. T. France notes that the USB Greek New Testament lists fifty-four direct citations and over 250 allusions in Matthew's Gospel, which he admits still may be a "conservative figure." R. T. France, *The Gospel of Matthew* (Grand Rapids, MI: Eerdmans, 2007), 10.
13. Hagner, *Matthew 1–13*, liv. France adds, "I have argued elsewhere that the central theme of Matthew's gospel is 'fulfillment.'" France, *The Gospel of Matthew*, 10.
14. Of this grouping of statements of prophetic fulfillment early in Matthew, Hays writes, "This clustering of fulfillment quotations near the beginning of the Gospel conditions readers to expect that nearly everything in the story of Jesus will turn out to be the fulfillment of something prescripted by the prophets." Hays, *Echoes of Scripture in the Gospels*, 106.
15. "Indeed, Matthew leaves nothing to chance: he repeatedly erects highway signs in large letters to direct his readers, making it unmistakably explicit that Jesus is the fulfillment of Israel's Scripture." Hays, *Echoes of Scripture in the Gospels*, 106.
16. For a discussion of the identity of the "virgin" and "Immanuel," see J. D. W. Watts, *Isaiah 1–33* (Nashville: Thomas Nelson, 2005), 136–42.

17. For further discussion of this prophecy and its place in the New Testament, see Jason Combs, "From King Ahaz's Sign to Christ Jesus: The 'Fulfillment' of Isaiah 7:14" herein.
18. "Again, in retrospective language, God describes his people in terms of their origins" (Douglas Stuart, *Hosea–Jonah* [Dallas: Words Books, 1987], 177).
19. The Hebrew verb קָרָאתִי is a qal perfect tense. In the LXX, Hosea 11:1 uses the Greek aorist tense μετεκάλεσα. In Matthew's quotation, he uses εκάλεσα, also the aorist tense.
20. "A second special exodus from Egypt, that of the child Jesus after the death of Herod (Matt 2:15), comports precisely with the wording Hosea was inspired to use, and which therefore does double duty. It has its own meaning in Hosea 11:1, in a context which does not concern itself with the Messiah. It has as well a *sensus plenior*, deriving from the double potential of the specific wording chosen. Events in Jesus' life thus *fulfill* (i.e., complete the potential meanings of) the wording of v 1b, while not constituting its sole referent" (Stuart, *Hosea-Jonah*, 178). See also discussion in Raymond Brown, *The Birth of the Messiah: A Commentary on the Infancy Narratives in the Gospels of Matthew and Luke*, rev. ed. ABRL (New York: Doubleday, 1993), 219–21.
21. The question of how many animals Jesus actually rode upon (one or two) has been the topic of much debate among scholars, some of who question whether or not Matthew misread the synonymous parallelism in Zechariah 9:9. Hays writes, "Matthew, on the other hand, is so eager to draw his readers' attention to the intertextual link that he quotes the Zechariah passage in full and explicitly points out that Jesus' action is the fulfillment of the prophecy. Furthermore, he reshapes the story to include *two* animals, a donkey and a colt, both mentioned in Zechariah 9:9, thereby underscoring the fulfilled prophecy but also creating for his readers the notoriously baffling image of Jesus somehow astride both creatures." Hays, *Echoes of Scripture in the Gospels*, 106. See also the discussion in Hagner, *Matthew*

1–13, 594–95, and David Instone-Brewer, "The Two Asses of Zechariah 9:9 in Matthew 21," *TynBul* 54 (2003): 87–98.

22. "Jesus's donkey ride was a matter of deliberate choice, and indeed probably of careful planning, rather than a matter of necessity." France, *The Gospel of Matthew*, 774.
23. "But in deliberately presenting himself before Jerusalem as its messianic king, Jesus has chosen an OT model which subverts any popular militaristic idea of kingship. The meek, peaceful donkey-rider of Zech 9:9 is not a potential leader of an anti-Roman insurrection." France, *The Gospel of Matthew*, 775.
24. For a useful discussion of Matthew's different approaches to prophecy, including the three discussed in this section, see David L. Turner, *Matthew* (Grand Rapids, MI: Baker Academic Books, 2008), 68–73. See also Jason Combs, "From King Ahaz's Sign to Christ Jesus: The 'Fulfillment' of Isaiah 7:14" herein.
25. James M. Hamilton Jr., "'The Virgin Will Conceive': Typological fulfillment in Matthew 1:18–23," in *Built upon the Rock: Studies in the Gospel of Matthew*, ed. Daniel M. Gurtner and John Nolland (Grand Rapids, MI: Eerdmans, 2008), 233.
26. John Nolland, *The Gospel of Matthew* (Grand Rapids, MI: Eerdmans, 2005), 123.
27. Hays, *Echoes of Scripture in the Gospels*, 284. See also Moyise, *The Old Testament in the New*, 6.
28. In the OT, the title "Son of God" is applied to Israel as God's people (Hos 11:1), the king at his coronation (Ps 2:7), the angels (Job 38:7), and the suffering righteous person (Wisdom 2:18). In Mark's Gospel, "Son of God" is a very prominent title for Jesus. John R. Donahue and Daniel J. Harrington, *The Gospel of Mark* (Collegeville, MN: Liturgical Press, 2002), 25. Robert A. Guelich adds, "Mark's story relates Jesus' mission as the divine Son who passes incognito through the realm of time and space." Robert A. Guelich, *Mark* (Dallas, TX: Word Books, 1989), xxxix.

29. "This usage and the texts cited show that Mark's audience is familiar with both the content and mode of citation of the OT. It also suggests a high level of literacy among first-century Jews and Jewish Christians." Donahue and Harrington, *Mark*, 60.
30. While in English represented above it may appear that Malachi 3:1 parallels Mark's words more closely, in the Greek text (LXX) Exodus 23:20 is clearly the source of the quotation, and the same is true for the quotation from Isaiah 40:3. The quotation from Malachi 3:1, however, corresponds more closely to the Hebrew text (MT).
31. William L. Lane, *The Gospel of Mark* (Grand Rapids, MI: Eerdmans, 1974), 47.
32. The classic study on the "Messianic Secret" is William Wrede's *Das Messiasgeheimnis in den Evangelien*, published in 1901. "Many scholars since Wrede have offered explanations of the significance of Mark's messianic secret. Nevertheless, no scholarly consensus has emerged on this issue. Part of the reason that no consensus has emerged is that scholars do not agree on exactly which passages constitute the messianic secret. The term functions essentially as a cipher: scholars have used it to refer to a wide variety of Marcan themes and passages. In general, some combination of the following sets of passages have been thought to constitute the messianic secret. Many scholars focus on only one or a few of these: 1:40–45, 5:21–24, 7:31–37, 8:22–26. . . . Together, these passages form a unified motif, a 'messianic secret,' in which Jesus' messianic identity and the necessity of his suffering, death and resurrection are kept hidden from all but a small group of his followers." David F. Watson, *Honor Among Christians: The Cultural Key to the Messianic Secret* (Minneapolis: Fortress Press, 2010), 2–4. See also the discussion in Donahue and Harrington, *Mark*, 27–29.
33. The occasion for this specific question could be the cry of the crowd as Jesus entered Jerusalem: "Blessed is the coming kingdom of our ancestor David" (Mark 11:10).

34. Psalm 110:1 is the most-quoted Old Testament text in the New Testament, appearing over thirty times. See discussion in D. M. Hay, *Glory at the Right Hand: Psalm 110 in Early Christianity* (Nashville/New York: Abingdon Press, 1973), 15, 45–47.
35. See, for example, Isaiah 9:2–7; 11:1–9; Jeremiah 23:5 f., 30:9, 33:15, 17, 22; Ezekiel 34:23 f., 37:24; Hosea 3:5; and Amos 9:11. See also the discussion in France, *Mark*, 435–36.
36. See, for example, *Psalms of Solomon*, 17:21. Cf. 2 Samuel 7:12–16.
37. See Konrad Schaefer, *Psalms* (Collegeville, MN: The Liturgical Press, 2001), 272–75.
38. France, *Mark*, 127. France continues: "therefore the distinctive use of 'the Son of Man' by Jesus derives from his own choice of a term with clear messianic overtones but without a ready-made nationalistic content such as was carried by 'Messiah' or 'Son of David."
39. 2:10, 28; 8:31, 38; 9:9, 12, 31; 10:33, 45; 13:26; 14:21, 41, 62.
40. See Geza Vermes, "The Use of שנ רב אשנ רב in Jewish Aramaic," Appendix E in M. Black, *An Aramaic Approach to the Gospels and Acts* (Oxford: Oxford University Press, 1967), 310–28; see also discussion in Lane, *Mark*, 296–303.
41. For a useful discussion, see Delbert Burkett, *The Son of Man Debate: A History and Evaluation* (Cambridge: Cambridge University Press, 2004). See also Kelli S. O'Brien, *The Use of Scripture in the Markan Passion Narrative* (London: T&T Clark, 2010), 172–189. For a general discussion of the title in the New Testament, see Larry W. Hurtado, *Lord Jesus Christ: Devotion to Jesus in Earliest Christianity* (Grand Rapids, MI: Eerdmans, 2003), 290–306. For a discussion of how the title is used specifically in Mark's Gospel, see Adela Yarbro Collins and John J. Collins, *King and Messiah as Son of God* (Grand Rapids, MI: Eerdmans, 2008), 150–52.
42. R. T. France, *The Gospel of Mark* (Grand Rapids, MI: Eerdmans, 2002), 534.
43. As Hays eloquently frames the riddle posed by the use of the "Son of Man" title, "The story moves on swiftly to Jesus' condemnation and crucifixion, but the reader who understands the force of the Daniel citation is left with

a stunning revelation: this prisoner being led away to execution is the eschatological Son of Man who will be revealed in his full glory in due course—or, at least, the reader is forced to decide whether this is true. Is this Jesus, the Messiah of Israel, also a transhuman figure of greater glory and dignity than any merely human king? Will he receive an everlasting dominion that shall not pass away?" Hays, *Echoes of Scripture in the Gospels*, 61.

44. Hays, *Echoes of Scripture in the Gospels*, 284. For a further breakdown of Luke's usage of the Old Testament, see Beale and Carson, *Commentary on the New Testament Use*, 251–53. See also Moyise, *The Old Testament in the New*, 6.
45. Darrell L. Bock, *Proclamation from Prophecy and Pattern: Lucan Old Testament Christology* (Sheffield: JSOT Press, 1987), 274–77.
46. Cf. Acts 3:13 and 25, where Luke also writes in terms of the Abrahamic covenant.
47. For a full discussion, see Joel B. Green, *The Gospel of Luke* (Grand Rapids, MI: Eerdmans, 1997), 51–58.
48. Green, *The Gospel of Luke*, 57. Richard Hays adds, "The evocation of this easily recognizable scriptural pattern does alert the reader to expect connections between God's gracious saving actions for Israel in the past and in the present: the same God who fulfilled his promise to Abraham is now at work again in the events of Luke's story." Hays, *Echoes of Scripture in the Gospels*, 198.
49. R. L. Smith, *Micah–Malachi* (Dallas: Word Books, 1998), 342.
50. According to John Nolland, this omission "may be no more than accidental agreement in economizing so as to make room for an added generalizing statement." John Nolland, *Luke 1–9:20* (Dallas: Word Books, 1989), 31.
51. There is some debate as to whether Gabriel (Luke) was claiming that John the Baptist was *the* fulfillment of Malachi's prophecy, or whether John the Baptist was *a* fulfillment of Malachi's prophecy. Raymond Brown argues for the former (*The Birth of the Messiah*, 276–77), while I. Howard Marshall argues for the latter. *The Gospel of Luke* Grand Rapids, MI: Eerdmans, 1978, 59.

52. Marshall, *The Gospel of Luke*, 60.
53. Green, *The Gospel of Luke*, 77.
54. Nolland, *Luke 1–9:20*, 31.
55. L. C. Allen, *Psalms 101–150 (Revised)* (Dallas: Word Books, 2002), 163.
56. Allen, *Psalms 101–150 (Revised)*, 167.
57. "Though deemed unimportant by imperial neighbors, Israel plays a distinguished role in the architecture of God's reign. . . . With the dawn of redemption, all nations will realize that Israel is the "cornerstone" of world redemption." Schaefer, *Psalms*, 291. See also the discussion in Beale and Carson, *Commentary on the Old Testament Use of the New Testament*, 337.
58. Cf. Acts 4:11 and 1 Peter 2:7.
59. Green, *The Gospel of Luke*, 817. Green adds, "Echoing Hosea, Jesus anticipates that those who have rejected God's salvific purpose by rejecting Jesus and his divinely ordained mission will articulate a similar death wish" (816).
60. At this eschatological moment, "the terror of Yawheh, which they (the Israelities) treated with such disdain, overwhelms them inescapably." Francis I. Anderson and David Noel Freedman, *Hosea* (Garden City, NY: Doubleday & Company, 1980), 559.
61. "Language from Hos 10:8 is called upon to evoke the full horror of that future. People will long for death as the only relief from the terrible suffering of that time." John Nolland, *Luke 18:35–24:53* (Dallas, TX: Word Books, 1993), 1139.
62. "In the midst of this coming calamity the natural values of the present will be reversed, and so, women who have been denied motherhood will consider themselves fortunate." Nolland, *Luke 18:35–24:53*, 1139.
63. Hays, *Echoes of Scripture in the Gospels*, 199.
64. In Luke's writings, "The fate of individuals in this judgment hangs upon their response to the proclaimed word; those who reject it judge themselves 'unworthy of eternal life.'" Hays, *Echoes of Scripture in the Gospels*, 219.

65. See Craig Blomberg, *The Historical Reliability of John's Gospel* (Downers Grove, IL: InterVarsity Academic Press, 2001).
66. These are John 2:17; 6:31; 6:45; 7:38; 10:34; 12:38; 13:18; 15:25; 19:24; 19:36; 19:37. See Moyise, *The Old Testament in the New*, 92–93.
67. Hays, *Echoes of Scripture in the Gospels*, 284.
68. Hays, *Echoes of Scripture in the Gospels*, 284.
69. "The first contribution of John's Gospel to the theology of the New Testament takes us back to where we began. It is the notion of Jesus as God's unique Envoy or messenger, simultaneously claiming for himself both Deity and obedient submission to Deity." J. Ramsey Michaels, *The Gospel of John* (Grand Rapids, MI: Eerdmans, 2010), 39.
70. "In any event, the words 'In the beginning' unmistakably echo Genesis 1:1, 'In the beginning God made the heaven and the earth.'" Michaels, *The Gospel of John*, 46.
71. "Our text (John 1:51) clearly alludes to Jacob's vision, but it contains no explicit reference to Jacob himself. . . . Still, we are certainly not dealing here, any more than in similar allusions, with imagery arbitrarily borrowed from the Old Testament." Herman Ridderbos, *The Gospel of John: A Theological Commentary* (Grand Rapids, MI: Eerdmans, 1997), 94. Also, "the Evangelist adds a saying addressed to all the disciples. Its imagery is complex; Jacob's dream is clearly in the foreground, but there are reminiscences of the baptism of Jesus, possibly of his temptation, and of the eschatological and apocalyptic picture language used of the Son of Man, such as appears in the synoptic Gospels." George R. Beasley-Murray, *John* (Dallas: Word Book, 1999), 28. However, compare Michaels, "The allusion in Jesus' pronouncement to Jacob's dream at Bethel (Gen 28:12) is neither as direct nor as unmistakable as is commonly assumed." Michaels, *The Gospel of John*, 136.
72. "Through these remarks, the Lord reveals himself to be the very same God who spoke to Abraham, and what is more, confirms that Jacob is the chosen line, who will henceforth enjoy divine protection. And even more,

though he is now fleeing Canaan, he will eventually return there. For what chiefly distinguishes this pronouncement of the promises from the earlier statements is their setting: the promises were first made to Abraham as he was settling in the land, but they are reaffirmed to Jacob as he is fleeing from it." Gordon J. Wenham, *Genesis 15–50* (Dallas, TX: Word Books, 1998), 223.

73. "Gate of heaven" occurs only here in the OT, but the idea that heaven, the divine abode, has one or more entrances is a familiar idea in ancient thought." Wenham, *Genesis*, 223.

74. "It is not clear whether the 'ladder' describes a ladder or 'a ramp or stairway,' or whether there is Egyptian or Babylonian influence on the imagery. What matters is that the 'ladder' links earth and heaven and has been placed on the earth presumably where Jacob is lying." Wenham, *Genesis*, 221–22.

75. "Thus, in short, Jesus is Jacob's ladder, the one who mediates between God in heaven and his servant Jacob on earth; thus the 'true Israelite' may receive the revelation of God as his ancestor did. As Jacob's ladder, he is also Bethel, God's house, an image that naturally connects with Jesus as the new temple." Craig S. Keener, *The Gospel of John: A Commentary* (Peabody, MA: Hendrickson, 2003), 489–90). See also Wayne Meeks, "The Man from Heaven in Johannine Sectarianism," *JBL* 91, no. 1 (March 1972): 44–72, esp. 51–52.

76. "What Jesus tells Nathanael, then, is that he himself will be the place of much greater divine revelation than that given at previous occasions. . . . Jesus is the 'new Bethel,' the place where God is revealed, where heaven and earth, God and humankind, meet." Andreas Kostenberger, *John* (Grand Rapids, MI: Baker Academic Books, 2008), 86). See also D. A. Carson, "Jesus is the new Israel. Even the old Bethel, the old 'house of God', has been superseded. It is no longer *there*, at Bethel, that God reveals himself, but in Jesus (*cf.* Davies, p. 298)—just as later on Jesus renders obsolete such holy places as the temple (2:19–22) and the sacred mountains of the

Samaritans (4:20–24)." D.A. Carson, *The Gospel according to John* (Grand Rapids, MI: Eerdmans, 1991), 164).

77. "From here on it is not so much a question of what Jesus will give as of who Jesus is, and that is where controversies in John's Gospel most often begin." Michaels, *John*, 373.
78. While this interpretation is a strong possibility, other scholars see God's condemnation aimed at angels who have abused their divine station or perhaps at Israel herself. See discussion in Kostenberger, *John*, 315.
79. "The 'divine council' or 'gods' are judges or governors who share God's responsibility to administer justice and protect the rights of the down-trodden and defenseless. . . . The drama is the opposition of good and evil. The repetition of 'the wicked' illustrates the dichotomy; the evil potentates are unfair in their dealings with the defenseless. The 'gods' support the oppressors instead." Schaefer, *Psalms*, 202.
80. "Yahweh expects judges and leaders to protect the marginalized people in society: the poor, the oppressed, and those without family support." Marvin E. Tate, *Psalms* 51–100 (Dallas: Word Books, 1998), 336.
81. "The gods will become vulnerable to the destructive "falls" of tyrants, chieftains, princes, generals, and other kinds of leaders and officials. They are to be deposed from their divine prerogatives." Tate, *Psalms 51–100*, 338.
82. "A very old stream of interpretation interprets the "gods" as human judges or officials. . . . Despite its exegetical weakness, however, the old tradition of relating Psalm 82 to human actions has a strong element of truth in it." Tate, *Psalms 51–100*, 341. For a useful discussion of the various ways this passage has been understood, see Beasley-Murray, *John*, 176–77.
83. "A single clear idea is in mind as Jesus cites this scripture: In the "Law" (i.e., the OT, of which the Law is the chief part; cf. 12:34; 15:25), the term "god" is applied to others than God himself; if those addressed by God in this passage can be called gods (and sons of God), how much more can he whom the Father consecrated and sent into the world be so termed?" Beasley-Murray, *John*, 175. D. A. Carson adds, "As Jesus uses the text, the

general line of his argument is clear. This Scripture proves that the word 'god' is legitimately used to refer to others than God himself." Carson, *The Gospel according to John*, 397.

84. Notably, this is one of only two fulfillment quotations from the mouth of Jesus in the Gospel of John (the other being John 15:25).
85. "Even the good friend, the one with whom so many a pleasant meal had been passed, would "raise up his heel" against the sick person." Peter C. Craigie, *Psalms 1–50*, 2nd ed. (Nashville: Nelson Reference & Electronic, 2004), 321.
86. See Beale and Carson, *Commentary on the New Testament Use*, 486.
87. "The quotation from Ps. 41:9—'Even my bosom friend in whom I trusted, who ate of my bread, has lifted the heel against me'—refers to what is still an extremely rude gesture in many Mediterranean cultures. The disciples have reluctantly had to make this gesture as Jesus washed their feet. Whereas Jesus's words to the disciples have nullified the offense, he does not grant the same pardon to Judas." Jo-Anne Brant, *John* (Grand Rapids, MI: Baker Academic Books, 2011), 203.

7

Understanding Micah's Lament for Judah (Micah 1:10–16) through Text, Archaeology, and Geography

George A. Pierce

George A. Pierce is an assistant professor of ancient scripture at Brigham Young University.

Martin Luther once stated that the prophets "have a queer way of talking, like people who, instead of proceeding in an orderly manner, ramble off from one thing to the next, so that you cannot make head or tail of them or see what they are getting at."[1] This is especially true for Micah 1:10–16, in which Micah's prophetic lament employs several forms of Hebrew wordplay, termed *paronomasia,* a literary device found throughout the Old Testament that employs the phonology and meaning of words to give added emphasis to a persuasive argument.[2] The prophets have the highest occurrences of this rhetorical device when compared to other genres in the Hebrew Bible, such as law, history, or wisdom literature, and in this passage, the wordplay of the prophet's lament draws on the names of towns or villages in the rural Judean countryside to illustrate impending judgment and destruction. This chapter seeks to explicate the word-play Micah used in lamenting the cities around him by surveying the geographical and historical settings behind Micah's oracle as related within biblical and Assyrian texts, by considering archaeological and geographic information, and by examining the mechanics of the text. Thus text, archaeology, and geography should not only give perspective to Micah's lament but also inform the potential application of the text in addition to the larger theological message of Micah for the modern reader. By understanding Micah's world, we may understand Micah's words much better.

Overview of Micah and His Ministry

To determine the themes and purposes within this record of prophecy, the questions of author, audience, subject, context, and relevance should be applied. To answer the first two, the main speaker within this book is Micah the Moreshite, the mouthpiece of Jehovah who addressed the Northern Kingdom of Israel and the Southern Kingdom of Judah in the second half of the eighth century BC, during the reigns of Jotham, Ahaz, and Hezekiah, kings of Judah (Micah 1:1). Little is known about Micah, except for his origin in Moresheth-gath, a settlement in the low hill country of Judah, a region known as the Shephelah. As a contemporary of Isaiah, he identified with the poor, which is evident in his proclamations against the prophets, priests, and judges.[3] Hans Wolff has suggested that Micah may have been an elder of Moresheth-gath, an opinion reached by examining Micah's focus on judges and elders rendering appropriate mercy and justice, but there is little internal evidence from the biblical text to support this claim.[4] It is also unknown if Micah was ever associated officially with the Jerusalem temple and the prophets there or with any prophetic guild, although scholars suggest that Micah spent much of his life in Jerusalem and may have delivered his oracles there.[5] While Micah the person may have disappeared from history, the message of Micah was remembered despite its unpopular laments and foretelling of judgments upon Israel and Judah. When Jeremiah was sentenced to death for prophesying against Jerusalem (Jeremiah 26:11–19), certain elders saved Jeremiah by recalling the prophecy of Micah of Moresheth against Jerusalem and Zion (Micah 3:12).

Considerations of subject and relevance for these oracles can be addressed by a brief overview of Micah's prophecy as a whole.[6] Micah proclaimed the impending downfall of Samaria, the capital of the Northern Kingdom of Israel, as well as the destruction awaiting Judah. Samaria's fall mainly resulted from the idolatry and apostasy of the northern Israelites (1:5–7), but Micah also made other indictments against the house of Jacob while addressing Judah. Judah's judgment came because of its prophets and elders, or judges, who practiced injustice and profited from their service to their God and nation (3:11). Micah's oracles are rife with war and exile,[7] yet God's condemnation was not without hope. The book of Micah contains a prophecy focused on a later time when the mountain of the Lord's house would be exalted, the nations would again worship him, and the people would learn from him in a time of peace (4:2–4).[8] In contrast to what the Judahites considered as safety, such as fortified cities on Judah's borders or chariot teams, the Lord's presence and justice would provide the ultimate security so that every man would be able to sit "under his vine and under his fig tree and no one shall make them afraid" (4:4). After proclaiming the Babylonian exile, Jehovah's redemption was again stated, and the promise of a ruler being born in Bethlehem-Ephrathah was issued (5:2; Matthew 2:6).

Micah's critiques of the Judahite elite centered on justice, employing legal terms, and initiating a prophetic lawsuit by Jehovah against Israel. Words with legal connotation are used throughout the book, such as justice (3:1, 8–9; 6:8), judgment (3:11, 7:9), judge (4:3, 5:1, 7:3), witness (1:2), and indictment (6:1–2). The climax of Micah's prophecy is the legal indictment by God against all of Israel, ending with what the Lord required, namely, to do justly, to love mercy, and to walk humbly before God (6:8).

Exposition of Micah 1:10–16

Although the preceding overview of the book of Micah may satisfy straightforward inquiries about author, audience, and subject, the context of Micah's prophecies—specifically his initial lament in the second half of Micah 1—requires an understanding of the section's linguistic features, especially form and wordplay within the passage under consideration. Subsequently, the historical and geographic settings of Micah's ministry also facilitate a textual and archaeological exposition of Micah 1:10–16 that may further our understanding of this enigmatic passage and its modern relevance and application.

Linguistic Considerations

While prophetic utterances can be divided into many subgenres, Micah's words here form a prophetic dirge, or funeral lament, performed "barefoot and naked" (1:8), symbolizing the shame that would be felt by Judah's inhabitants when conquered and treated as captives.[9] This lament is an early component of a so-called "Book of Doom" (1:2–3:12), which focused on judgment against both the Northern Kingdom of Israel and the Southern Kingdom of Judah.[10] Micah's dirge foresaw the results of a campaign by the Assyrian king Sennacherib in 701 BC to quell a rebellion by the confederate Judahite and Philistine kings.[11] The list of towns in the lament has been interpreted as the Assyrian line of march for Sennacherib's campaign, with emphasis on the extensive destruction in the Judean countryside, although Nadav Na'aman cogently argues against this interpretation and asserts that the names were chosen on their suitability for paronomasia.[12]

Dirges usually follow a form that includes a call to hear, the dirge itself, a messenger formula, and a prediction. James L. Mays proposed that the beginning of the lament and the call to hear are found in Micah 1:8, with "For this, I will lament . . ." looking forward in the text rather than the opposite.[13] However, using this identification of the announcement, we can identify that Micah 1:10–15 would form the lament and the prediction would follow in verse 16, with the command to shave their heads because of their children's exile. The expected messenger formula ("Thus says the Lord") between the lament and prediction is absent in the passage, unless it is associated with "The word of the Lord that came to Micah of Moresheth" (1:1). Smith suggests that Micah is actually performing a mourning ritual to accompany this verbal expression of grief.[14]

Within the dirge format, Micah employs paronomasia based on the names of towns that he is lamenting.[15] In addition to allusions to biblical history, four techniques are employed to create the desired effect, including direct wordplay, antithetical wordplay, alliteration, and rhyme. [16] Exploring the wordplay communicated in Micah's message in conjunction with the historical and geographical contexts of the prophet's activity leads to an appreciation of some of the cognitive effects Micah's lament would have had on its original audience as he used puns based on place names to prophesy of each site's doom.

Historical and Geographical Contexts

Israel and Judah's history is uniquely tied to the concept of it being a land bridge or the "Land Between."[17] The "Land Between" refers to the land's position as a crossroads between the kingdoms of Aram and Assyria to the north and Egypt to the south, as well as the merchants and traders of Arabia in the east and the Mediterranean world lying to the west. Interregional dynamics within this land and specific regional characteristics shaped history and affected its inhabitants'

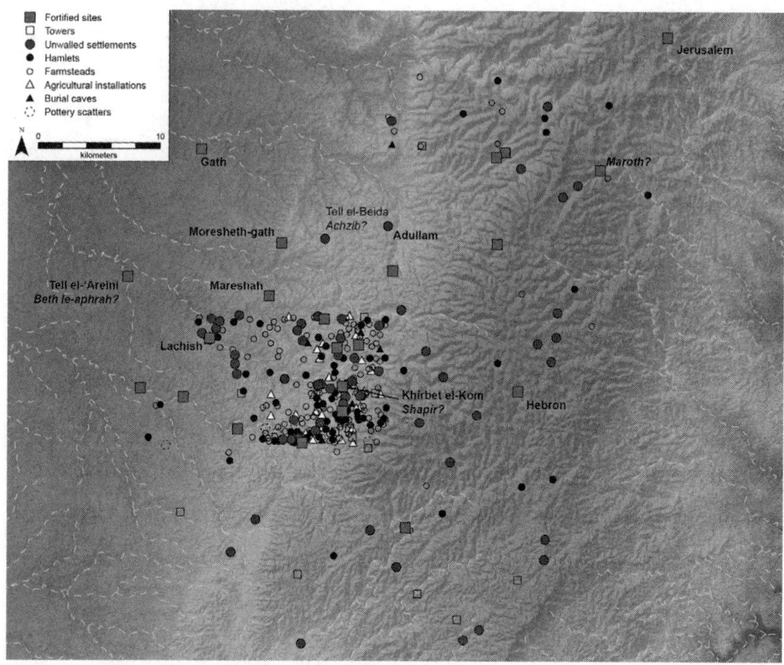

Figure 1. Settlement types and distribution in Judah at the time of Micah during the eighth century BC. (Areas of denser settlement reflect published intensive archaeological surveys; areas with less dense distribution await further study.)

lives as much as the external forces of warfare, politics, or trade with neighboring kingdoms and larger empires affected its inhabitants.

Micah's region, the Judean Shephelah, is situated between the coastal plain to the west and the hill country of Judah to the east and is composed of low hills and many valleys, allowing for more extensive agriculture than the higher hills eastward. Archaeological surveys and excavations reveal that in addition to the main fortified Judahite cities, the Shephelah during the eighth century BC was dotted with villages, farmsteads, and agricultural installations like wine and oil presses, threshing floors, and kilns (Figure 1). The Shephelah formed a valuable part of the Judahite kingdom since this area was a gateway to the Judean hills.[18] Conflict with the Philistines occurred in this area as Israel gained strength during the United Monarchy (1 Samuel 17).

Recognizing the threat to Judah's safety, Rehoboam fortified the cities of the Shephelah against attack (2 Chronicles 11:5–11). The importance of the Shephelah lay not only in its agricultural capabilities but also in the roads that allowed Judah to access the coastal plain and take part in the international commerce that traveled the coastal highway. The Assyrian king Sennacherib, to whom Micah is probably referring in his lament (1:9, 12), realized the strategic importance of the region and laid siege to its villages and fortified cities as a punishment for Hezekiah's rebellion against Assyrian domination. The most notable and well-documented battle of this campaign mentioned in 2 Kings 18:13 is that of Lachish, chronicled by Sennacherib's scribes on a hexagonal clay pillar, known as Sennacherib's Prism, and his artists in the reliefs from his throne room, which are now on display at the British Museum.[19] With the seizure of Lachish and the Shephelah, Hezekiah's routes to potential allies like Egypt were closed. Sennacherib boasted that he had made Hezekiah "a prisoner in Jerusalem, his royal residence, like a bird in a cage."[20]

The accounts and renderings of Sennacherib's siege of Lachish provide not only a needful lesson in regional geography but also a lesson in politics of the eighth century BC and historical setting in which Micah ministered. The opening verse of Micah states that the Lord spoke to Micah "in the days of Jotham, Ahaz, and Hezekiah, kings of Judah" (1:1). Philip J. King lists the dates for these rulers collectively between 750–687 BC, starting with Jotham's regency (2 Kings 15:5) and ending with the death of Hezekiah (2 Kings 20:21; 2 Chronicles 32:33).[21] No mention is made of the Syro-Ephraimite war or the deportation of the Galilean tribes such as Zebulun or Naphtali, leading some scholars to suggest that Micah prophesied after 734 BC.[22] Wolff dates Micah's prophecy somewhere between 734–728 BC based on the foretelling of Samaria's fall, dated to 722 or 721 BC.[23] Micah's activity as a prophet during the reign of Hezekiah, which commenced circa 727 BC, is confirmed by the account in

Jeremiah 26:18, and scholars generally agree that the lament in Micah 1 predates Sennacherib's campaign of 701 BC.

During the eighth and seventh centuries BC, Judah and Israel were linked with the dominant powers of Aram and Assyria—sometimes as vassal states, other times as enemies allied to Egypt. When these two powers weakened, Israel and Judah were able to prosper, though they would not reach the former glory or prosperity of Solomon. Instability within the northern kingdom, coupled with God's judgment against Samaria for her idolatry, led to Israel's fall and deportation at the hands of Shalmaneser V and Sargon II of Assyria (2 Kings 18:9–12). To the south, Hezekiah was successful in organizing a rebellion against Assyrian rule (2 Kings 18:7), but this was checked by Sennacherib's campaign in 701 BC. Micah lamented this campaign and concomitant destruction probably a few years before it occurred. When Micah began his ministry, the kingdoms of Israel and Judah were teetering on a precipice above the gaping maw of the Assyrian empire, ready to seize their land, deport their families, and execute the judgment the Lord had rendered upon these idolatrous peoples. Geopolitical intrigue and religious syncretism fill the world of Micah and the kingdom of Judah, a world in which the righteous Judge of the universe would make a ruling against his people.

Textual and Archaeological Exposition

The lament over the destruction foretold for the Judean Shephelah incorporates the names of eleven sites, some confidently identified, some with tentative identifications, and the rest remaining unidentified.[24] This does not account for the possibility that some sites are fictive or that the site names are symbolic and merely devices for wordplay. While it would seem unlikely that Micah would deliver a lament for a nonexistent site in Judah, Na'aman has suggested that Micah chose the place names based on their suitability for paronomasia.[25]

Exploring the site names, the wordplay associated with them, and the archaeology of the sites, together with suggested identifications for the unknown sites, will facilitate an understanding of the historical geography of the region. Only "after the reader is made to understand the relationship between the various places mentioned can he begin to comprehend the true meaning of the text, both on a literal-historical and on an allegorical-exegetical level."[26]

Micah 1:10 bĕgat ʾal-taggîdû bākô ʾal-tibkû bĕbêt lĕʿaprâ ʿāpār ḥitpallāštî

Tell it not in Gath, weep not at all; in Beth-leaphrah, roll yourselves in the dust.

The dirge that Micah performs for the impending destruction of Judah's countryside, as a result of transgressions similar to Samaria and the Northern Kingdom of Israel, starts with the proclamation of a lament in Micah 1:8–9. In 1:10, Micah begins the geographic portion of his lament with a plea to "Tell it not in Gath." Gath means a "press" for oil or wine, and while presses are common features of agricultural sites in the biblical period, the site referred to as Gath is commonly known as one of the major Philistine cities and the home of the Philistine champion Goliath (1 Samuel 17:4). The site of Tell es-Safi has been identified as biblical Gath since 1887, although this identification was still subject to debate until excavations from the late twentieth century to the present unearthed strong evidence of a Canaanite and Philistine center that was eventually destroyed by the Aramean king Hazael in the ninth century BC.[27] The period of Micah, the second half of the eighth century BC, is represented at Safi by architecture resembling a four-room house, a type of house characteristic of Israelite and Judahite dwellings in the Iron Age, which points to a "strong Judahite presence" at Tell es-Safi during the ministry of Micah.[28] Archaeological finds from this period include a pillar figurine, an Assyrian stele, shekel weights, and jar handles stamped with the Hebrew word *lmlk*, meaning "(belonging) to the king" dating to the time of Hezekiah.[29]

Micah makes the admonition to not tell the news of Judah's impending defeat in Gath, clearly referencing David's lament over the deaths of Saul and Jonathan: "Tell it not in Gath, publish it not in the streets of Ashkelon, lest the daughters of the Philistines rejoice, lest the daughters of the uncircumcised triumph" (2 Samuel 1:20). This is a direct play on the name *Gath* against the Hebrew imperative verb *taggîdû*, "you (pl.) do not tell/exult."[30] Yet just as the lament contrasts Gath with a reversed initial syllable, *tag*, a comparison to David's statement may also be adduced. While David did not want the news of Saul and Jonathan's defeat to reach Philistia, he encouraged the women of Israel to weep and mourn for the fallen leaders. In stark contrast, Micah proscribed weeping. As Anderson and Freedman noted, this passage, where silence and weeping are both encouraged as signs of lament, is parallel to Isaiah 23:1–2, where the imperative for the ships of Tarshish to wail is followed by an injunction for the merchants of Sidon to be silent.[31]

In the second half of the verse, Micah also uses another direct approach with some rhyming with the name of the second town, Beth-leaphrah (*bêt le'aprâ*), the "House of Dust." Here, the wordplay results in the "House of Dust" being commanded to roll in dust (*'apar*), a symbol of mourning (Job 16:15, Jeremiah 6:26).[32] Beth le-aphrah was previously identified tentatively with et-Taiyibeh, although no archaeological material confirms this identification. Recently, Matthew Suriano posits that Beth le-aphrah should be located at Tell el-'Areini, using historical place names and the presence of eighth century BC archaeological remains.[33] Tell el-'Areini is located on the border of the Shephelah and the coastal plain between ancient Judah and Philistia, so the wordplay involved with the verbal root of rolling one's self in the dust (*plš*) and its similarity to Philistia and the Philistines seem apt.

Micah 1:11 ʿibrî lākem yôšebet šapîr ʿeryâ-bōšet lōʾ yāṣĕʾâ yôšebet ṣaʾănān mispad bêt hāʾēṣel yiqqaḥ mikkem ʿemdātô

Pass on your way, inhabitants of Shaphir, in nakedness and shame; the inhabitants of Zaanan do not come forth; Beth-ezel is wailing and shall remove its support from you.

In this verse, Micah first applied an antithetical wordplay and then rhyme to enforce his lament over Judah's towns whose identification and even existence are debated. Saphir, also rendered as Shapir, has been identified as Khirbet el-Qôm, southwest of Hebron, based on the toponymic work of F. M. Abel who related it to the Arabic site name Wadi es-Saffar.[34] Archaeological finds from the eighth and seventh centuries BC, such as pottery sherds, *lmlk* jar handles, and part of a city wall, help to corroborate this recognition. Inscriptions discovered at the site refer to Asherah, a Canaanite fertility goddess, sometimes depicted as a consort of Yahweh. The religious syncretism of the Judahites and their neighbors, which included veneration of Asherah and the use of fertility objects like pillared figurines found at Tell es-Safi, Khirbet el-Qôm, Lachish, and other sites discussed here, engendered God's judgment and resulted in a declaration of destruction (see Micah 5:13–14). The name Shaphir has been translated as "beautiful" and stands in direct contrast to the "nakedness and shame" that lies ahead for exiled people.[35] The rhyming pun in this verse involves the town of Zaanan (*ṣaʾănān*), an unidentified site, with the verb "come forth" (*yāṣĕʾâ*). According to Anderson and Freedman, there is no wordplay associated with Beth-ezel (*bêt hāʾēṣel*) and they doubt its historicity, although Beth-ezel is tentatively identified as Deir al-Asal.[36] Na'aman also regards Beth-ezel, which he translates as "House of No Shade," not as an actual town but as "a mocking designation" for the Assyrian empire, contrasting the concept of the protective "shadow of the king" seen in Assyrian literature against the destruction prophesied by Micah.[37] As Allen notes, regardless of the accuracy of archaeology or historical geography to identify the sites, the fact remains that the lament illustrates the destruction of the Shephelah's cities and villages that would be conquered in the Assyrian campaign.[38]

Micah 1:12 kî-ḥālâ lĕṭôb yôšebet mārôt kî-yārad rāʿ mēʾēt yhwh lĕšaʿar yĕrûšālēm

For the inhabitants of Maroth wait anxiously for good, yet disaster has come down from the Lord to the gate of Jerusalem.

The idea of antithetical wordplay is hinted with the name of another unidentified site, Maroth, meaning "bitter," which is contrasted with "good." It is again unclear if this is an actual village or if the places names are fictive and created solely for this lament to emphasize Micah's message, as suggested by Na'aman. A divinely sent catastrophe was at the gates of Jerusalem, and this passage forms "the most intelligible sentence in the entire piece," according to Anderson and Freedman.[39] Concerning the disaster at the gate of Jerusalem, the use of the term "gate" is likely symbolic for the entire city of Jerusalem and could be alluding to Sennacherib's siege of Jerusalem detailed in 2 Kings 19 and 2 Chronicles 32.

Micah 1:13 rĕtom hammerkābâ lārekeš yôšebet lākiš rēʾšît ḥaṭṭāʾt hîʾ lĕbat-ṣiyyôn kî-bāk nimṣĕʾû pišʿê yiśrāʾēl

Harness the steeds to the chariots, inhabitants of Lachish; it was the beginning of sin to Daughter Zion, for in you were found the transgressions of Israel.

Lachish was a principal city of Judah, second only to Jerusalem, and a sign of stability and safety in the Shephelah.[40] Micah's wordplay here is a rhyme between Lachish and the term for a team of horses (*rekeš*), which is probably a critique of the perceived might and power of Lachish and Judah. There is a curious phrase concerning "the beginning of sin to Daughter Zion" at Lachish. Is this a possible polemic against the horses and chariots at Lachish?[41] Was the beginning of sin connected to pride and a false sense of security offered by the city's fortifications? The prophets warn against trusting in military might for salvation rather than God.[42] Daniel Smith-Christopher has also interpreted this passage about the expenses of chariotry and fortifications in light of the social justices ignored in Judah, and by extension in the modern world.[43]

When this passage is considered in light of the sins of the kings of Israel and the sins of Judahite kings preceding Hezekiah, a diatribe against idolatry may be discerned.[44] In context with the sin of Samaria affecting Judah (1:5, 9), it may be that idolatry in connection with Asherah or another fertility cult had infiltrated Judah from Samaria via Lachish. A recent archaeological discovery at Lachish illustrates this facet of Micah's prophecy. Within the gate of the city dated to the eighth century BC, excavators discovered numerous stamped *lmlk* jar handles and a shrine consisting of a staircase leading to a room with a bench, presumably for votive offerings.[45] An opening in the corner of the room leads to what the excavators have deemed a "holy of holies" for the shrine in which they recovered ceramic lamps, bowls, vessel stands, and two four-horned altars, all of which were commonly used in cultic rituals in the biblical period. The excavators note that the horns on the altars were intentionally truncated and the shrine desecrated by the installation of a latrine, measures that are likely evidence of Hezekiah's religious reforms (see 2 Kings 18:4). Although the modern reader may be left perplexed concerning the "beginning of sin," Micah's audience could immediately recognize what the sin at Lachish was, and idolatry fits the context just as well as the Lord's wrath at chariots, Judahite fortifications, or perceived security in the Shephelah as evinced in the later proclamation against all these elements in Micah 5:10–14:

> *In that day, says the Lord, I will cut off your horses from among you and will destroy your chariots;*
>
> *And I will cut off the cities of your land and throw down all your strongholds;*
>
> *And I will cut off sorceries from your hand, and you shall have no more soothsayers;*
>
> *And I will cut off your images and your pillars from among you, and you shall bow down no more to the work of your hands;*
>
> *And I will uproot your sacred poles from among you and destroy your towns.*

Micah 1:14 lākēn tittĕnî šillûḥîm ʿal môrešet gat bāttê ʾakzîb lĕʾakˇzāb lĕmalkê yiśrāʾēl

Therefore you shall give parting gifts to Moresheth-gath; the houses of Achzib shall be a deception to the kings of Israel.

Here Micah proclaims God's judgment against his own town of Moresheth-gath. According to Wolff, "genuine prophetic activity results from . . . accusations raised in the name of justice and wholehearted sharing in the judgment that is striking [others]."[46] Therefore, Micah is also indicting himself with Judah and sharing in their punishment. There seems to be a direct wordplay technique with the use of Moresheth (related to "betrothed") and the term "parting gifts" or what may be considered a "dowry."

Most scholars agree that Moresheth-gath is Tell ej-Judeideh, northeast of Lachish. The compound site name suggests that it was within the political sphere of Gath at some point.[47] Aharoni argued that Tell ej-Judeideh was probably fortified as part of Rehoboam's efforts due to its natural elevation and strategic position on a route between Lachish and Azekah.[48] Archaeological excavations during the early twentieth century revealed at least one complete house and the remains of other storage buildings with silos for grain storage associated with each building, but fortifications associated with this phase of occupation were not discovered.[49] The pottery assemblage, including *lmlk* stamped jar handles and ceramic pillar figurines, are contemporary with assemblages from other sites discussed here and date to Micah's time in the eighth century BC.[50] The site suffered conflagration as evinced by ash deposits and burnt debris associated with the architectural remains, and it is almost certain that this destruction was the result of the Assyrian campaign in 701 BC. Alternatively, scholars argue that Moresheth-Gath should be identified with Tel Ḥarasim instead.[51] Situated to the northwest of Tell es-Safi/Gath, the site would fall within the territory controlled by Gath during the Philistine period, and it exhibits tenth–ninth century BC fortifications, possible evidence of the fortifications commissioned by Rehoboam. However, eighth century BC remains were not found according to the excavator.[52]

The place name Achzib (*'akzîb*) is a clear, direct pun with the word (ʾ*akzāb*), meaning "lie, falsehood, deceptive thing." Therefore, this site would be deceptive to kings of Israel, but it is not clear how that deception acts. Achzib is mentioned in the cities list for this region in Joshua 15:44 and an identification with Tell el-Beida has been proposed.[53]

Micah 1:15 ʿōd hayyōrēš ʾābî lāk yôšebet mārēšâ ʿad-ʿădullām yābôʾ kĕbôd yiśrāʾēl

I will again bring a conqueror upon you, inhabitants of Mareshah; the glory of Israel shall come to Adullam.

In this verse, Micah utilizes another case of direct and rhyming correlation between the situation described and the site name. Not to be confused with Micah's hometown, the site of Mareshah, identified with Tell Ṣandaḥanna, is known from Hellenistic and Roman sources. Excavations have recovered seventeen *lmlk* stamped jar handles from Micah's time.[54] While the verse is rendered in the KJV as "Yet will I bring an heir unto thee, O inhabitant of Mareshah," the word translated as "heir" (*yôrēš*) is better translated as "conqueror" or "plunderer." Thus, Micah's lament is not providing a promise of hope but a declaration of judgment as God would bring a conqueror (*yôrēš*) to Mareshah (*mārēšâ*).

In the second half of this verse, the "glory of Israel" is prophesied to come to Adullam, and Micah again evokes the Davidic past. A cave at the site afforded David protection in his flight from Saul (1 Samuel 22:1) and featured in the narrative about David's mighty men (2 Samuel 23:13). In both cases, Adullam has a sense of refuge in the face of trouble. However, the meaning of "glory of Israel" is unclear. Scholars have suggested that the term could refer to Jehovah himself, the Israelite army,[55] a particular class of Judahites or a group of David's descendants,[56] a conceptual idea about what makes a nation glorious rather than material wealth,[57] or even Adullam itself as a fortified city.[58] The voice of Micah lamenting Judah's fate seems to get lost in the din of all these opinions, and the focus is no longer on the destruction of Judah. Whatever the full meaning of "glory of Israel," places of refuge like Adullam are reminiscent of David's life on the run from an aggressor, and the Judahites will become refugees like David in the face of their Assyrian invaders.

Micah 1:16 qorḥî wāggōzî ʿal-bĕnê taʿănûgāyik harḥībî qorḥātēk kannešer kî gālû mimmēk

Make yourselves bald and cut off your hair for your pampered children; make yourselves as bald as the eagle, for they have gone from you into exile.

Micah tells his audience to "enlarge thy baldness as the eagle" because their children in whom they delight are going into exile. Here the prophet draws upon the shared cultural context, evoking a response in his audience with the implications within his utterance. While the process of mussing one's hair and being disheveled was a common expression of mourning in the ancient Near East, intentional shaving of the head was also a treatment for captives of military action sent into exile. Additionally, part of the expression of grief, and a way to honor the dead, involved shaving one's head hair (and beard if applicable), tearing one's clothes or wearing sackcloth, sitting or wallowing in ashes, putting dirt on one's head, and wailing.[59] Ezekiel 27:29–32 presents an excellent biblical example of this practice, combining all the elements as the Tyrian mariners weep for the loss of a ship by shaving their heads, wearing sackcloth, and throwing dust on their heads. Manufactured baldness is proscribed for Israel and its priests outside of the act of mourning for immediate relatives (Leviticus 19:27; 21:1–5; see also Deuteronomy 14:1). Appearing "barefoot and naked" (1:8) and uttering this dirge, Micah by his actions urged the Judahites to carry out this shameful task in earnest lamentation for the impending exile. This is not the false, hired grief that Jeremiah 9:16–17 mentions; rather this is to be actual, heart-felt sorrow at the prediction of their beloved children being captured by the Assyrian invaders.

A brief note is also needed to clarify Micah's command or prediction and eagle imagery at the close of this lament. For the North American reader, the likeness of a bald eagle, with its striking white head plumage, usually springs to mind. However, the Hebrew word translated as "eagle," *nešer*, would be better translated as "vulture," specifically, the Griffon vulture (*Gyps fulvus*), whose modern range includes Israel.[60] The appearance of these vultures, which also have a white head contrasting with their brown bodies, would have produced a clear illustration of baldness within the minds of Micah's audience.

Conclusion

Micah's oracle against Judah and Samaria involves assessment of what Jehovah was trying to teach the family of Israel about himself and the appropriate response to sin through the lens of language and material culture readily known to his audience. First, the main theme of this book is Jehovah's holiness and the need for justice. The prophets, especially Micah, portray Jehovah as a judge over Israel, executing his judgment by means of the Assyrian invader. Within the larger context of this passage, the Lord is seen coming down to touch the mountains and having them melt away as he judged both the northern and southern kingdoms in his righteousness because of their injustice to each other and their syncretism with fertility cults (1:3–7). Micah's lament countered Judah's response of trusting in the safety of their fortified cities by emphasizing their lack of safety in the face of impending doom. It is interesting to note that the elders in Jeremiah's time recognized that Hezekiah heeded Micah's prophecy and saved Jerusalem from destruction (Jeremiah 26:18–19).

This paper has examined Micah's lamentation for the towns of the Judean Shephelah recorded in Micah 1:10–16. As Daniel Smith-Christopher notes,

> There are many allusions to ideas, prejudices, or opinions about local political realities and regional struggles that we may never fully comprehend—some of which may even

> include made-up locations in the Shephelah simply to express the idea of local villages and their issues of concern . . . or even local nicknames lost to history.[61]

While the precise meaning of each component within this dirge cannot be fully clarified, textual considerations, geography, history, and archaeology have proven beneficial in the study of this passage. By grasping a small part of the larger concepts of judgment, hope, and mercy within the book of Micah, the prophets become more manageable, and Micah's world and words become clearer to the modern mind. Although we may not have Assyrians, Arameans, or Babylonians poised to invade our lands, we still have a responsibility to be just in our personal relationships and have the appropriate response to sin. The unchanging God still commands his elect to be just in their dealings with each other and exclusive in their relationship to him.

Notes

1. Quoted in Gerhard von Rad, *Old Testament Theology,* vol. 2 (New York: Harper & Row, 1965), 33n1.
2. See Anthony J. Petrotta, *Lexis Ludens: Wordplay and the Book of Micah* (New York: Peter Lang, 1991), 5–8 for a comprehensive discussion of the definitions of "wordplay," "pun," and "paronomasia," with the latter primarily concerned with phonology. Following Petrotta's introduction, wordplay and paronomasia are used interchangeably within this paper.
3. Philip J. King, *Amos, Hosea, Micah–An Archaeological Commentary* (Philadelphia: Westminster Press, 1988), 27–28.
4. Hans Walter Wolff, *Micah the Prophet,* trans. R. Gehrke (Philadelphia: Fortress Press, 1981), 4; but Francis I. Anderson and David Noel Freedman, *Micah: A New Translation with Introduction and Commentary,* The Anchor Bible 24E (New York: Doubleday, 2000), 109–10 see no support from the biblical language or overall message of Micah to support Wolff's suggestion.

5. Otto Eissfeldt, *The Old Testament: An Introduction* (New York: Harper and Row, 1965), 407; see also Ralph L. Smith, *Micah–Malachi*, Word Biblical Commentary 32nd ed. (Waco, TX: Word Books, 1984), 14; and Anderson and Freedman, *Micah*, 109.
6. Although scholars debate Micah's authorship of the last four chapters, overall, the book of Micah is probably best viewed as an anthology of Micah's oracles; see R. K. Harrison, *Introduction to the Old Testament* (Grand Rapids, MI: Eerdmans, 1969), 922–25 for a summary of the literary criticism of Micah since the nineteenth century that has attempted to distinguish "genuine" passages within the book.
7. See for example Micah 1:6–7, 15–16; 3:12; 4:10; 5:5–6, 10–15; and 6:16.
8. See Isaiah 2:2–4 for a contemporary parallel prophecy later quoted in 2 Nephi 12:2–4.
9. Hans Walter Wolff, *Micah: A Commentary* (Minneapolis, MN: Augsberg, 1990), 58; see also Mignon R. Jacobs, *The Conceptual Coherence of the Book of Micah* (Sheffield, UK: Sheffield Academic Press, 2001), 107. Isaiah (20:2–4) also delivered oracles concerning Egyptian and Nubian captives of Assyria in this state of undress.
10. Anderson and Freedman, *Micah*, 130–31.
11. Bernhard W. Anderson, *The Eighth Century Prophets: Amos, Hosea, Isaiah, Micah* (Philadelphia: Fortress Press, 1978), 5. Nadav Na'aman, "'The House-of-No-Shade Shall Take Away Its Tax from You' (Micah I 11)," *Vetus Testamentum* 45 (1995): 525 construes this section as an invitation "to lament the imminent catastrophe" of Sennacherib's campaign, a position grammatically sustained by the use of perfect verbs "interpreted as indications of the prophetic future."
12. Anderson, *The Eighth Century Prophets*, 16; Na'aman, "Micah I 11," 523; see also John H. Walton, Victor H. Matthews, and Mark W. Chavalas, *The IVP Bible Background Commentary: Old Testament* (Downers Grove, IL: IVP Academic, 2000), 782, who interpret the list as an indicator of order of the Assyrian campaign.

13. James L. Mays, *Micah: A Commentary* (Philadelphia: Westminster Press, 1976), 51.
14. Smith, *Micah–Malachi*, 20.
15. Petrotta, *Lexis Ludens*, 84–85.
16. Wolff, *Micah the Prophet*, 40–41.
17. Yohanan Aharoni, *The Land of the Bible*, trans. A. Rainey (Philadelphia: Westminster, 1979), 6; see also James Monson, *Regions on the Run: Introductory Map Studies in the Land of the Bible* (Rockford, IL: Biblical Backgrounds, 2009), 6–7.
18. Aharoni, *Land of the Bible*, 23.
19. James B. Pritchard, *Ancient Near Eastern Texts Relating to the Old Testament*, 3rd ed. (Princeton: Princeton University Press, 1969), 287–88; see David Ussishkin, *The Conquest of Lachish by Sennacherib* (Tel Aviv: The Institute of Archaeology, 1982) for details of the reliefs depicting the Assyrian siege and capture of Lachish.
20. Pritchard, *Ancient Near Eastern Texts*, 288.
21. King, *Amos, Hosea, Micah*, 30.
22. J. M. P. Smith, W. H. Ward, and J. A. Brewer, *A Critical and Exegetical Commentary on Micah, Zephaniah, Nahum, Habakkuk, Obadiah, and Joel* (New York: Charles Scribner's Sons, 1911), 19.
23. Wolff, *Micah the Prophet*, 3.
24. Matthew J. Suriano, "A Place in the Dust: Text, Topography and a Toponymic Note on Micah 1:10–12a," *Vetus Testamentum* 60 (2010): 433–46.
25. Na'aman, "Micah I 11," 523.
26. Yigal Levin, "The Search for Moresheth-Gath: A New Proposal," *Palestine Exploration Quarterly* 134 (2002): 28.
27. Ephraim Stern, "Ẓafit, Tel," in *New Encyclopedia of Archaeological Excavations in the Holy Land*, vol. 4, ed. E. Stern (Jerusalem: Carta, 1993), 1522; Aren Maeir, "Ẓafit, Tel," in *New Encyclopedia of Archaeological Excavations in the Holy Land*, vol. 5, ed. E. Stern (Jerusalem and Washington, DC: Israel Exploration Society and Biblical Archaeological Society), 2079–81.

28. Alexander Zukerman and Aren Maeir, "The Stratigraphy and Architecture of Area A: Strata A1–A5," in *Tell es-Safi/Gath I: The 1996–2005 Seasons*, ed. A. Maeir, Agypten und Altes Testament 69 (Berlin: Harrassowitz Verlag, 2012), 208.
29. Stern, "Ẓafit, Tel," 1524; storage jars with such stamped handles are widely considered to be indicators of the administrative measures of Hezekiah to collect and redistribute foodstuffs throughout Judah in preparation for the rebellion against Assyrian control.
30. Some scholars do not see evidence of wordplay in the initial portion of verse 10; see Smith, *Hosea, Amos, Micah*, 453, and Anderson and Freedman, *Micah*, 213.
31. Anderson and Freedman, *Micah*, 216.
32. L. Allen, *The Books of Joel, Obadiah, Jonah, and Micah* (Grand Rapids, MI: Eerdmans, 1976), 279.
33. Suriano, "A Place in the Dust," 441–43.
34. William G. Dever, "Qôm, Khirbet el-," in *New Encyclopedia of Archaeological Excavations in the Holy Land*, vol. 4, ed. E. Stern (Jerusalem: Carta, 1993), 1233; see also King, *Amos, Hosea, Micah*, 59.
35. Allen, *The Books of Joel, Obadiah, Jonah, and Micah*, 280.
36. Anderson and Freedman, *Micah*, 209, 213.
37. Na'aman, "Micah I 11," 520.
38. Allen, *The Books of Joel, Obadiah, Jonah, and Micah*, 280.
39. Anderson and Freedman, *Micah*, 225.
40. Occupied for most of the Bronze and Iron Ages, Lachish has a history of human habitation stretching back to the fourth millennium BC; see David Ussishkin, ed., *The Renewed Archaeological Excavations at Lachish (1973–1994)*, 5 vols. (Tel Aviv: Sonia and Marco Nadler Institute of Archaeology, Tel Aviv University, 2004). During Sennacherib's campaign, the Assyrians built a large siege ramp that is still visible today. The fall of Lachish in 701 BC was devastating, as it virtually spelled doom for Jerusalem, but not insurmountable as Lachish was rebuilt and destroyed again during the Babylonian assault on Judah in 586 BC.

41. For chariots as the sin of Lachish, see Allen, *The Books of Joel, Obadiah, Jonah, and Micah*, 281; Mays, *Micah*, 58; and George Adam Smith, *The Book of the Twelve Prophets*, vol. 1 (New York: George H. Doran, 1894), 383; see also B. Vawter, *Amos, Hosea, Micah with an Introduction to Classical Prophecy* (Wilmington, VA: Michael Glazier, 1981), 135.
42. See Hosea 10:13, 14:3; Isaiah 2:7, 30:16, and 31:1.
43. Daniel Smith-Christopher, *Micah: A Commentary* (Louisville, KY: Westminster John Knox Press, 2015) 75.
44. Anderson and Freedman, *Micah*, 230.
45. "An Important Archaeological Discovery: A Gate-Shrine Dating to the First Temple Period was Exposed In Excavations of the Israel Antiquities Authority in the Tel Lachish National Park," http://www.antiquities.org.il/Article_eng.aspx?sec_id=25&subj_id=240&id=4221.
46. Wolff, *Micah the Prophet*, 8.
47. Aharoni, *Land of the Bible*, 109.
48. Aharoni, *Land of the Bible*, 330.
49. Frederick Jones Bliss and R. A. Stewart Macalister, *Excavations in Palestine During the Years 1898–1900* (London: Palestine Exploration Fund, 1902), 50.
50. Shimon Gibson, "The Tell ej-Judeideh (Tel Goded) Excavations: A Re-Appraisal Based on Archival Records in the Palestine Exploration Fund," *Tel Aviv* 21 (1994): 230.
51. Levin, "The Search for Moresheth-Gath," 28–36.
52. Shmuel Givon, "Ḥarasim, Tel" in *New Encyclopedia of Archaeological Excavations in the Holy Land*, vol. 5, ed. E. Stern (Jerusalem and Washington, DC: Israel Exploration Society and Biblical Archaeological Society), 1767.
53. King, *Amos, Hosea, Micah*, 60.
54. Michael Avi-Yonah, "Mareshah (Marisa)" in *New Encyclopedia of Archaeological Excavations in the Holy Land*, vol. 3, ed. E. Stern (Jerusalem and New York, NY: Carta and Simon & Schuster, 1993), 948.
55. Anderson and Freedman, *Micah*, 213.
56. R. Chisholm, *Interpreting the Minor Prophets* (Grand Rapids, MI: Zondervan, 1990), 137; see also Mays, *Micah*, 59.

57. Smith, *Hosea, Amos, Micah*, 454.
58. W. McKane, *The Book of Micah: Introduction and Commentary* (Edinburgh: T&T Clark, 1998), 48
59. Philip J. King and Lawrence E. Stager, *Life in Biblical Israel* (Louisville, KY: Westminster John Knox Press, 2001), 373; Texts with these mourning elements also include 2 Samuel 1:11–12, 3:31; Jeremiah 6:26, 7:29, 9:16–17; Lamentations 2:10; and Isaiah 15:2.
60. Oded Borowski, *Every Living Thing: Daily Use of Animals in Ancient Israel* (Walnut Creek, CA: AltaMira Press, 1998), 150.
61. Smith-Christopher, *Micah*, 70.

8

"O Lord God, Forgive!"

Prophetic Intercession in Amos

Joshua M. Sears

Joshua M. Sears is a doctoral candidate in
Hebrew Bible at The University of Texas at Austin.

Prophets are commonly defined as messengers or spokesmen who represent God and make known his will to people on earth. Less familiar, however, are scriptural depictions that flip this image and show prophets representing humans before God. For example, "Samuel told all the words of the LORD unto the people," but then he also "heard all the words of the people, and he rehearsed them in the ears of the LORD" (1 Samuel 8:10, 21). One important way the prophets act as emissaries *to* God is by engaging in intercession, that is, speaking to God in behalf of others in order to defend or assist them.[1] Their pleas for their fellow mortals respond to or anticipate some calamity, often at God's own hand. In one account, "the LORD sent thunder and rain that day . . . And all the people said unto Samuel, Pray for thy servants unto the LORD thy God, that we die not" (12:18–19). Not only did Samuel agree to take their plea to the Lord but also told them, "God forbid that I should sin against the LORD in ceasing to pray for you" (12:23). Samuel saw such prayers as a crucial part of his prophetic ministry.[2]

Although Samuel, Moses, and Jeremiah are the Bible's most famous prophet-intercessors, in this chapter I will focus on the intercessory activity of a less well-known figure, the prophet Amos. I will begin by analyzing relevant passages in the book of Amos line by line, attempting to clarify their context for those less familiar with them. I will then explore how these passages use intercession to advance the message of God's coming judgment. Like many texts describing intercession, the rhetoric of Amos's experiences can be difficult, even troubling, for modern readers, and so I will close with a more theologically oriented reflection on how we might understand that rhetoric.

Introduction to Amos

The prophet Amos lived in the eighth century BC, a contemporary of Isaiah, Hosea, and Micah. He describes himself as a "herdman, and a gatherer of sycomore fruit" (Amos 7:14), before "the LORD took me as I followed the flock, and . . . said unto me, Go, prophesy unto my people Israel" (7:15). This call brought him from his native Tekoa, in the Southern Kingdom of Judah (1:1), to prophesy to those living in the Northern Kingdom of Israel.

The book of Amos consists of just nine modern chapters, but its internal structure is quite complex, and theories about its composition and editing vary considerably.[3] Amos's intercessory petitions appear in the context of four visions, found in Amos 7:1–3, 7:4–6, 7:7–9, and 8:1–3. The first two visions form a complementary pair, as do the last two, and the four together form two contrasting pairs.[4] The book contains an additional vision in 9:1–4, but it does not share the same structural connections as the first four; therefore, I do not include it in the discussion below.[5]

The First and Second Visions: Amos Successfully Intercedes for Israel

The first and second visions (7:1–3 and 7:4–6) have a very similar structure. Each opens with Amos beholding a terrible disaster: a plague of locusts and a devouring fire, respectively. That Amos would be privileged to preview God's plans is in harmony with a statement from elsewhere in his book: "Surely the Lord GOD will do nothing, but he revealeth his secret unto his servants the prophets" (3:7). As these visions unfold, Amos reacts to the scenes of destruction by interceding in Israel's behalf. For the locusts he pleads, "O Lord GOD, forgive" (7:2), and for the fire he changes a single word—"O Lord GOD, cease" (7:5). Both "forgive" and "cease" are commands, even in Hebrew, suggesting Amos's urgency.[6]

Following his pleas to either forgive or stop, the first two visions proceed with Amos offering the same brief explanation: "By whom shall Jacob arise? for he is small" (7:2, 5). "Small" is perhaps best understood as a relative description, acknowledging that however powerful Israel may be, it would be irreversibly devastated by the "firepower" God proposes sending against it. Some have interpreted Amos's words as an emotional appeal, revealing a tender heart within a man often characterized as a prophet of doom. Others see this as a forceful accusation that total annihilation would violate God's covenant promises. Whether his words are a sympathetic response or a suit for breach of contract (or both), it is significant that Amos does not appeal to the people's righteousness or repentance—and given the tone of the rest of the book, there does not appear to be much evidence for either.

Following Amos's intercessions comes the Lord's response. After the first intercession, the account reports: "The LORD repented for this: It shall not be, saith the LORD" (7:3). The report after the second intercession varies only slightly: "The LORD repented for this: This also shall not be, saith the Lord GOD" (7:6). The King James Version's phrasing of "the LORD repented" is problematic for modern readers. "Repented" translates the Hebrew verb *nḥm*, a theologically rich word with a variety of possible meanings, including "to regret," "to feel sorrow or sympathy," "to comfort," or "to relent or forebear." Rather than God "repenting" (with that word's modern connotation of sinfulness), a better contextual translation in Amos 7:3, 6 might be "the Lord relented" or "the Lord changed his mind."[7] Thus Amos's intercessions during the first and second visions meet with success—at least for a time.

The Third and Fourth Visions: Amos Does Not Intercede for Israel

Just as the first and second visions share a similar structure, the third and fourth visions (7:7–9; 8:1–3) can be read in parallel. Each vision opens with God showing Amos an object: first, "a plumbline in his [God's] hand" (7:7), and second, "a basket of summer fruit" (8:1). In each case God then asks, "Amos, what seest thou?" (7:8; 8:2). To both queries Amos gives a brief response: "A plumbline" and "A basket of summer fruit." These answers are Amos's final words in these two visions; God does all the talking from this point forward.

In response to Amos's identification of the plumbline—a tool used to make a vertical reference line during construction—God states, "Behold, I will set a plumbline in the midst of my people Israel: I will not again pass by them any more: And the high places of Isaac shall be desolate, and the sanctuaries of Israel shall be laid waste; and I will rise against the house of Jeroboam with the sword" (7:8–9). The plumbline indicates that Israel's behavior is not aligned with God's commands, and it will consequently be destroyed.[8] This time, Amos offers no intercessory protest.

In response to Amos's identification of the basket of summer fruit, God states, "The end is come upon my people of Israel; I will not again pass by them any more. And the songs of the temple shall be howlings in that day, saith the Lord GOD: there shall be many dead bodies in every place; they shall cast them forth with silence" (8:2–3). A Hebrew word-play connects the "summer fruit" (*qāyiṣ*) with God's pronouncement of the coming "end" (*qēṣ*). Again, Amos offers no challenge to this plan.[9]

In both the third and fourth visions, God repeats the key line, "I will not again pass by them any more" (7:8; 8:2). The phrase "pass by" translates the Hebrew *'br,* a common verb that usually refers to spatial movement, such as "to pass through" or "go, come, or cross over." The word *'br* also has a number of figurative meanings, one of which is the forgiving of sin (for examples, see 2 Samuel 12:13, 24:10, Micah 7:18, Job 7:21, or Zechariah 3:4). Something like "forgive" or "pardon" is the most likely fit for the context of Amos 7:8 and 8:2.[10]

The final Hebrew word at the end of the fourth vision, *has,* presents some interpretive challenges. In the King James Version, it appears as the adverbial phrase "with silence," as in, "there shall be many dead bodies in every place; they shall cast them forth *with silence* [*hās*]" (Amos 8:3; emphasis added to show how the Hebrew and English words relate). This interesting little word appears in only six other contexts:

> Judges 3:19: "[The king] said [to his courtiers], *Keep silence* [*hās*]."
>
> Nehemiah 8:11: "The Levites stilled all the people, saying, *Hold your peace* [*hassû*]."
>
> Amos 6:10: "Then shall [the survivors] say, *Hold thy tongue* [*hās*]."
>
> Habakkuk 2:20: "*Let* all the earth *keep silence* [*has*] before [the LORD]."
>
> Zephaniah 1:7: "*Hold thy peace* [*has*] at the presence of the Lord GOD."
>
> Zechariah 2:13: "*Be silent* [*has*], O all flesh, before the LORD."

All six of these other examples use *has* in an imperative or jussive (command) sense, that is, "hush!" or "be quiet!" We should probably therefore take *has* in Amos 8:3 as a command as well. Most modern-English translations do render it as a command, such as in this example from the New Revised Standard Version: "'The songs of the temple shall become wailings in that day,' says the Lord GOD; 'the dead bodies shall be many, cast out in every place. Be silent!'"

So if the last word at the end of the four visions commands silence, who does the commanding? The meaning of Amos 8:3 "has been differently perceived by different translators and interpreters" because the difficult Hebrew makes it less than clear how to tie together "the formal, logical, and syntactic connections among the various parts [of the verse]."[11] The most common approach among commentators is to compare this verse to Amos 6:9–10, a passage that also speaks of calamity and also uses the word *has*:

> And it shall come to pass, if there remain ten men in one house, that they shall die.
>
> And a man's uncle shall take him up, and he that burneth him, to bring out the bones out of the house, and shall say unto him that is by the sides of the house, Is there yet any with thee? and he shall say, No. Then shall he say, *Hold thy tongue* [*hās*]: for we may not make mention of the name of the LORD.

Some scholars understand the command for silence in this passage as reflecting a superstitious fear that speaking the name of the deity—who has destroyed large numbers of people already—will bring down death upon those who have survived.[12] Because Amos 8:3 also uses the word *has* in the context of widespread death, commentators then interpret *has* in Amos 8:3 the same way, as the cry of humans responding to the carnage. And if the final word of 8:3 is spoken by humans, then that word opens the door for the entire second half of the verse to be human speech as well, speech providing the content of the "howlings" mentioned in the first half of the verse. This is the logic behind such translations as this example from the English Standard Version: "'The songs of the temple shall become wailings in that day,' declares the Lord GOD. 'So many dead bodies!' 'They are thrown everywhere!' 'Silence!'"

I question this common interpretation of Amos 8:3 for two reasons. First, I am unconvinced that Amos 6:10 and 8:3 share such a "similar context"[13] as many have proposed. Yes, each involves mass death, but Amos 6:9–10 describes men at a house, while Amos 8:3 describes singers at the temple. Apart from the words *has* and *yhwh* ("the LORD"), the two passages share not a single vocabulary word, even in cases where words very easily could have been identical, such as *ləhôṣî'* ("bring out") or *'ăṣāmîm* ("bones") in 6:10, compared with *hišlîk* ("cast out") or *happeger* ("corpses") in 8:3. Second, I believe the grammatical evidence from Amos 8:3 points away from a change of speakers midway through that verse, meaning God is still speaking clear to the end.[14] Given those reasons, and although it runs against most commentaries, I suggest it is the Lord who commands "Silence!" at the close of the fourth vision.

If God commands silence in Amos 8:3, whom does he command? The most recent indicator of who speaks to whom appeared in the previous verse, where Amos stated, "Then said the LORD unto me . . ." If no change of speaker occurs in 8:3, then the most logical conclusion is that God continues to address Amos. His intentions will be addressed below.

The Message of the Visions

Having surveyed each of the visions, we can now examine them together. Indeed, most scholars have concluded that the reports of these visions were composed together and that "there is a certain development and progression between them."[15] While we cannot recover all the details about the experiences that lay behind the vision reports—whether they occurred on separate occasions or in succession, for example—the literary presentations of those visions in Amos 7:1–9 and 8:1–3 probably "form a single composition with its own message which can be discerned only when the separate elements are viewed together in their interrelationship."[16] Unfortunately for Amos's contemporaries, that unified message seems to be that Israel is headed toward an irreversible doom. Prophetic intercession, or the lack of it, functions as a rhetorical tool to reinforce that message.

This message of inevitable destruction begins to take shape in the first and second visions. Although Amos successfully intercedes during both of them, it does not bode well that (as presented) the first successful intercession is followed immediately by a second proposal of disaster. In addition, the change from "forgive" in the first vision to "cease" in the second may reveal a subtle but important shift in Amos's approach. "Forgive" is translated from the Hebrew verb *slḥ*, "to forgive or pardon." This verb appears forty-six times in the Old Testament, and in every instance, God is the subject of the verb, the one doing the forgiving.[17] "Cease" is translated from the Hebrew verb *ḥdl*, "to stop, cease, or desist." This verb appears fifty-seven times in the Old Testament, but, in contrast to *slḥ*, this is the only instance where God is the subject of the verb.[18] Thus, Amos moves from asking God to do something perfectly routine to asking for something completely unprecedented (at least within the literary corpus of the Bible). This strange shift may be deliberate. "Forgive" gets back to the root problem of sin, while "cease" targets only the punishment and leaves sin unresolved.[19] The second request seeks to gain less than the first and perhaps represents an awkward compromise as Amos continues to defend a people who reject his prophetic critiques.

If Amos's transition from "forgive" to "cease" represents a retreat, then that trajectory is made explicit in the shift to the third and fourth visions. As we have seen, God states in that final pair of visions that "I will not again pass by them any more," meaning he will not pardon the people. Structurally, this denial of forgiveness foils the clemency shown in the first and second visions, in which God stated that "it [the punishment] shall not be." The words "again" and "any more" presuppose that forgiveness was granted previously and thus connect the third and fourth visions with the first and second. This deliberate tie back to Amos's successful intercessions suggests that God, more than simply denying forgiveness, is also denying any new attempts to intercede.

God's denial of intercession to Amos—his message of irreversible doom—may also be reflected in how their dialogue is portrayed in these texts. A count of the number of Hebrew words each party speaks to the other reveals a striking pattern:[20]

First vision:	Amos, 10	God, 2
Second vision:	Amos, 10	God, 4
Third vision:	Amos, 1	God, 26
Fourth vision:	Amos, 2	God, 28

In contrast to the first pair of visions, God has almost completely monopolized the conversation in the second pair. Given the intercessory content of Amos's words in the first two visions, his diminished speaking role in the final two visions highlights that the option to intercede has been withdrawn.

God's denial of intercession may also be emphasized by the final word of the final vision, *has*, "silence!" I argued previously that God gives this command to Amos. Assuming that reading is correct, I find it plausible that the purpose of this order is to cut off any further intercession. This is, after all, the final word of a vision series that is very much shaped by its intercessory dynamic. This is also perhaps the point where Amos might most wish to intercede. The first vision saw the destruction of "the grass of the land" (7:2);

the second vision, "the great deep" and "a part [of the land]" (7:4); and the third vision, "the high places," "the sanctuaries," and "the house of Jeroboam" (7:9)—but only in the fourth vision are the people *themselves* the direct target, and Amos is forced to behold "many" of them, all "dead bodies" (8:3). While the text records no open protest in the third and fourth visions, it is telling that God must state yet again that the time for discussion is past.[21]

Intercession and the Character of God

Amos's experience being denied intercession highlights the theological discomfort that may arise when modern readers study intercessory accounts in scripture. Defensive arguments like Amos's make the prophet sound very much like a legal advocate, which leaves God playing the role of prosecutor—and in some depictions, a very vengeful prosecutor. As readers, are we to piously identify with God, to mentally seek acceptance of the people's well-deserved penalty? Or can we not help but feel a kinship with our fellow humans and thus see the prophet as "our" hero? Bible readers over the centuries have often resorted to two interpretive extremes, either condemning Jehovah as a cruel and bloodthirsty deity on the one hand or apologizing for God on the other by arguing ad extremum that the people very much deserve to suffer. Both views fail to grasp the full dynamics of the intercessory experience.

Prophetic intercession involves a dialogue between the prophet and God, a give-and-take flow of ideas and identities. Because prophets tap into the mind of God, even as they remain mortal men, the roles both parties play in relation to one another are not always what they seem. We may ask, if God were solely interested in prosecuting Israel, why bother holding conversations with the defense in the first place? God also serves as judge, and judgment would certainly be easier without the debate. But easier is not what he chooses.

"Shall I hide from Abraham that thing which I do[?]" God asks, before deciding no (Genesis 18:17). He tells Abraham of his plans to destroy Sodom, Abraham balks, and the intercessory probing begins (see 18:20–33). One cannot help but sense that God had intended this all along. The invitation to be challenged hints that the prosecution has more in mind than winning. Furthermore, the fact that God the judge so often decides *against* God the prosecutor suggests that, despite all the talk of death and doom, God the judge really isn't rooting for God the prosecutor after all. The division between judge, prosecution, and defense begins to break down.

Despite their literary presentation as such, intercessory episodes are not really a fight to change God's mind. Perhaps it is better to understand them as creative explorations into one of the marvelous paradoxes of our theology: the simultaneous operation of both justice and mercy within God himself. Exodus 34:6–7 records God's own description of this duality: "The Lord, The Lord God, merciful and gracious, longsuffering, and abundant in goodness and truth, Keeping mercy for thousands, forgiving iniquity and transgression and sin, and that will by no means clear the guilty; visiting the iniquity of the fathers upon the children, and upon the children's children, unto the third and to the fourth generation." Latter-day revelation provides equally poignant depictions of this internal contradiction: "And the fire of mine indignation is kindled against them; and in my hot displeasure will I send in the floods upon them, for my fierce anger is kindled against them. . . . Wherefore should not the heavens weep, seeing these shall suffer?" (Moses 7:34, 37).

As Amos and other prophets speak out against God's plans for punishment, they may actually personify God's own desire to grant mercy. Jewish scholar Yochanan Muffs argues the following:

> If there is no balance in the divine emotion, if justice gets the upper hand over mercy, then the world is placed in great danger. Therefore, God allows the prophet to represent in

> his prayer His own attribute of mercy, the very element that enables a calming of God's feelings. . . . Even at the moment of His anger, He manifests His love by listening to the prayers of the prophets, prayers that control and calm His anger.[22]

As prophets give voice to God's own desire to forgive, the literary dialogues may serve a didactic purpose—that is, the story may be there to teach us something. God could have simply told Abraham he would spare Sodom if he could find ten righteous people. But that would not have the same rhetorical effect as our actual text—eleven verses of Abraham pleading for a lower and lower and lower threshold, while God shows mercy again and again and again.[23]

This perspective might also be helpful to Latter-day Saints who wish to read these texts through a doctrinal lens that understands prophetic intercession as typological for the role of Jesus. Several scriptural passages pick up this imagery, describing Christ as one who "make[s] intercession" (Hebrews 7:25, 2 Nephi 2:9, Mosiah 15:8) or one who is our "advocate with the Father" (1 John 2:1, D&C 29:5, 32:3, 110:4), "who is pleading [our] cause before him—saying: . . . Father, spare these my brethren" (D&C 45:3–5). The rhetoric of advocacy does not force the conclusion that God, as judge and prosecutor, delights in punishing people. Indeed, Elder Jeffrey R. Holland taught that one of the great purposes of Christ's ministry was to act as the Father's love personified, to teach the people through his actions what the Father's own compassion looks like.[24]

What about circumstances where intercession fails? Amos, after all, was successful only in diverting judgment for so long. As God explained with his plumbline analogy, those who fail to align with his covenant standards cannot forever escape the consequences. Most of the rest of the book of Amos consists of a series of indictments against the Israelites, such as his skewering of the upper class for exploiting the poor (Amos 2:6–7, 4:1, 5:11–12, 6:4–7). In such circumstances, blame for the penalty lies not with God for acting nor with the intercessor for failing to act but with the people who have refused to repent. Seen in this light, God's command for Amos not to intercede anymore becomes an ironic echo of the Israelites who told Amos, "O thou seer, go, flee thee away . . . [and] prophesy not again any more" (Amos 7:12–13).

Still, when justice does demand that God act, prophetic literature often records a promise of renewal; even as bleak a book as Amos ends with hope for better days (Amos 9:11–15).[25] Jeremiah, another prophet who was denied intercession, promised:

> For thus saith the LORD, That after [the penalty] be accomplished . . . , I will visit you, and perform my good word toward you. . . .
>
> For I know the thoughts that I think toward you, saith the LORD, thoughts of peace, and not of evil, to give you an expected end.
>
> Then shall ye call upon me, and ye shall go and pray unto me, and I will hearken unto you.
>
> And ye shall seek me, and find me, when ye shall search for me with all your heart. (Jeremiah 29:10–13)

Notes

1. Although the definition of intercessory prayer has been debated, most scholars maintain that the petition must be offered in behalf of another and that it must invite God to act in response (i.e., simple lamenting is not enough). See Yochanan Muffs, *Love and Joy: Law, Language and Religion in Ancient Israel* (New York: Jewish Theological Seminary of America, 1992), 9–48; Samuel E. Balentine, "The Prophet as Intercessor: A Reassessment," *Journal of Biblical Literature* 103 (1984): 161–73; and Patrick D. Miller, *They Cried to the Lord: The Form and Theology of Biblical Prayer* (Minneapolis: Fortress, 1994), 262–80.

2. Other biblical texts involving prophetic intercession include Genesis 18:22–32; 20:7, 17; Exodus 32:7–14, 30–32; Numbers 11:1–2; 12:13; 14:11–20; 16:20–22; Deuteronomy 9:14, 18–20, 25–29; 10:10; 1 Samuel 7:5, 8–13; 15:11; 1 Kings 17:20–22; 18:41–45; 2 Kings 4:32–35; 6:17–20; Isaiah 37:4; Jeremiah 4:10; 7:16; 11:14; 14:11–12; 15:1; 18:20; 21:1–2; 27:18; 37:3; Ezekiel 9:8; 11:13; 13:5; 14:14, 20; 22:30; Amos 7:1–6; John 17; Acts 7:60; and possibly also Habakkuk 1:2–4, 12–13; 2:1; Joel 1:19; and Hosea 9:14. Some relevant texts from Restoration scripture include 1 Nephi 1:4–6; 18:21; 2 Nephi 33:3–4; Jacob 5:26–28, 49–51; Enos 1:9–12; Mosiah 27:14; Alma 14:10–11; 15:10–11; 30:54; 31:32–33; Helaman 11:3–4, 8–18; Ether 1:34–37; Moroni 9:21–22; D&C 109:47–53; 121:1–6; Official Declaration 2; and Moses 7:49–51.
3. For a well-written and relatively up-to-date review, see Tchavdar S. Hadjiev, *The Composition and Redaction of the Book of Amos*, Beihefte zur Zeitschrift für die alttestamentliche Wissenschaft 393 (Berlin: de Gruyter, 2009).
4. A story describing Amos's clash with Amaziah the priest at Beth-el interrupts between the third and fourth visions (7:10–17). This narrative may have been placed after the third vision (either originally or by a later editor) because the story describes the negative reaction to Amos's announcement in the third vision that king Jeroboam would die by the sword.
5. The first four visions begin with the same opening line: "Thus hath the Lord GOD shewed unto me: and, behold . . ." (The third vision lacks the title "Lord GOD.") By contrast, the fifth vision begins "I saw . . ." and features several other differences. Scholars have never reached a consensus regarding the relationship between the four visions and this final vision. See Hadjiev, *The Composition and Redaction of the Book of Amos*, 60–73.
6. The King James Version follows both "forgive" and "cease" with the phrase "I beseech thee," which attempts to translate a Hebrew particle, *nāʾ*, that follows each verb. This word has traditionally been translated with meanings like "please" or "I pray" based on the understanding that it makes a request more polite, but its exact nuance is rather enigmatic, and

many authorities now recommend that it is better left untranslated. See Bruce K. Waltke and M. O'Connor, *An Introduction to Biblical Hebrew Syntax* (Winona Lake, IN: Eisenbrauns, 1990), §34.7.

7. The Joseph Smith Translation contains significant reinterpretations of these two verses. For Amos 7:3 the JST manuscript reads, "And the Lord said, concerning Jacob, Jacob shall repent for this, therefore I will not utterly distroy him, saith the Lord." And for verse 6 it says, "And the Lord said, concerning Jacob, —Jacob shall repent of his wickedness; therefor; I will not utterly distroy him, saith the Lord God." See Scott H. Faulring, Kent P. Jackson, and Robert J. Matthews, eds., *Joseph Smith's New Translation of the Bible: Original Manuscripts* (Provo, UT: Religious Studies Center, 2004), 847; strikeouts and brackets removed.

How should these readings affect a Latter-day Saint interpretation of the text of Amos? We must remember that the JST was produced by studying and revising the King James Version of the Bible in English. Latter-day Saint scholars have proposed that these changes fall into at least five categories, including restoring the original text, revealing true but unrecorded events, editing and modernizing to make the KJV more understandable, harmonizing theology, and providing latter-day commentary. See a full explanation in *Joseph Smith's New Translation of the Bible*, 8–11; see also Ben Spackman, "Why Bible Translations Differ: A Guide for the Perplexed," *Religious Educator* 15, no. 1 (2014): 51–53. Of these five categories, editing to make the KJV more understandable for modern readers seems to account for "more individual corrections . . . than . . . any other [category]." Kent P. Jackson, "New Discoveries in the Joseph Smith Translation of the Bible," *Religious Educator* 6, no. 3 (2005): 153. I believe this is also the best lens through which to understand the JST emendations to Amos 7:3 and 7:6. The changes made to the KJV in these verses fit within a larger pattern seen in several passages of the Old Testament in which the KJV says that God "repents" (which, as noted, is an unfortunate translation of the verb *nḥm*), and the JST responds not by changing the word *repent* itself (the strategy taken by most modern-English translations) but by creatively rewriting the sentence so that some other party becomes the subject of the verb *repent*. See Robert J. Matthews, *"A Plainer Translation": Joseph Smith's Translation of the Bible—A History and Commentary* (Provo, UT: Brigham Young University Press, 1985), 311–13. Thus I interpret the Prophet's revisions in Amos 7:3, 6 as a response to an idiosyncrasy in the KJV and not as a restoration of original text, and for that reason I do not give priority to the JST readings in my discussion of the text of Amos.

8. Beginning with a 1965 article that examined comparative evidence from Akkadian sources, several modern interpreters have suggested that the Hebrew word *'ănāk* means "tin" rather than "plumbline," though the traditional translation still has its defenders. For a survey of positions, see H. G. M. Williamson, "The Prophet and the Plumb-Line: A Redaction-Critical Study of Amos 7," in *"The Place Is Too Small for Us": The Israelite Prophets in Recent Scholarship*, ed. Robert P. Gordon (Winona Lake, IN: Eisenbrauns, 1995), 459–67. The overall meaning of the third vision is clear in either case.
9. Some have taken Amos's brief responses (just one word and two words in Hebrew) to mean that he was in the dark about what these objects signified until God explained their meaning to him. For example, Tzvi Novick has argued that "God rigs the third and fourth visions so that the prophet will unwittingly sentence Israel, and thus preclude himself from again intervening on their behalf." "Duping the Prophet: On אנך (Amos 7.8b) and Amos's Visions," *Journal for the Study of the Old Testament* 33 (2008): 127. However, Amos may understand more than it first appears. Consider that, in the third vision, Amos's answer could have focused on the wall, the plumbline, or God himself, but "a plumbline" correctly identifies the component most crucial for understanding God's point. Similarly, in the fourth vision, Amos could have described the number of fruit or any other detail, but Amos's precise wording was the only possible answer that could have provided the wordplay God was looking for. As a prophet, Amos does not just "see" what others cannot see; he intuitively sifts the significant from the ancillary. See Samuel A. Meier, *Themes and Transformations in Old Testament Prophecy* (Downers Grove, IL: IVP Academic, 2009), 38–51.

10. H. F. Fuhs, "עָבַר *'āḇar*," in *Theological Dictionary of the Old Testament*, ed. G. Johannes Botterweck, Helmer Ringgren, and Heinz-Josef Fabry, trans. Douglas W. Stott (Grand Rapids, MI: Eerdmans, 1999), 10:421–22. Context is extremely important in establishing this interpretation, because while "passing by" means to pass through *without taking action* in this situation, *'br* can also be used with the opposite meaning; see Amos 5:17, where "I will pass through [*'e'ĕbōr*] thee" is God's warning that he will pass through *punishing as he goes*.
11. Francis I. Andersen and David Noel Freedman, *Amos: A New Translation with Introduction and Commentary* (New York: Doubleday, 1989), 798.
12. See Hans Walter Wolff, *Joel and Amos: A Commentary on the Books of the Prophets Joel and Amos* (Philadelphia: Fortress, 1977), 282–83; and Shalom M. Paul, *Amos: A Commentary on the Book of Amos* (Minneapolis: Fortress, 1991), 214–17.
13. Andersen and Freedman, *Amos*, 799.
14. The phrase "saith the Lord God" appears in the middle of Amos 8:3, and its position there is often used to justify the interpretation that God's voice, which began in 8:2, effectively ends at this point in 8:3 and that the rest of the verse switches to quoting terrified mortals. I disagree with this position. The word translated "saith" in the KJV is actually a noun, *nə'ūm*, which means "utterance (of)" or "declaration (of)." It appears 376 times in the Old Testament, most often in prophetic texts and usually preceding a divine title such as "the Lord"; in fact, only eleven times is *nə'ūm* used to refer to something spoken by a mortal. H. Eising, "נְאֻם *ne'um*," in *Theological Dictionary of the Old Testament*, ed. G. Johannes Botterweck, Helmer Ringgren, and Heinz-Josef Fabry, trans. David E. Green and Douglas W. Stott (Grand Rapids, MI: Eerdmans, 1998), 9:110. Many scholars have said that *nə'ūm* normally comes at the end of direct speech, but a more careful analysis reveals "this stance to be without support," as *nə'ūm* actually appears with "extreme variability" at the beginning, middle, and end of quoted material. Samuel A. Meier, *Speaking of Speaking: Marking Direct Discourse in the Hebrew Bible* (Leiden: Brill, 1992), 310; for the full

discussion, see pages 298–314. Because of this variability, "context is the only means of discriminating when [*nəʾūm*] functions as a marker of the close of speech, the beginning of speech, or a medial marker in the midst of speech." Meier, *Speaking of Speaking*, 309. Unless we predetermine that *has* in Amos 8:3 *must* be human speech due to its alleged connection to Amos 6:10, there is little contextual indication that *nəʾūm* in Amos 8:3 marks the end of God's discourse. Additionally, among the twenty other appearances of *nəʾūm* in the book of Amos specifically, seven of which also appear mid-verse, the word never indicates a switch from one speaker to another.

Of course, one could understand God continuing to speak in the second half of the verse while *quoting* what humans will say, but I also find this unlikely. The book of Amos is extremely attentive to distinguishing divine and mortal speech (see Meier, *Speaking of Speaking*, 226–29), which is especially remarkable given that the trend for prophets of Amos's era was to more loosely blend those voices (see Meier, *Themes and Transformations*, 70–77). An ambiguous change of voices in Amos 8:3 would thus be highly unusual. The lack of markers for such a change of speakers is even more striking when we compare Amos 8:3 with the other *has* passage in 6:10, where *wəʾāmar*, "he will say," appears three times to indicate a change of speaker (all human).

15. Hadjiev, *The Composition and Redaction of the Book of Amos*, 60.
16. Hadjiev, *The Composition and Redaction of the Book of Amos*, 60. Some scholars do attempt to link the vision reports to various places in Amos's life story. Andersen and Freedman, for example, interpret the first and second visions as belonging to an early stage in Amos's ministry when repentance was still possible and intercession could successfully win a reprieve from the plagues afflicting Israel. In their reconstruction, the third and fourth visions belong to a later stage when Amos's calls to repentance have been rejected and punishment becomes inevitable. Further, they divide Amos chapters 1–6 into sections that correspond with the historical setting of each vision. See Andersen and Freedman, *Amos*, 5–6, 83–88. While proposals such as these are interesting, they must ultimately remain speculation.

17. I derived this count from the list in Gerhard Lisowsky, *Konkordanz zum Hebräischen Alten Testament*, 3rd ed. (Stuttgart: Deutsche Bibelgesellschaft, 1993), 998. Thirteen times the verb is used passively (the *niphal* stem), but God is still the implied agent providing pardon.
18. Lisowsky, *Konkordanz zum Hebräischen Alten Testament*, 464.
19. See J. Hausmann, "סָלַח *sālaḥ*," in *Theological Dictionary of the Old Testament*, 10:258–65.
20. The Hebrew text consulted here and throughout is the Masoretic Text as presented in *Biblia Hebraica Quinta, Fascicle 13: The Twelve Minor Prophets*, ed. Anthony Gelston (Stuttgart: Deutsche Bibelgesellschaft, 2010).
21. This interpretation of "silence!" is strengthened by the fact that God explicitly forbids prophetic intercession elsewhere in scripture; see Exodus 32:10; Deuteronomy 9:14; Jeremiah 7:16; 11:14; 14:11; 15:1; Ezekiel 14:14, 20; Alma 14:11; 30:54–55; and Moroni 9:21.
22. Muffs, *Love and Joy*, 33.
23. See Anson Laytner, *Arguing with God: A Jewish Tradition* (Northvale, NJ: Jason Aronson, 1990), 3–8. Nathan MacDonald has characterized the exchange between Abraham and God as "a learning incident" for Abraham: "Abraham does not appeal to the mercy of God and ask for full forgiveness; instead, presuming [God] to be a harsh judge, he prepares to barter with him. His strategy is undone by [God's] persistent acceptance of Abraham's offer; [God] turns out to be far more merciful than Abraham imagines." "Listening to Abraham—Listening to Yhwh: Divine Justice and Mercy in Genesis 18:16–33," *Catholic Biblical Quarterly* 66, no. 1 (2004): 40.
24. See Jeffrey R. Holland, "The Grandeur of God," *Ensign*, November 2003, 70–73.
25. Scholars usually identify the final five verses of Amos as an editorial insertion coming from a time much later than the time of the eighth-century prophet, the optimistic tone being one feature that contrasts with the rest of the book (other differences include a sudden focus on the house of David, which the passage assumes has already fallen). See Hadjiev, *The*

Composition and Redaction of the Book of Amos, 31–32; and Andersen and Freedman, *Amos,* 893. Whether these verses go back to Amos or whether they were added later, the present text fits within a pattern found in prophetic literature of following judgment with a message of hope. See D. Kelly Ogden, "The Book of Amos," in *Studies in Scripture,* vol. 4, *First Kings to Malachi,* ed. Kent P. Jackson (Salt Lake City: Deseret Book, 1993), 59–60.

9

The Prophet's Remnant Theology

A Latter-day Saint Perspective

Joseph M. Spencer

Joseph M. Spencer is visiting assistant professor of ancient scripture at Brigham Young University.

For many reasons, Latter-day Saints tend to be more familiar with the Book of Mormon than with the Old Testament. A curious consequence of this fact is that we are sometimes aware of Old Testament *ideas* but unaware of the *sources* for and the *contexts* of those ideas. Readers of the Book of Mormon thus know from the volume's title page that it was "written to the Lamanites, who are a remnant of the house of Israel." But without substantial familiarity with the Old Testament, we might not feel the full force of this claim. The fact is that the Book of Mormon's emphasis on Israel's remnant is something it consciously borrows from the Israelite prophets. Thus, if we wish to understand better the basic purposes of the Book of Mormon, we would profit from deeper understanding of the Israelite prophets from whom the Nephite prophets drew inspiration. That is, because the first listed purpose of the Book of Mormon—again on the volume's title page—is "to show unto the remnant of the house of Israel what great things the Lord hath done for their fathers," we committed readers of the Book of Mormon would do well to become much more familiar with what the writings of the prophets have to say about the remnant idea.

Essential to understanding the larger implications of both the Bible's and the Book of Mormon's remnant theologies is the way they differ from what might be called *replacement* theologies. Replacement theologies—often called "supersessionist"—claim that Israel, although once God's chosen covenant people, was at some point replaced by another chosen covenant people, usually the Christian church. According to this viewpoint, the covenant with Israel was either temporary or transferable.[1] But according to most remnant theologies, God's covenant with Israel was inviolable, and so God can be expected to continue to work with Israel.[2] Rather than eliminating or replacing Israel as the covenant people, God consistently focuses on just the part of Israel—the remnant—that exhibits or might be taught true faithfulness. Israel *itself* is to be redeemed, beginning with whatever remnant of it remains.

My purpose in this essay is to outline the remnant theology the Nephites seem to have found in the Old Testament, albeit without giving direct attention to how the Book of Mormon interprets particular passages.[3] Because the Book of Mormon, in its development of the remnant theme, draws primarily on the books of Micah and Isaiah (see, of course, "the Isaiah chapters" of 2 Nephi 11–24, but also the uses of Micah in 3 Nephi 20–21), I will focus on them, as well as on the book of Amos, which interpreters have generally taken to provide a major source for Micah and Isaiah. Further and by way of preparation, I will look briefly at references to the remnant idea in the books Israel produced to explain its history and its prehistory. Seeing how this theme is developed in key places in the Hebrew Bible's prophetic books should help Latter-day Saints see how the Book of Mormon is part of a long history of prophetic reflection on the idea of the remnant.

Laying a Foundation

The idea of the remnant can be found already in the stories ancient Israel had to tell about its own prehistory—that is, about Abraham's predecessors—and a theological reading of these stories can prepare for a study of what the books of Amos, Micah, and Isaiah have to say. Israel seems to have inherited the theme of the remnant in large part from its neighbors in the ancient near east, where notions of a divinely-saved remnant appear in various forms in different cultures and contexts.[4] Israel often inherited its basic view of the world from the larger cultural context in which it found itself, and this seems to have been the case with the idea of the remnant. But, as it often did with ideas it borrowed from its neighbors, Israel developed the remnant theme in unique and—as the Book of Mormon insists—importantly inspired ways. These developments are what deserve theological attention, and they are found in a kind of foundational form in the stories Israel told about its origins.

Every reader of the Bible is familiar with the story of Noah, through whom God preserved life on earth. In one summary description of the flood, Genesis describes Noah's survival by using the verbal form of the Hebrew noun (šĕʾār) that is later consistently used by Micah and Isaiah to speak of Israel's remnant: "And every living substance was destroyed which was upon the face of the ground, both man, and cattle, and the creeping things, and the fowl of the heaven; and they were destroyed from the earth: and Noah only remained alive [*yišāʾer*], and they that were with him in the ark" (Genesis 7:23). In this passage, D. M. Warne interprets that the author of Genesis "has made the concept of the remnant an integral part of primitive history."[5] In other words, from the point of view of Genesis, the whole of humankind can be understood to be a remnant, just a fragment of what *might* have been. Human beings as we know them after the flood are, in their very being, *survivors*.[6]

This idea—that all human beings since the flood are part of a divinely delivered remnant—is of peculiar theological significance.[7] Inasmuch as I recognize that I live only because of God's goodness in the past, I am prepared to recognize my weakness as a human being and my consequent dependence on divine grace at every moment. Significantly, according to Genesis, God's action immediately following the flood was to give to surviving humanity not only a well-known covenant but also a new law that focused them on the fragility of life (see Genesis 9:1–17). On one reading, the story thus indicates that it is only as humankind is reduced to a remnant that it might be prepared to live according to divine laws. If human beings see themselves as survivors, preserved from destruction only by God's grace, they might prove humble enough to receive guidance from their Creator.[8]

Of course, as the stories in Genesis that follow after that of the flood suggest, human beings quickly forget their dependence on God. They find supposed strength and pretended sufficiency in their national identities, propped up by their national deities. Thus, after the flood, Genesis recounts the rise of the great nations (see Genesis 10:1–32), with the chief of them organized around a misguided form of worship (see Genesis 11:1–9). The result, it seems, is a world full of human beings who seek not God but "a name" for themselves. They appear to find strength only in numbers, and what they seem to fear above all else is the possibility that they might "be scattered abroad upon the face of the whole earth." And yet, despite their fears, they exhibit what seems to be remarkable arrogance, seeking to produce a human construction with its top near heaven (see Genesis 11:4)! Disregarding the lesson of the flood, humankind refuses to see its life and preservation on the earth as a gift of God. We fail to see that we are only a remnant of humankind, just as we consistently fail to live the law God has given to us all.

The narrative sequence of Genesis suggests that it was in part to solve this problem that God called on Abraham and Sarah, promising to make of them a nation that might serve as a light to other nations (see Genesis 12:1–3). Through Abraham and Sarah there thus came into the world a nation apparently meant to be unlike the other nations: a nation fully aware of the true God and therefore attuned to its own weakness (a nation that exists only inasmuch as it remains bound to God by covenant). Abraham's and Sarah's experiences certainly seem tailored to teach them their absolute dependence on God—for example, through the impossible but promised birth of Isaac or through the impossible but real commandment to offer Isaac in sacrifice (which Isaac survives and so himself becomes a remnant). If their example of care for divine instruction, coupled with recognition of their dependence on God, could be put on display before the world, then it might be that "all families of the earth" could "be blessed" (Genesis 12:3).[9] Unfortunately, however, it took only a few generations for Abraham's descendants to fall in with other traditions. At one point they explicitly sought to be "like all the nations" (1 Samuel 8:5), and from almost the beginning they "served other gods" and hoped that the true God would "not reign over them" (1 Samuel 8:7–8). Eventually, then, there arose an Israelite prophet who could lament before the Lord in utter despair: "The children of Israel have forsaken thy covenant, thrown down thine altars, and slain thy prophets with the sword; and I, even I only, am left; and they seek my life, to take it away" (1 Kings 19:10).

These last words are those of the prophet Elijah, uttered, according to the biblical text, a hundred years before Amos, Micah, and Isaiah.[10] Significantly, the text presents the Lord as gently rebuking Elijah for his despair. "Yet I have left me [*hiš'artî*] seven thousand in Israel," the Lord says to the frustrated prophet, "all the knees which have not bowed unto Baal, and every mouth which hath not kissed him" (1 Kings 19:18). It is true enough that the covenant people fall short of their responsibilities. They too seldom see their weakness, too seldom acknowledge their dependence on God. Those bound by the covenant spend much of their time seeking to be like the nations from among which they are summoned. Yet, as God's words to Elijah make clear, even at the worst moments in history, there is at least a part of Israel—a remnant—attuned in the right way to the Lord's intentions. In this passage, as in the flood story, the noun used in Micah and Isaiah to describe the Israelite remnant (šĕʾār) appears in verbal form. But here it seems to mark something new. In the Lord's word to Elijah, he does not refer to the remnant of *all* humanity (as in the Flood); he refers to only a remnant of *Israel*. As Gerhard Hasel notes, "We meet in this passage for the first time in the history of Israel the promise of a future remnant that constitutes the kernel of a new Israel."[11]

This narrowing of emphasis—from the Flood story's emphasis on the remnant of all humanity to an emphasis on the remnant just of Israel—opens onto the books of Amos, Micah, and Isaiah. These books concern themselves primarily with the remnant of Israel, rather than with the remnant of humanity. And yet the larger history from the Flood to the time of Elijah helps to clarify the theological stakes of the remnant theme in these books. In narrowing Israel down to a preserved remnant—a group of Israelite survivors finally fully prepared to live the divine law—God brings the covenant people to see their weakness and dependence. And inasmuch as God succeeds in bringing Israel to see its true relationship to him, he makes it possible for the Israelite remnant to bring the remainder of humanity to see its own weakness and its dependence on God. It is perhaps only as Israel becomes a mere remnant of itself that it can earnestly call the rest of humankind to a recognition of the fact that all human beings are survivors, the beneficiaries of God's goodness and grace.

In light of these precedents, on the reading outlined here, it is possible to consider what the prophets on whose books the Book of Mormon draws have to say about Israel's remnant.

The Book of Amos

Amos, originally a shepherd from the small Judahite village of Tekoa (see Amos 1:1), is a fiery prophet with an uncomfortable message for the northern kingdom of Israel. Although the book of Amos occasionally speaks of hope and redemption, it much more consistently condemns the prophet's hearers. And the style with which it does so is devastating. Amos deploys theological themes of Israel's historical self-understanding (they are the elect to whom God has bound himself, and therefore they will be delivered from their enemies). But he provides these themes—the theme of the remnant's deliverance included—with "a radical reinterpretation."[12] "You only have I known of all the families of the earth," the Lord says through Amos; but the consequence of this special relationship with God is a unique sense of responsibility and therefore a unique judgment: "*Therefore* I will punish you for all your iniquities" (Amos 3:2; emphasis added). Readers are meant to understand that where Israel had come to trust that its covenantal relationship to the Lord would secure its preservation, Amos announces that this promise is unstable.

Accordingly, in the first allusion to the remnant in Amos, the prophet addresses the wealthy in ancient Samaria with a creative refashioning of the well-known[13] remnant theme: "As the shepherd rescueth from the mouth of the lion two legs, or a piece of an ear; so shall the children of Israel be rescued that dwell in Samaria, only with the corner of a bed, and with the foot of a couch" (Amos 3:12, translation modified).[14] While this prophecy might seem at first to indicate that wicked Israelites can look forward to a partial deliverance from their enemies, one possible reading suggests that Amos uses the remnant theme *against* Israel. According to Hans Walter Wolff, Amos's "example presupposes a specific statute drawn from the laws governing shepherds," in which physical evidence of a wild beast's attack excused a domesticated animal's caretaker of any responsibility for the loss of property. "Two thin splint-bones or merely the tip of an ear would constitute admissible pieces of evidence." But, of course, Wolff goes on to point out, "those little bits of 'rescued' evidence" legally serve only as "proof that *total loss* was unavoidable."[15] In parallel, the bits of furniture in Amos's prophecy—"the corner of a bed," "the foot of a couch"—serve not as symbols of Israel's survival but as tokens of their eradication. Amos's readers know of the promises that God will preserve a remnant from Israel, but Amos predicts that the only remnant one can expect will be material possessions left behind in death.

Similarly negative prophetic words regarding an Israelite remnant appear in Amos 6:9–10 and 9:1–4. In the latter,[16] more or less at the conclusion of the book,[17] Amos provides his most extreme statement. Elsewhere, Amos concedes the promise of a remnant while criticizing those who use it to justify their wickedness and corruption. But in Amos 9:1–4, the prophet suggests the possibility that Israel might ultimately be left without any remnant at all. "He that fleeth" and "he that escapeth," Amos says, referring to those who could constitute a preserved remnant of Israel, are both to end up dead. "I will slay the last of them with the sword," the Lord says through the prophet; although some might "go into captivity before their enemies," the Lord announces that he will "command the sword, and it shall slay them" as well (Amos 9:1, 4).[18]

This worry, expressed at the close of the book of Amos, seems to lie at the root of the indecision Amos expresses in his most explicit statement regarding Israel's remnant—a key passage where he employs the term used more consistently by Micah and Isaiah to describe the remnant (šĕʾērīt). Tying promises to commandments (to "seek" and to "love" the good), Amos hopes that "the Lord God of hosts will be gracious unto the remnant of Joseph" (Amos 5:14–15). But he expresses this hope as just a possibility: "It may be [ʾûlay, perhaps] that the Lord God of hosts will be gracious unto the remnant of Joseph" (Amos 5:15).[19] Paul Noble points out that Amos's "perhaps" focuses less on the "existence" of the remnant than on "whether or not it will enjoy God's favor"; Amos "in fact takes it for granted that there will be a remnant."[20] This seems right, but of course any continued existence for a remnant of Israel *without* God's gracious attention would be *mere* survival—not *life*. Amos's "perhaps" thus underscores the prophet's "extremely paradoxical notion of a remnant: Its unconditional survival is immediately juxtaposed to equally unconditional images of total destruction."[21]

It is this paradox that the book of Amos ultimately presents in connection with the remnant. It draws on an idea that readers are led to see as already developed into a well-known theme, but it expresses inspired skepticism that the promises associated with the remnant should be used by Israelites without fear and trembling. Amos exhibits confidence that God will be true to his word, but he simultaneously despairs of Israel being true enough to their word to see the promises fulfilled as popularly anticipated. What good would it do to reduce Israel to a preserved remnant if it were no more committed to living the divine law than those whom it survives? Before Micah and Isaiah, prophets whose books are more naturally optimistic with respect to the remnant, Amos sounds an important note of caution regarding the theme.

The Book of Micah

Where the book of Amos arguably exhibits a relatively loose organization, the book of Micah reads as rather tightly ordered, especially in light of the remnant theme. The book divides into three sequences (chapters 1–2, chapters 3–5, and chapters 6–7), each concluding with a reflection on the theme of the remnant.[22] Where Amos either expresses ambivalence or outlines a paradox concerning the remnant, Micah provides a near-systematic theology along with a theological perspective consistently rooted in hope for Israel. But Micah's hope focuses primarily on just a *part* of Israel: the southern kingdom of

Judah. During the period of Micah's prophecy, the northern kingdom of Israel was destroyed while the southern kingdom, Judah, survived. For Micah, then, Judah itself comes eventually to serve as a kind of remnant of Israel, the focus of promise and hope.

The first two chapters of Micah present a devastating prophecy of doom and destruction. "The Lord cometh forth out of his place," the prophet announces, "and the mountains shall be molten under him . . . as wax before the fire" (Micah 1:3–4). Samaria, the capital of Israel's northern kingdom is to become "an heap of the field" (1:6), and Jerusalem, the parallel capital of Israel's southern kingdom of Judah, is to receive a "wound" that "is incurable" (1:9). And this announcement distresses the prophet. "I will wail and howl," he cries out; "I will go stripped and naked" in mourning (1:8). Naturally, what Micah condemns in Israelite and especially Judahite culture is what all the prophets of the eighth century condemn: obsession with wealth and gain, mistreatment of the marginalized and underprivileged, and a tendency toward substance abuse (see Micah 2:1–11). It is for all these clear wrongs, amounting to systematic abandonment of the Abrahamic heritage, that the covenant people deserve Micah's strong rebuke. But there follows a word of hope from the Lord: "I will surely assemble, O Jacob, all of thee; I will surely gather the remnant of Israel" (2:12).[23] The passage even promises that the remnant either will be large from the beginning or will grow, since "they shall make great noise by reason of the multitude of men" (2:12). Leading the remnant, moreover, is "their king," and at their head stands "the Lord" himself (2:13).[24]

Chapters 1–2 establish the pattern for the book of Micah. Chapters 3–5 also present prophecies of doom and destruction but then work their way toward anticipations of the remnant's redemption. And then chapters 6–7, with a rather different tone and style, do the same. In the last section, the plight of Israel is presented more personally than it is in Micah 1–5, through a series of laments about the impossibility of commending the covenant people to God. These conclude with the question of whether there is any God like Israel's God "that pardoneth iniquity, and passeth by the transgression of the remnant of his heritage" (Micah 7:18). The book of Micah thus concludes on a particularly hopeful and worshipful note, with confidence in God's "mercy to Abraham" (7:20). But it is in the central portion of the book, in chapters 3–5, that the most remarkable of Micah's treatments of the remnant theme appear. And what is especially significant is the way that, in these chapters, Micah attempts to discern a previously unrecognized divine purpose for the winnowing of Israel down to a remnant.

In Micah 3, the prophet again focuses on the sins of Judah but now with an intense focus on corruption, both in Judah's political institutions (especially in the courts) and in Judah's religious institutions (thanks especially to false prophets). Micah describes the judicial system in Jerusalem as cannibalistic, with judges who not only "hate the good, and love the evil" but who also "eat the flesh of [God's] people, and flay their skin from off them" (Micah 3:2–3). He then condemns "the prophets that make [the Lord's] people err" because they falsely cry "peace" when they have "no answer of God" (3:5, 7). All this amounts to a building up of Jerusalem "with blood" and "with iniquity" rather than with truth and justice (3:10), and the prophet announces that the city will consequently "be plowed as a field" and "become heaps" (3:12). But then, as before, Micah interrupts these harsh words with a prophetic message of promise. Destruction will serve to purify the covenant people by reducing them to a remnant that might be gathered and finally prepared to do God's real work. But what, according to Micah, is this work?

The message of promise opens with Micah's famous words regarding the establishment of "the house of the Lord . . . in the top of the mountains" (Micah 4:1). To this place where the true God might be worshiped Micah sees "many nations" gathering, "beat[ing] their swords into plowshares, and their spears into pruninghooks" (4:2–3).[25] Here the prophet begins to indicate the purpose of singling out a band of Israelite survivors for divine purposes. Producing a remnant requires that Israel come into contact with non-covenantal peoples—that is, with *gentiles*. (The Hebrew word translated "nations" in the passage just cited, *gôyīm*, is the same often translated as "gentiles" in the King James Version. The gentiles *are* the nations.) It is in the wake of Israel's winnowing that it is possible for the covenant people to serve as a light to non-covenant peoples, at last implicitly inviting them to live "the law" that "go[es] forth of Zion" (Micah 4:2). (Presumably this is in part because the winnowed remnant of Israel is itself finally prepared to live quite fully the law gracefully given to it.) Seeing themselves as a remnant dependent on God's goodness for their survival, and forced by history to be in contact with non-covenantal peoples, the remnant of Israel can serve as instructive examples for gentiles of what it might mean for them to understand their own dependence on the true God.[26]

Thus Micah next prophesies of what Israel's remnant will do "in that day" (Micah 4:6), that is, in the day when the nations might be summoned to worship in "the house of the Lord" (4:1). God promises to "make her that halted a remnant, and her that was cast far off a strong nation: and the Lord shall reign over them in mount Zion from henceforth, even for ever" (4:7). God gathers the survivors of Israel's difficult history as a remnant over which he might finally rule in righteousness—as Hans Walter Wolff puts it, "the Lord is still king over the heap of ruins"[27]—and they are therefore prepared to receive the gentiles that are to "flow" in God's direction (Micah 4:1). But then, as Micah continues his prophecy, he uses two related images to describe the negative consequences to come upon all gentile peoples who do *not* give up their warfare against God and each other. Both images are meant to describe Israel's place "in the midst of many people" (5:7–8), though they seem at first to differ drastically in nature.[28]

The first image is that of dew: "And the remnant of Jacob shall be in the midst of many people as a dew from the Lord, as the showers upon the grass, that tarrieth not for man, nor waiteth for the sons of men" (Micah 5:7). Most commentators have assumed that this image is a positive one,[29] but some more astutely note a possible negative meaning, one more in line with the obvious meaning of the second image. The remnant, Micah says in presenting the second image, will also be "among the Gentiles . . . as a lion among the beasts of the forest, as a young lion among the flocks of sheep: who, if he go through, both treadeth down, and teareth in pieces, and none can deliver" (Micah 5:8). Aligning the two images, Delbert Hillers points out that the image of dew appears in a military context in 2 Samuel 17:12, which concludes with the complete eradication of an enemy: "So shall we come upon [the enemy] in some place where he shall be found, and we will light upon him as the dew falleth on the ground: and of him and of all the men that are with him there shall not be left so much as one."[30] Micah's two images of dew and lion, which at first appear opposed or contrasting, then seem in the end to serve as closely parallel ways of envisioning the unfortunate end for all who oppose God's work. Micah imagines Israel as visiting divinely appointed destruction on those who insist on perpetuating violence.

This is, in many ways, an unfortunate note upon which to end Micah's reflection. It nonetheless underscores the seriousness of the Lord's intervention in the history of the world, as envisioned in the Israelite prophets. Those who refuse to see their fundamental dependence on God cannot be allowed to hold sway forever. However it might have to be achieved, universal peace is that toward which the writings of the prophets look. This is true of the book of Micah. It is truer still of the book of Isaiah.

The Book of Isaiah

Scholars working on the book of Isaiah have increasingly come to see how much it is shaped by theological concerns. A major theological concern throughout the book—but most forcefully in the first twelve chapters, where this discussion will be focused—is the theme of the remnant.[31] But before whatever processes the book may have undergone in reaching its final form,[32] Isaiah himself took the remnant theme seriously, the clearest indication being simply that he named one of his sons Shear-jashub, "The Remnant shall Return" (Isaiah 7:3). Thus, while it might be that some passages from Isaiah focused on the remnant are editorial additions rather than the prophet's own words (but this remains a point of controversy), all interpreters agree that Isaiah himself had important things to say about the remnant theme, and thus that any potential editorial additions to the book are essentially developments of Isaiah's own prophetic views.[33] For their part, Latter-day Saints, with their own unique faith commitments, might respond to Isaiah scholarship in a variety of ways, even raising questions about certain conclusions regarding authorship.[34] But whatever one decides about the authorship of Isaiah, the Book of Mormon clearly draws on long stretches of Isaiah as they are found in the received biblical text, and it is the biblical text in its final form that interests me here.

The theme of the remnant appears already in the first chapter of Isaiah, which serves as a kind of introduction to the whole book. There, in the wake of terrible devastation in Israel, the prophet says, "Except the Lord of hosts had left unto us a very small remnant, we should have been as Sodom, and we should have been like unto Gomorrah." He then calls on the "rulers" and "people" of the devastated Israelite cities to "hear the word of the Lord" and to "give ear unto the law of [their] God" (Isaiah 1:9–10). This passage announces to the reader of Isaiah in advance that the remnant theme is a major feature of the book—Edward Kissane calls it "the most characteristic feature of [Isaiah's] teaching"[35]—and that the remnant theme is to be found in Isaiah's preaching in the form found elsewhere in the prophets. A remnant of Israel has been spared, and it is to them that the divine law is ultimately addressed.

Isaiah's prophecies proper begin in his second chapter, with the vision of "the mountain of the Lord's house" (Isaiah 2:2) analyzed previously in connection with its appearance in the book of Micah. In the book of Micah, this vision follows prophecies of destruction and devastation and draws the reader's attention to the promise of a preserved remnant of Israel, a remnant that will assist in the redemption of the gentile nations during the promised "last days" (Micah :1). In the book of Isaiah, however, this vision *precedes* prophecies of destruction and devastation, such that it poignantly contrasts Israel's prophetic future with their sinful state at the time of the prophecy. Thus, where the book of Micah uses the vision to mark a transition from destruction to promise, the book of Isaiah uses it to highlight the distance between present difficulties and future redemption. Nonetheless, the Isaiah text does come eventually to dwell on the remnant theme as well. At the end of the textual unit that begins with the vision, a prophecy predicts the day when "he that is left [*ha-nišʾār*] in Zion, and he that remaineth in Jerusalem, shall be called holy, even every one that is written among the living in Jerusalem" (Isaiah 4:3).[36] From Isaiah's perspective, the remnant is to be regarded as holy, and he explicitly notes that their names are to be written—"written among the living" in the King James rendering, but "recorded for life" according to a more literal rendering of the Hebrew.[37] Commentators routinely note the likelihood that "the registry of names, which preserves the identity of the holy ones, may refer to God's book of life."[38] From early in the book of Isaiah, therefore, the remnant is regarded as holy and foreordained, prepared for a divinely appointed responsibility in history. As Gerhard Hasel notes, this remnant is not made up of "those who are left behind after the ruin of the city" but of "those who remain after the purifying judgment."[39]

This last point is clarified further along when Isaiah reports on the experience in which he was commissioned to pursue his prophetic task. After seeing the Lord and being cleansed by a seraph (see Isaiah 6:1–8), the prophet receives a commission to preach to a people who will reject his message (see 6:9–10). When he asks "how long" he should pursue this task (6:11), he is told to preach "until the cities be wasted without inhabitant . . . and the Lord have removed men far away" (6:11–12). Isaiah's message is to serve as God's word to Israel through a period of destruction and exile. But then the Lord makes clear that this period of destruction and exile is also one of purification, because he promises Isaiah (in a very difficult passage) that at least a portion of those taken away "shall return." This remnant of Israel, which Isaiah pictures as a stump (suggestively translated as "substance" in the King James Version), is a "holy seed" that can sprout again to give new life to Israel (6:13).[40] And just a few chapters later, the book of Isaiah indeed predicts the moment when "a branch" does "grow out" of these once-dead "roots" (11:1).

Between the report of Isaiah's commission and the later prediction concerning the remnant-stump sprouting new life, one of Isaiah's best-developed discussions of the remnant appears. It finds its original setting during the dangerous approach of the Assyrian empire during the late eighth century—a situation during which Judah's survival was seriously threatened.[41] Due to the Judahite king's lack of faith, the nation faced serious danger, namely "the king of Assyria," who would "pass through Judah" like a flood; Assyria would "overflow and go over" and "reach even to the neck" (Isaiah 8:7–8), as another passage puts it. Judah, Isaiah thus predicts, would be ravaged by Assyria until the Lord has "performed his whole work upon mount Zion and on Jerusalem," at which point he would "punish the fruit of the stout heart of the king of Assyria" (10:12). Then the prophet announces, "The remnant shall return, even the remnant of Jacob, unto the mighty God" (10:21).[42] The remnant in question is to be made up of those who "are escaped of the house of Jacob," and they "shall stay upon the Lord, the Holy One of Israel, in truth" (10:20). Isaiah here does not hesitate to announce a "consumption" that has been "determined," one that shall bear consequences for "all the land" (10:23), yet he firmly states also that "the consumption decreed shall overflow with righteousness," since "a remnant of [Israel] shall return" (10:22). Destruction and devastation for the covenant people eventually give way to the existence of a winnowed remnant fully prepared to receive instruction from the Lord.[43]

It is *as* this finally holy remnant returns that the remnant-stump from Isaiah's prophetic commission springs forth with new life (see Isaiah 11:1).[44] The stump or "root" in question, according to the prophet, "shall stand for an ensign of the people; to it shall the Gentiles seek: and his rest shall be glorious" (11:10). Here Isaiah echoes the prophet Micah, anticipating the role Israel's remnant is to play in the redemption of the whole world and of all its peoples. Further, Isaiah now predicts a "second time" of recovery for Israel: "The Lord shall set his hand again the second time to recover the remnant of his people, which shall be left" (11:11).[45] As in Micah's prophecy, the still-rebellious nations are to be destroyed: "They shall spoil them of the east together: they shall lay their hand upon Edom and Moab; and the children of Ammon shall obey them" (11:14). But above all, the time of the remnant's full redemption is a time of immense peace. "The wolf also shall dwell with the lamb, and the leopard shall lie down with the kid; and the calf and the young lion and the fatling together; and a little child shall lead them" (11:6). In Brevard Childs's words, "the remnant will experience all the terrors of judgment, but the promise of new life through the destruction is affirmed," and this new life comes in the shape of "an age of universal peace."[46]

Thus, the book of Isaiah, rather like Micah and more optimistically than Amos, develops in its opening chapters a near-systematic theology of the remnant. Isaiah is, interestingly, not averse to more traditional formulations of the remnant idea (formulations of the sort Amos seems to have set about to criticize).[47] But the first twelve chapters of the book of Isaiah develop the traditional notion of the Israelite remnant rather far beyond such traditional formulations. Further, what in Micah's book remains a prophetic *idea* becomes in Isaiah's prophecies a fully developed prophetic *history*. The book of Micah anticipates the *role* the remnant is to play in redemption, but the book of Isaiah outlines a long and detailed *story* about how that remnant-based redemption is to unfold.[48] Isaiah shares with Amos a certain skepticism about Israel's self-honesty in understanding the promises given to it as a covenant people, and he shares with Micah an interest in more fully formulating a better understanding of what those promises might really mean. But it is Isaiah, perhaps uniquely, who sees how the remnant lies at the center of God's intentions in world history.

Conclusion

Both prophets and Jesus Christ himself recommend to the Book of Mormon's readers that the words of the Israelite prophets be taken seriously—Isaiah chief among them (see 2 Nephi 11:2, 8; 25:1–8; 3 Nephi 23:1–2; Mormon 8:23). And among the themes the Nephite prophets and the Savior draw consistently from the Israelite prophets is that of the remnant. When the resurrected Lord appeared among Lehi's descendants anciently, he used his pierced hands to point his people to the writings of Isaiah and Micah, among others (see 3 Nephi 20–26). And he highlighted passages addressed to and focused on the fate of Israel's remnant. Similarly, when Nephi decided to place at the very center of his second book a lengthy quotation from Isaiah (see 2 Nephi 11–24), he decided to copy down the chapters in which the book of Isaiah develops the historical importance of the Israelite remnant. If we are to understand these choice teachings, brought to our attention by the miraculous coming forth of the Book of Mormon, we would do well to search the ancient Israelite prophets. Amos, Micah, and Isaiah provide an important place to start.

Notes

1. For an overview of replacement theology, along with a critical assessment, see Michael J. Vlach, *Has the Church Replaced Israel? A Theological Evaluation* (Nashville, TN: B&H Publishing, 2010).
2. For a good study of early Jewish thought with sustained reflection on the remnant theme, see Mark A. Elliott, *The Survivors of Israel: A Reconsideration of the Theology of Pre-Christian Judaism* (Grand Rapids, MI: Eerdmans Publishing, 2000).
3. Methodologically, I follow the lead of two related subdisciplines within the field of biblical studies. First, both because I work and write as a philosopher and theologian and because the Book of Mormon interprets biblical texts in a theological fashion, I read the biblical text from the perspective of biblical theology. For helpful explanations of the history and current situation of biblical theology, see James K. Mead, *Biblical Theology: Issues, Methods, and Themes* (Lousiville: Westminster John Knox Press, 2007); and Edward W. Klink III and Darian R. Lockett, *Understanding Biblical Theology: A Comparison of Theory and Practice* (Grand Rapids, MI: Zondervan, 2012). Second, both because I see as important the distinction between the Bible as text and the Bible as scripture and because the Book of Mormon consistently draws on certain biblical passages as these are couched in their canonical contexts, I follow the lead of canonical criticism. For a good introduction to canonical criticism, see James A. Sanders, *Canon and Community: A Guide to Canonical Criticism* (Philadelphia: Fortress Press, 1984). Because I borrow from these two methodologies, I refer often to biblical *books* and *texts*, rather than to specific prophetic *persons* (although I do that as well). This is meant to draw attention to the final

form of the text, rather than to what can be reconstructed, historically, of the actual persons behind the biblical text.

4. See the helpful survey in Gerhard F. Hasel, *The Remnant: The History and Theology of the Remnant Idea from Genesis to Isaiah* (Berrien Spring, MI: Andrews University Press, 1974), 50–134.
5. D. M. Warne, "The Origin, Development, and Significance of the Concept of the Remnant in the Old Testament" (PhD diss., University of Edinburgh, 1958), 45. Interestingly, a similar interpretation of the passage can be found anciently among the writings of the Qumran community. See the discussion in Dorothy M. Peters, *Noah Traditions in the Dead Sea Scrolls: Conversations and Controversies of Antiquity* (Atlanta: Society of Biblical Literature, 2008), 70.
6. This idea of humanity as remnant is developed in Giorgio Agamben, *Remnants of Auschwitz: The Witness and the Archive*, trans. Daniel Heller-Roazen (New York: Zone Books, 2002).
7. Gerhard Hasel develops the theological significance of the flood's remnant theme by arguing that it indicates "a union of judgment and salvation." See Hasel, *The Remnant*, 138.
8. "The catastrophe purges the community of its impurities, and the remnant is called to exemplary life. . . . Thus, the appointment and rescue of the remnant, making possible the continuation of the life of the community, may be viewed as themselves constituting the saving activity of Yahweh [Jehovah]." Lester V. Meyer, "Remnant," in *The Anchor Yale Bible Dictionary*, ed. David Noel Freedman (New York: Doubleday, 1992), 5:670.
9. Such a connection is made explicitly in the Book of Mormon, in 1 Nephi 22:10. There, Nephi says to his wondering brothers that "all the kindreds of the earth cannot be blessed unless [the Lord God] shall make bare his arm in the eyes of the nations." (In addition to alluding to Genesis 12:3, this passage alludes to Isaiah 52:10.)
10. For a good outline of the relevant chronology, see Richard Neitzel Holzapfel, Dana M. Pike, and David Rolph Seely, *Jehovah and the World of*

the Old Testament: An Illustrated Reference for Latter-day Saints (Salt Lake City: Deseret Book, 2009), 246–61, 278–97.

11. Hasel, *The Remnant,* 172. Hasel overstates his point by speaking of "a new Israel."
12. James Luther Mays, *Amos: A Commentary* (Philadelphia: Westminster Press, 1969), 8.
13. As mentioned before, the remnant theme seems to have been known well throughout the ancient near east. Given its popularity across a variety of cultural contexts, it seems clear that Amos's words assume familiarity with the theme—and likely even familiarity with its application to Israel.
14. Unfortunately, the King James Version of this passage is almost incomprehensible, in large part due to the difficulties of the underlying Hebrew. In altering it, I have here drawn on the translation in Shalom M. Paul, *Amos: A Commentary on the Book of Amos* (Minneapolis: Fortress Press, 1991), 115. For some discussion of the difficulty of the Hebrew text, see Francis I. Andersen and David Noel Freedman, *Amos: A New Translation with Introduction and Commentary* (New Haven: Yale University Press, 2008), 408–10.
15. Hans Walter Wolff, *Joel and Amos: A Commentary on the Books of the Prophets Joel and Amos,* trans. Waldemar Janzen, S. Dean McBride Jr., and Charles A. Muenchow (Philadelphia: Fortress Press, 1977), 197–98. For the legal texts in question, see especially Exodus 22:9–12.
16. The former text is problematic and obscure. For some helpful commentary on its general meaning, see Andersen and Freedman, *Amos,* 573–74; and on its message concerning the remnant, see Hasel, *The Remnant,* 183–84.
17. Jörg Jeremias, *The Book of Amos,* trans. Douglas W. Stott (Louisville, KY: Westminster John Knox Press, 1998), 158, suggests that the book of Amos originally ended with this devastating announcement. In final form, Amos contains another eleven verses.
18. This may, of course, be primarily overheated rhetoric, used principally for effect. Just a few verses later (in what may well be a later addition), the text

claims just that "all the sinners" of the covenant people "shall die by the sword," thanks to a process of "sift[ing]" (Amos 9:9–10).

19. Mays nicely underscores the implications of this "perhaps": "'Perhaps' characterizes the prospect of Yahweh's [Jehovah's] gracious help as a matter beyond human control and guarantee. The Lord is no national god of Israel; he will be gracious toward whomever he wills to be gracious (Ex. 33.19). He is not bound to Israel by any kind of cultic or legal guarantee; rather, Israel is completely in the hands of his sovereignty." Mays, *Amos*, 102.
20. Paul R. Noble, "The Remnant in Amos 3–6: A Prophetic Paradox," *Horizons in Biblical Theology: An International Dialogue* 19, no. 2 (1997): 129.
21. Noble, "The Remnant in Amos 3–6," 138. Noble's words are overly strong here. There is reason to think that Amos's more extreme statements are primarily for rhetorical effect. Jeremias notes that Amos's "'perhaps' has undergone a significant history of influence within the Old Testament," citing passages in Zephaniah, Joel, and Jonah, along with rabbinical teachings. Jeremias, *The Book of Amos*, 96.
22. See Kenneth H. Cuffey, *The Literary Coherence of the Book of Micah: Remnant, Restoration, and Promise* (New York: Bloomsbury, 2015), 153–63, 215–345.
23. As James Luther Mays notes, because this note of hope seems out of place in Micah 1–2, "There is general agreement that the oracle [of 2:12–13] is a late addition to the Micah collection." James Luther Mays, *Micah: A Commentary* (Philadelphia: Westminster Press, 1976), 74. Certainly, the placement of the passage in the book of Micah is suggestive of theological shaping.
24. Some interpreters have suggested that this passage should be read either as an awkwardly worded prophecy of doom or as a quotation of the false prophets against whom Micah contends. None of these arguments is ultimately compelling. See Daniel L. Smith-Christopher, *Micah: A Commentary* (Louisville, KY: Westminster John Knox Press, 2015), 104–105.
25. This same passage, with a few differences, appears also in Isaiah. Scholars have long debated which prophet borrows from which, but there has

emerged a kind of consensus that there are more interesting questions to address concerning the place of the prophecy in each of the two books, regardless of which (if either) prophet first uttered the words. See the helpful discussion in Brevard S. Childs, *Isaiah* (Louisville, KY: Westminster John Knox Press, 2001), 28–31.

26. One peculiarly Latter-day Saint interpretation of Micah 4:11–13 might suggest this, despite the passage's transparent war imagery in the Hebrew text. See the discussion in Joseph M. Spencer, *For Zion: A Mormon Theology of Hope* (Salt Lake City: Greg Kofford Books, 2014), 81–94.
27. Hans Walter Wolff, *Micah the Prophet*, trans. Ralph D. Gehrke (Philadelphia: Fortress Press, 1981), 163.
28. Philip Jensen notes "the almost identical repetition of the first lines" in the two verses, but he concludes that this repetition is meant to highlight "the contrast" between the two images. Philip Peter Jensen, *Obadiah, Jonah, Micah: A Theological Commentary* (New York: T&T Clark, 2008), 161.
29. Daniel Smith-Christopher, for instance, follows the tradition in noting simply that "'dew' is always a positive image" in the Hebrew scriptures. In somewhat compelling support of his position, he notes "the similar contrast of dew and lions in Prov[erbs] 19:12." Smith-Christopher, *Micah*, 177–78.
30. See Delbert R. Hillers, *Micah: A Commentary on the Book of the Prophet Micah*, eds. P. D. Hanson and L. R. Fisher (Philadelphia: Fortress Press, 1984), 71. Hans Walter Wolff, *Micah: A Continental Commentary*, trans. Gary Stansell (Minneapolis: Augsburg Fortress, 1990), 156, notes other occasions in the Israelite prophets' writings where dew can "mean something negative."
31. I limit this discussion to Isaiah 1–12 because it is there that the theological theme of the remnant appears most consistently and in its most developed form. The theme is arguably developed further, but without direct reference to "the remnant," in Isaiah 40–55, major portions of which appear in the Book of Mormon. But because these later chapters do not directly address the remnant idea, I have left them out of this discussion.

32. The formation of Isaiah has become a major focus for researchers working on Isaiah. For a representative and particularly important work, see H. G. M. Williamson, *The Book Called Isaiah: Deutero-Isaiah's Role in Composition and Redaction* (New York: Oxford University Press, 1994).
33. See, for instance, the discussion in E. W. Heaton, "The Root ראש and the Doctrine of the Remnant," *Journal of Theological Studies* 3.1 (1952): 27–39. As can be seen in the notes for the following discussion, many passages that have been generally regarded as late additions have been reevaluated in important recent work—especially that of J. J. M. Roberts—and the possibility of their having originated with Isaiah himself has been defended.
34. For a traditional approach to Isaiah authorship from a Latter-day Saint perspective, see Sidney B. Sperry, *Answers to Book of Mormon Questions* (Salt Lake City: Bookcraft, 1967), 73–97; or, more recently but in a similar vein, Kent P. Jackson, "Isaiah in the Book of Mormon," in *A Reason for Faith: Navigating LDS Doctrine and Church History*, ed. Laura Harris Hales (Salt Lake City and Provo, UT: Deseret Book and Religious Studies Center, 2016), 69–78. For an enumeration of a wider range of possible approaches to Isaiah authorship from a position of faith, see Grant Hardy, *Understanding the Book of Mormon: A Reader's Guide* (New York: Oxford University Press, 2010), 291–92.
35. Edward J. Kissane, *The Book of Isaiah: Translated from a Critically Revised Hebrew Text with Commentary*, 2 vols. (Dublin: Richview Press, 1941), 1:10.
36. Commentators almost universally recognize the whole of Isaiah 2–4 as a larger literary unit, albeit made up of several oracles. See, for instance, the helpful discussion of literary units in Marvin A. Sweeney, *Isaiah 1–39 with an Introduction to Prophetic Literature* (Grand Rapids, MI: Eerdmans, 1996), 44–46. Although there has long been general agreement that the oracle of Isaiah 4:2–6 is a late addition to the text, J. J. M. Roberts has recently outlined an argument for its being original to Isaiah. See J. J. M. Roberts, *First Isaiah: A Commentary* (Minneapolis: Fortress Press, 2015), 67–68.
37. This is how the passage is rendered in Joseph Blenkinsopp, *Isaiah 1–39: A New Translation with Introduction and Commentary* (New Haven: Yale University Press, 2000), 202.

38. Gary V. Smith, *Isaiah 1–39* (Nashville, TN: B&H Publishing, 2007), 157–58.
39. Hasel, *The Remnant*, 266.
40. According to Hasel, *The Remnant*, 240, this passage outlines a destruction "in two stages," since a *first* remnant—described in the text as "a tenth"—will be reduced even further upon its return to its lands. The holy Israelite remnant may thus be understood best as a remnant of a remnant. A similar interpretation can be found in Sweeney, *Isaiah 1–39*, 141. Here again there has been a general consensus that the word of hope in the Isaiah text is a late editorial addition. But also here again J. J. M. Roberts has recently made an important case that the text might be traced back to Isaiah himself. See Roberts, *First Isaiah*, 101–2.
41. For an introduction to the relevant historical events, see Edward F. Campbell Jr., "A Land Divided: Judah and Israel from the Death of Solomon to the Fall of Samaria," in *The Oxford History of the Biblical World*, ed. Michael D. Coogan (New York: Oxford University Press, 1998), 206–41. For some discussion of the dating of the passage, see Blenkinsopp, *Isaiah 1–39*, 257–58.
42. John Oswalt finds significance in the fact that Assyrian texts use the remnant motif "in a wholly negative sense to describe the thoroughness of their conquest." He consequently sees Isaiah as deliberately repurposing the Assyrian use of the image: "Isaiah takes the Assyrian term, agreeing with their estimate of the situation, but then shows that even a remnant, in God's hand, is more enduring than all Assyria's might." John N. Oswalt, *The Book of Isaiah: Chapters 1–39* (Grand Rapids, MI: Eerdmans Publishing, 1986), 269–70.
43. I have provided a much more detailed analysis of Isaiah's account of the production of the Israelite remnant in Joseph M. Spencer, *The Vision of All: Twenty-Five Lectures on Isaiah in Nephi's Record* (Salt Lake City: Greg Kofford Books, 2016), 191–201.
44. Numerous dates have been assigned to the oracles in Isaiah 11, some of them very late (for a recent argument for a later date, see Blenkinsopp, *Isaiah 1–39*, 263–64; for a recent interpretation that places the oracle

within Isaiah's own lifetime, see Roberts, *First Isaiah*, 177–83). On the whole, however, Brevard Childs seems right that "the importance of precisely dating 11:1–9 needs to be greatly relativized" because "the movement of the text within the larger context of the preceding chapters" presents itself as organized "in theological terms." Childs, *Isaiah*, 100–101.

45. This passage especially has generally been regarded as a late addition to the book of Isaiah. See, however, the important rebuttal in Roberts, *First Isaiah*, 188–89.
46. Childs, *Isaiah*, 95, 103. See his discussion also on p. 102: "Chapter 11 has been editorially positioned to form the culmination of a theological direction that commenced at chapter 6."
47. See references in Isaiah 14:22, 30; 15:9; 16:14; 17:3; 37:4, 31, 32; and 46:3.
48. Isaiah most fully develops this long and detailed story in passages that do not directly refer to Israel's remnant—at least by that term. These are to be found, significantly, much later in the book of Isaiah—especially in chapters 40–55, the portion of the book often called Second Isaiah.

10

Old Wine in New Bottles

Exploring the Use of the Old Testament in the Doctrine and Covenants

Nicholas J. Frederick

Nicholas J. Frederick is an assistant professor of ancient scripture at Brigham Young University.

From its opening verses, the Doctrine and Covenants demonstrates a close reliance upon the language of the Old Testament. D&C 1:1–2 contains two allusions to the words of Isaiah (D&C 1:1/Isa. 51:4; D&C 1:2/Isa. 6:10).[1] D&C 2 is a restatement by Moroni to Joseph Smith of Malachi 4:5–6, with significant theological changes. D&C 3, a remarkable revelation that records the Lord's chastisement of Joseph Smith after his loss of the 116 pages, contains an allusion to 1 Samuel 15:24, Saul's confession to Samuel that he has "transgressed the commandment of the Lord" (cf. D&C 3:6). D&C 4 begins with an allusion to Isaiah 29:14 and its discussion of a "marvelous work and a wonder" that, the Lord reveals, is about "to come forth among the children of men" (D&C 4:1).

This appropriation of Old Testament language appears at length throughout the Doctrine and Covenants and tends to take one of two forms (or in some cases both). The first form is *structure*, meaning that the language of the Old Testament provides the textual building blocks for the various texts of the Doctrine and Covenants. These various sections adopt and utilize phrases or sentences from the Old Testament and then adapt them into a new text. The second form is *meaning,* occurring when the Old Testament language is adopted and adapted in a manner that reflects or expands the Old Testament context. Sometimes a phrase or sentence from the Old Testament will appear in the Doctrine and Covenants in a way that mirrors the Old Testament context. However, at other times the revelations will adopt words or phrases from the Old Testament and place them in a new context, one that alters or adapts the original context. By exploring the different ways in which the Doctrine and Covenants interacts with the Old Testament, we can gain a deeper appreciation for both texts.[2] The clear and obvious presence of the Old Testament throughout the Doctrine and Covenants suggests that this important book of scripture is just as relevant to an understanding of the restored gospel as the New Testament or the Book of Mormon. This paper will proceed as follows: It will first look at how the Doctrine and Covenants adopts and adapts the *structure* of the Old Testament in its own construction. It will then look at passages where the Old Testament *meaning* or *context* is reflected or expanded. It will then offer some concluding observations on the general role of the Old Testament in the Doctrine and Covenants.

I. Structure[3]

When discussing how the Old Testament contributes to the *structure* of the Doctrine and Covenants, we can perhaps do it in three basic ways: simple, expanded, and condensed. An example of a "simple" structure would be an instance when a phrase or sentence from the Old Testament is appropriated into the Doctrine and Covenants without any real changes to the Old Testament text. Simple allusions can be fairly easy to identify and make up the majority of structural forms. One example of a simple structure can be seen in this comparison between D&C 66:11 and Isaiah 35:10. Isaiah 35:10 is a verse describing the eschatological redemption of Jerusalem, when those liberated by Yahweh will safely find sanctuary in Zion.[4]

> Keep these sayings, for they are true and faithful; and thou shalt magnify thine office, and push many people *to Zion with songs* of *everlasting joy upon their heads.* (D&C 66:11)
>
> And the ransomed of the Lord shall return, and come *to Zion with songs and everlasting joy upon their heads:* they shall obtain joy and gladness, and sorrow and sighing shall flee away. (Isaiah 35:10)

With the exception of only one word change, "and/of," the phrase from Isaiah 35 has been seamlessly appropriated into D&C 66. Another example can be seen when comparing D&C 71:9 with Isaiah 54:17:

> Verily, thus saith the Lord unto you—there is *no weapon that is formed against you shall prosper;* (D&C 71:9)
>
> *No weapon that is formed against thee shall prosper; and every tongue that shall rise against thee in judgment thou shalt condemn.* This is the heritage of the servants of the Lord, and their righteousness is of me, saith the Lord. (Isaiah 54:17)

Again, with the exception of a single word change, "you/thee," the statement from Isaiah 54 has been fully appropriated into the structure of D&C 66, although the careful preservation of the language from Isaiah 54 does make D&C 71:9 read a little awkward due to the addition of "there is" at the beginning of the phrase.

In some instances, the simple structure is altered slightly by inverting a series of phrases. For example, Isaiah 58:1, a verse instructing God's prophet to loudly and publically call Israel to repentance, reads:

> Cry aloud, *spare not, lift up thy voice* like a trumpet, and shew my people their transgression, and the house of Jacob their sins. (Isaiah 58:1)

In D&C 34:10, the two italicized phrases from Isaiah 58:1 are repeated, but in an inverted order:

> Wherefore, *lift up your voice and spare not*, for the Lord God hath spoken; therefore prophesy, and it shall be given by the power of the Holy Ghost. (D&C 34:10)

There is a similar phrasal inversion in D&C 98:12, which contains an allusion to Isaiah 28:10:[5]

> For he will give unto the faithful *line upon line, precept upon precept*; and I will try you and prove you herewith. (D&C 98:12)
>
> For precept must be *upon precept, precept upon precept; line upon line*, line upon line; here a little, and there a little: (Isaiah 28:10)

A more nuanced inversion can be seen in D&C 84:69, which also contains an allusion to Isaiah, in this case Isaiah 35:5, another verse foreshadowing the eschatological redemption of God's people:[6]

> In my name they shall *open the eyes of the blind*, and *unstop the ears of the deaf*; (D&C 84:69)
>
> Then *the eyes of the blind shall be opened*, and *the ears of the deaf shall be unstopped*. (Isaiah 35:5)

In this instance, the phrases are preserved in the same order, with "blind" preceding "deaf," but the word order has been inverted. In Isaiah, the word order was "eyes of the blind," followed by "opened" and "ears of the deaf," then "unstopped." In D&C 84:69, the word order shifts to "open," followed by "eyes of the blind" and "unstop," then "ears of the deaf."[7]

On other occasions, the Doctrine and Covenants will adopt a phrase or sentence from the Old Testament, but rather than simply inserting it nearly word-for-word into the revelation, the language from the Old Testament will be *expanded*. This expansion is perhaps a way of furnishing new meaning or further explanation to the phrase appropriated from the Old Testament. D&C 128 is an 1842 letter written by Joseph Smith after he was forced to flee Nauvoo following an attempt by an unknown party to assassinate former Missouri governor Lilburn Boggs.[8] In this letter, Joseph celebrates the blessings of the Restoration, in particular the restoration of priesthood keys, with their power of sealing the living and the dead. Towards the end of this letter, he writes:

> Let the mountains shout for joy, and all ye valleys cry aloud; and all ye seas and dry lands tell the wonders of your Eternal King! And ye rivers, and brooks, and rills, flow down with gladness. Let the woods and all the trees of the field praise the Lord; and ye solid rocks weep for joy! And let the sun, moon, and *the morning stars sing together, and let all the sons of God shout for joy*! And let the eternal creations declare his name forever and ever! And again I say, how glorious is the voice we hear from heaven, proclaiming in our ears, glory, and salvation, and honor, and immortality, and eternal life; kingdoms, principalities, and powers! (D&C 128:23)

Compare the italicized portion above to Job 38:7, a verse that originates in an encounter between God and Job wherein God poses a series of rhetorical questions to Job, such as the following:

> When *the morning stars sang together, and all the sons of God shouted for joy?* (Job 38:7)

Joseph has taken the question posed by God to Job and changed it in two notable ways. First, he adds "sun" and "moon" to the "morning stars." Second, he has taken what was originally a rhetorical question highlighting the beauty and wonder of the natural world and turned it into a declarative statement celebrating the beauty and wonder of the Restoration.

A second example of structural expansion can be seen in D&C 109, which records the 1836 dedicatory prayer for the Kirtland Temple. Toward the end of the prayer, the following words are spoken:

> And whatsoever city thy servants shall enter, and the people of that city receive their testimony, let thy peace and thy salvation be upon that city; that they may gather out of that city the righteous, that they may *come forth to Zion*, or to her stakes, the places of thine appointment, *with songs of everlasting joy*; (D&C 109:39)

Now compare this with Isaiah 35:10, a verse celebrating the redemption of Jerusalem and a successful journey to Zion:

> And the ransomed of the Lord shall return, and *come to Zion with songs and everlasting joy* upon their heads: they shall obtain joy and gladness, and sorrow and sighing shall flee away. (Isaiah 35:10)

D&C 109:39 is clearly drawing upon Isaiah 35:10 for its language, but it has inserted two phrases, "or to her stakes" and "the places of thine appointment," in between the two phrases borrowed from Isaiah 35, "come forth to Zion" and "with songs of everlasting joy." The purpose of this structural expansion is to help the Saints understand that the process of gathering "to Zion" is not necessarily limited to a central gathering place but includes the "stakes" of Zion as well.

A third type of structural form is the appropriation of an Old Testament phrase or group of phrases in a manner in which the Old Testament language is *condensed* or shortened. For example, D&C 58:8 contains two allusions to Isaiah 25:6, a passage describing a future messianic banquet celebrating the victory of Yahweh:

> And also that a feast of fat things might be prepared for the poor; yea, *a feast of fat things, of wine on the lees well refined*, that the earth may know that the mouths of the prophets shall not fail; (D&C 58:8)
>
> And in this mountain shall the Lord of hosts make unto all people *a feast of fat things*, a feast of wines on the lees, of fat things full of marrow, *of wines on the lees well refined*. (Isaiah 25:6)

In D&C 58:8, the phrases "a feast of wines on the lees" and "of fat things full of marrow" have been omitted from Isaiah's words, while the phrases "a feast of fat things" and "of wine on the lees well refined" have been appropriated.

Readers encounter a similar "condensing" in D&C 133. In this eschatologically charged revelation, the Lord elaborates on the place of the gospel and the Saints as the arrival of the Kingdom of God grows nearer. Near the end of the revelation, the Lord declares that he sent forth the "fulness of his gospel" in order

> to prepare the weak for those things which are coming on the earth, and for the Lord's errand in the day when the weak shall confound the wise, and the *little one become a strong nation,* and two shall put their tens of thousands to flight. (D&C 133:58)

The phrase "little one become a strong nation" is an allusion to Isaiah 60:22, where Isaiah predicts that the influence of Israel will become so great that it will be disproportionate to her size:

> A *little one shall become a* thousand, and a small one a *strong nation*: I the Lord will hasten it in his time. (Isaiah 60:22)

Isaiah's words in this verse are an example of *synonymous parallelism,* a feature of Hebrew poetry in which the poet makes a statement and then restates it with different wording in the next line. For example,

> And he shall *judge among the nations,* and shall *rebuke many people*: and they shall *beat their swords into plowshares,* and *their spears into pruninghooks*: nation shall not lift up sword against nation, neither shall they learn war any more. (Isaiah 2:4)

In three separate places, Isaiah makes a statement and then restates it for poetic purposes. In D&C 60:22, the two parallel expressions are "a little one shall become a thousand" and "a small one a strong nation." In D&C 133, the two phrases have been combined to read "little ones become a strong nation." However, the remarkable element of this verse is that, after condensing Isaiah's two parallels into one phrase, the revelation adds a second phrase (from Deuteronomy) to maintain the synonymous parallelism:

> To prepare the weak for those things which are coming on the earth, and for the Lord's errand in the day when the weak shall confound the wise, and the little one become a strong nation, *and two shall put their tens of thousands to flight*. (D&C 133:58)
>
> How should one chase a thousand, and *two put ten thousand to flight*, except their Rock had sold them, and the Lord had shut them up? (Deuteronomy 32:30)

Textually, this is a remarkable feat, one requiring not only knowledge of verses from Isaiah and Deuteronomy but also recognition of the poetic structure behind Isaiah's words.[9]

II. Meaning

As hinted at in the discussion of structure, the explicit presence of the Old Testament in the text of the Doctrine and Covenants can have an influence on how the Doctrine and Covenants is interpreted. This section will explore four ways in which meaning is conveyed through the appropriation of Old Testament language by the Doctrine and Covenants. The first type of meaning is "modernization," referring to occasions when the Doctrine and Covenants appropriates language from the Old Testament but, either through addition or omission, places the Old Testament allusion in a modern context. The second type of meaning is "clarification," referring to occasions where the Doctrine and Covenants clarifies or illuminates the meaning behind an Old Testament text. The third and fourth types of meaning are primarily derived from how the *context* of the Old Testament passage being alluded to is itself adopted and adapted by the Doctrine and Covenants. On one hand, the context of the Old Testament passage may mirror or reflect the context of the Doctrine and Covenants verse it is placed within. In this instance, the Old Testament context can be read into the Doctrine and Covenants context and serve as additional or further *contextualization*. On the other hand, the context of the Old Testament passage being alluded to may be expanded or altered and thus *recontextualized* in the Doctrine and Covenants. This type of meaning focuses on allusions to passages from the Old Testament whose recontexualization in the Doctrine and Covenants goes "against the grain," so to speak, of how these passages are generally understood or read in their original context. This shouldn't be taken to mean that the Doctrine and Covenants is using these passages incorrectly. Rather, the recontextualization would be the result of modern revelation providing an alternate interpretation. It should be noted, however, that these categories can be rather fluid and will often overlap with one another. In other words, a category that attempts contextualization can also be providing modernization or clarification.

A. Modernization

The Old Testament is a text that was written many centuries before the birth of Joseph Smith. When the Doctrine and Covenants alludes to passages from the Old Testament, it is sometimes necessary to "modernize" certain elements of the Old Testament that wouldn't necessarily be familiar to a nineteenth-century American audience. One example of this modernization can be seen in D&C 133:46:

> And it shall be said: *Who is this that cometh down from God in heaven with dyed garments*; yea, from the regions which are not known, *clothed in his glorious apparel, traveling in the greatness of his strength?* And he shall say: I am he who spake in righteousness, mighty to save. (D&C 133:46–47)

This is an allusion to Isaiah 63:1:

> Who is *this that cometh from Edom, with dyed garments* from Bozrah? this that is *glorious in his apparel, travelling in the greatness of his strength?* I that speak in righteousness, mighty to save. (Isaiah 63:1)

For the most part, the language of D&C 133 matches that of Isaiah 63:1, with the notable omission of two words: "Edom" and "Bozrah." Isaiah 63 begins as a dialogue between a watchman and a warrior. The watchman sees the warrior approaching Jerusalem from the south in what appears to be red garments and in 63:1 asks him who he is. The warrior responds that he is one who speaks "in righteousness, mighty to save." This answer sparks a second question from the watchman: "Wherefore art thou red in thine apparel" (Isaiah 63:2), to which the warrior responds, "I have trodden the winepress alone; and of the people there was none with me: for I will tread them in mine anger, and trample them in my fury; and their blood shall be sprinkled upon my garments, and I will stain all my raiment" (Isaiah 63:3).

The direct meaning of Isaiah's words is unclear. Perhaps he is referring to Jehovah's execution of judgment against those who reject him[10] or perhaps to his protection of Jerusalem against her enemies (albeit without Jerusalem's assistance).[11] Reading Isaiah "backwards" yields perhaps a glimpse of Jesus's conquest of sin and death on the cross or perhaps of Jesus's Second Coming and conquest of the wicked.[12] Of interest here are the references to "Edom" and "Bozrah." Edom was situated southeast of Jerusalem, and its capital city was Bozrah. Additionally, "Edom was the perennial enemy of Judah, so much so that it came to represent all its enemies."[13] Isaiah's selection of Edom as the location of the warrior's conquest makes sense in an Old Testament context. As one scholar has noted, "The choice of Edom is dictated by the paradigmatic status of Edom as neighbor, related by kinship, yet unremittingly hostile, and also by the fact that traditionally, in heroic poetry, Edom is where YHWH first came from."[14] However, by the time D&C 133 was received, the symbolic nature of Edom and Bozrah would have been lost and more likely would have been confusing to a nineteenth-century American audience. Thus the allusion to Isaiah 63:1 eliminates the geographic symbolism but maintains the meaning behind Isaiah 63: the enemies of God will be destroyed.[15]

Another example of this modernization can be seen in D&C 65:2, a passage that contains two allusions to Daniel 2. In Daniel 2, Daniel offers an interpretation of a dream that had been given to Nebuchadnezzar, king of Babylon. Nebuchadnezzar's dream centered on a great image made of various types of metal and clay, which is then destroyed by a mysterious "stone." Here is the verse describing the stone:

> Thou sawest till that a *stone was cut out without hands*, which smote the image upon his feet that were *of* iron and clay, and brake them to pieces. Then was the iron, the clay, the brass, the silver, and the gold, broken to pieces together, and became like the chaff of the summer threshingfloors; and the wind carried them away, that no place was found for them: and the stone that smote the image became a great mountain, and *filled the whole earth*. (Daniel 2:34–35)

Daniel interprets Nebuchadnezzar's dream to be one of a vague succession of kingdoms, beginning with the Babylonians and continuing until they are broken by the stone. There remains a great deal of scholarly debate as to the identity of this image. Does it refer to the four ages of man? Does it refer to the rulers who will immediately succeed Nebuchadnezzar? Does it represent those empires that would follow the Baylonians, namely the Medes (silver), the Greeks (brass), and the Romans (iron)?[16] The true nature of the "stone" is also the topic of debate among scholars. Does it historically represent

Cyrus and the Persian overthrow of Babylon? Does it broadly speak to the sacred, divine nature of kingship and stand as a reminder that God can stand behind the rise and fall of any secular empire?[17] Early Christians, building off of passages that also spoke of a stone, such as Isaiah 8:14 and Psalms 118:22 (cf. Luke 20:17–18), began to interpret the stone as either referring to Jesus Christ (in either his first or second advent) or the eschatological kingdom he will establish in the final messianic age.[18]

In D&C 65, "a voice" declares to Joseph Smith that the keys of the kingdom have been restored and that the eschatological kingdom of God is prepared to come forth if the Saints would seek after it through prayer. D&C 65:2 then appropriates language from Daniel 2:35:

> The keys of the kingdom of God are committed unto man on the earth, and from thence shall the gospel roll forth unto the ends of the earth, as the *stone which is cut out* of the mountain *without hands* shall roll forth, until it has *filled the whole earth.* (D&C 65:2)

Significantly, there is no mention in D&C 65:2 of the image of metal and clay from Daniel's vision. One explanation for this absence is that the Doctrine and Covenants is *modernizing* Daniel's text. If the image of metal and clay represented either kings or empires that rose up in succession after the fall of Babylon, then they have very little relevance to a nineteenth-century restoration of God's church in America. Nebuchadnezzar was seeing something in the future, but by the time Joseph receives D&C 65, Nebuchadnezzar's visionary experience has become the distant past. There is no need to discuss ancient empires that have come and gone—the Lord's emphasis is on the present kingdom of God.

For this reason, the primary focus of D&C 65:2 is instead upon the stone, which the Lord likens to "the gospel" as it rolls "forth unto the ends of the earth." In this sense, D&C 65:2 also serves to *clarify* the mystery surrounding the stone: the stone appears to be the gospel of Jesus Christ, which will spread throughout the earth through missionary work. Joseph Smith further expounded on the image of the stone, stating that it revolved similar to "a grind stone" and that as "the Elders went abroad to preach the gospel and the people became believers in the Book of Mormon and were baptized," they would be "added to the little stone."[19]

B. Clarification

Clarification is similar to modernization, but instead of altering an appropriated Old Testament text in a manner that makes sense to a modern audience, clarification occurs when the Doctrine and Covenants alludes to an Old Testament text in a manner that helps to resolve or answer ambiguous Old Testament passages. Due to the nature of prophecy, it can sometimes be difficult to understand what or when a prophet is referring to. For example, consider Isaiah 63, the chapter discussed in the previous section. A warrior approaches Jerusalem from the south, and the watchman inquires about what appears to be red clothing. The warrior responds, "I have trodden the winepress alone; and of the people there was *none with me: for I will tread them in mine anger, and trample them in my fury; and their blood shall be sprinkled upon my garments, and I will stain all my raiment*" (Isaiah 63:3). It is often presumed that the warrior is Jehovah, his clothes stained with blood after his conquest of the wicked. However, Isaiah scholar John D. W. Watts has noted that "most interpreters have identified the bloody warrior as Yahweh himself, but the text does not so identify him." Watts argues that the warrior "is more likely a symbol of Persian imperial power fighting Jerusalem's and Yahweh's battles for them."[20]

Part of the complication behind this verse and others like it is that prophecy can often have *multiple* fulfillments. Prophecies given during Isaiah's lifetime can have certain elements fulfilled during his life yet also be fulfilled during the life of Jesus and during the era of the Church in the latter days, with each fulfillment being a valid result of the prophecy.[21] So, returning to the warrior prophesied about in Isaiah 63, the Doctrine and Covenants provides a possible clarification regarding *an* identity of the warrior. Consider this verse from D&C 88:

> And again, another angel shall sound his trump, which is the seventh angel, saying: It is finished; it is finished! The Lamb of God hath overcome and *trodden the wine-press alone*, even the wine-press of the fierceness of the wrath of Almighty God. (D&C 88:106)

With this allusion to Isaiah 63:3, the Lord reveals to Joseph Smith that an identity of the warrior who has "trodden the wine-press alone" is "the Lamb of God," or Jesus Christ, an identification that is also made in D&C 76:107. However, while D&C 88:106 may provide clarification as to an identity of the warrior, and while Jesus Christ may represent a valid fulfillment of this prophecy, this interpretation does not preclude Isaiah 63:1–6 from having an equally valid fulfillment during a prior dispensation.

Another clarification of an ambiguous identification occurs in D&C 116. D&C 116 is a revelation received by Joseph Smith in 1838 as to the location of Adam-ondi-Ahman:

> Spring Hill is named by the Lord Adam-ondi-Ahman, because, said he, it is the place where Adam shall come to visit his people, or *the Ancient of Days shall sit*, as spoken of by Daniel the prophet. (D&C 116:1)

The revelation specifically identifies Adam as being "the Ancient of Days," a mysterious figur who is mentioned in the book of Daniel:

> I beheld till the thrones were cast down, and *the Ancient of days did sit*, whose garment was white as snow, and the hair of his head like the pure wool: his throne was like the fiery flame, and his wheels as burning fire. (Daniel 7:9)

The true identity of the "Ancient of Days" has long been an enigma for Old Testament scholars. In the words of one, "The Ancient of Days has always been an intriguing yet obscure figure, though there is little doubt that in Daniel he can represent none other than Yahweh."[22] The equally mysterious "Son of Man," also mentioned in Daniel 7, provides another possible candidate for scholars.[23] However, D&C 116 provides some additional clarity to the question by suggesting that Adam, or Michael, is the "Ancient of Days" spoken of by Daniel.[24]

Two different types of clarification, *identity* and *time*, can be seen in D&C 110:14. D&C 110 is a record of the vision Joseph Smith and Oliver Cowdery received on 3 April 1836, during the dedication of the Kirtland Temple. The appearance of Jehovah is described first, followed by the appearances of Moses, Elias, and Elijah. When Joseph describes the vision of Elijah, he includes a statement by Elijah in which the Old Testament prophet directly alludes to Malachi 4:

> Behold, the time has fully come, which was spoken of by the mouth of Malachi—testifying that he *[Elijah] should be sent, before the great and dreadful day of the Lord come*— (D&C 110:14)

Here is the verse as it appears in Malachi:

> Behold, I will *send you Elijah the prophet before the coming of the great and dreadful day of the Lord*: (Malachi 4:5)

Two of the questions surrounding the Malachi passage deal with a literal versus figurative interpretation for Elijah and the timing of this appearance. Various interpretations for the identity of Elijah include

John the Baptist, Malachi himself, or an unnamed angelic messenger but not necessarily Elijah himself in a physically restored sense.[25] The timing of the "day of Yahweh" is usually linked with the Second Coming, when Jehovah will return and judge the nations. It constitutes "the ultimate theophany; all the signs, miracles, and cataclysms of nature marking Yahweh's previous encounters with humanity were but pallid foreshadowings of this most dramatic and momentous intervention of Yahweh in the human sphere for the sake of his people Israel."[26] According to Malachi, Elijah would appear at some point prior to this "day of the Lord," although Malachi gave no hint as to how long in the future this would be, allowing for anyone from John the Baptist to a future, unknown prophet to fit this description. D&C 110 clarifies both of these confusing issues. First, as to the identity of Elijah, D&C 110 states specifically that it was Elijah himself—not John the Baptist, Malachi, or another messenger—who appeared to Joseph Smith in the Kirtland Temple. Second, D&C 110 tells readers that this appearance of Elijah represents *a* fulfillment of the timing of Malachi's prophecy: "Behold, the time has fully come." Again, this does not mean that the only fulfillment of Malachi's prophecy is the Kirtland Temple dedication, but it does clarify that the dedication provided *one* instance of fulfillment.

C. *Reflection*

A third type of meaning that can be found in the use of Old Testament scripture by the Doctrine and Covenants is "reflection." What is meant by reflection is that an allusion by the Doctrine and Covenants to the Old Testament can sometimes reflect not only the *language* but also the *context* as well. An example of this reflection can be seen in D&C 10:27, where Satan is described:

> And thus he *goeth up and down, to and fro in the earth,* seeking to destroy the souls of men. (D&C 10:27)

D&C 10:27 is an inverted allusion to Job 1:7 and 2:2:

> Then Satan answered the Lord, and said, From *going to and fro in the earth*, and from walking *up and down* in it. (Job 1:7; cf. 2:2)

The context of Job 1:7 and 2:2 is a discussion between Yahweh and Satan and represents one of the few passages in the Old Testament where Satan appears to have a defined role, although not perhaps the one he assumes in later Christian texts.[27] Here Satan comes among the "sons of God" and makes his presence known in the council of Yahweh. Yahweh inquires of Satan, "Whence comest thou?" and Satan responds with the passage quoted above. Yahweh and Satan then begin a theological discussion that centers on the figure of Job, specifically whether Job is loyal to Yahweh in spite of his suffering or because Job hasn't yet been subjected to true suffering. In other words, is Job prosperous because he is pious, or is he pious because he is prosperous? If he loses his prosperity, will his piety fall away as well? In order to determine Job's true nature, Satan seeks and receives Yahweh's divine authorization to afflict Job in any fashion short of killing him.

The context of D&C 10 broadly reflects the context of Job, as again we encounter the Lord (Jehovah) and Satan, and again their point of focus appears to be the actions and responses of a single individual, in this case Joseph Smith, who repeatedly sought and was eventually granted permission to lend Martin Harris the 116 pages. The loss of the 116 pages by Martin Harris and the instruction received by Joseph to not retranslate the lost portion provide the immediate context for the allusion to Job 1:7 in D&C 10:27. The Satan described in D&C 10 is closer to the Satan familiar from the New Testament, the enemy of humanity who seeks to "lead their souls to destruction" and "destroy the work of God" (D&C 10:22–23). It is difficult to know how far to push this allusion. While in both cases the allusion refers to Satan, does this intertextual connection open the door to the possibility of understanding Joseph's loss of the 116 pages as the result of a "test" conceived by God and Satan? Probably not, as the likely placement of the allusion to Job 1:7 in D&C 10:27 is to allude to Satan in general and not necessarily in a specific way.

A second example of a textual reflection can be seen in D&C 84:5:

> For verily this generation shall not all pass away until an *house shall be built unto the Lord,* and a *cloud shall rest upon it, which cloud shall be even the glory of the Lord,* which shall *fill the house.* (D&C 84:5)

This verse is an allusion to a passage from 1 Kings:

> And it came to pass, when the priests were come out of the holy place, *that the cloud filled* the *house* of *the Lord,* So that the priests could not stand to minister because of the cloud: for *the glory of the Lord had filled the house* of the Lord. (1 Kings 8:10–11)

The context of D&C 84:5 is the building of a temple by "this generation," presumably on the temple site in Independence, Missouri, which Joseph had already purchased and dedicated a year earlier on 3 August 1831 (cf. D&C 57:1–3). This temple context is reflected in 1 Kings 8:10–11, which refers to Solomon's temple and more specifically to the *Shekinah,* or presence of God, which inhabited the temple of Solomon during periods of Israel's righteousness. The comparison of the "glory" or presence of God to a "cloud" is also noteworthy, as it was the presence of God in a pillar of "cloud" and "fire" that led the children of Israel through the wilderness (cf. Exodus 13:21–22). The implication of this allusion in D&C 84:5 is that the temple built in this dispensation will be the restoration of Solomon's temple, perhaps in fulfillment of Ezekiel's vision where he witnessed the return of the *Skekinah* to the temple in the latter days (Ezekiel 43:2–3).

A third reflection can be seen in this verse from D&C 130:

> Joseph, my son, if thou livest until thou art eighty-five years old, thou shalt see the face of the Son of Man; *therefore let this suffice, and trouble me no more on this matter.* (D&C 130:15)

The Old Testament source of this allusion is likely the book of Deuteronomy:

> But the Lord was wroth with me for your sakes, and would not hear me: and the Lord said unto me, *Let it suffice thee; speak no more unto me of this matter.* (Deuteronomy 3:26)

This allusion is an interesting one and raises an important hermeneutical issue: How much of the Old Testament context can be brought to bear on the interpretation of a verse from the Doctrine and Covenants? The context for most of D&C 130 is a series of instructions given by Joseph Smith to a group of Saints in Ramus, Illinois, in 1843. The immediate context of D&C 130:15 appears to be Joseph talking about an occasion in which he had made an inquiry of the Lord regarding the timing of the Second Coming of Jesus Christ.[28] The Lord's response to Joseph's inquiry is D&C 130:15, the verse quoted above. D&C 130:15, as we can see, is an allusion to Deuteronomy 3:26. In Deuteronomy 3:26, Moses relates an experience he had where he prayed to the Lord and begged to be able to see the promised land, which had been forbidden to him as a result of Israel's wickedness. Moses had apparently been rather persistent in his seeking this favor from the Lord, to the point where the Lord responds with the passage quoted above. The King James translation of Deuteronomy 3:26 doesn't fully convey the Lord's frustration with Moses, and some modern scholars have chosen to translate this verse as "Enough!

Never speak to me of this matter again!"[29] or "Enough of You! Do not continue speaking to me."[30]

Deuteronomy 3:26 shows the Lord frustrated with Moses for his repeated inquiries to enter the promised land. The enigmatic element of D&C 130:15 is whether we can interpret a similar tone when the Lord is speaking to Joseph Smith. We have seen how the Doctrine and Covenants can appropriate the language of the Old Testament, and we have seen how the Doctrine and Covenants can appropriate the general context of the Old Testament. The question here, as with the Job passage discussed above, is how much context is being reflected. In the Job passage discussed above, the question was raised of how far a text can be pushed beyond it limits, but here the context invites readers to pursue a deeper meaning. D&C 130:15 suggests that what Joseph is relaying to his audience is that he, like Moses, persisted in a request that the Lord was unwilling to grant, to the point that the Lord finally responded with an answer (albeit a confusing one) and then ordered Joseph to not broach the subject again. Whether Joseph is describing the exchange with the Lord in this specific language because this is how the Lord said it or because Joseph is linking his experience with that of Moses's experience takes us into the realm of speculation. But the allusion itself demonstrates that the role of the Old Testament in the Doctrine and Covenants goes beyond simply inserting a biblical phrase here and there. Each allusion must be identified and carefully explored in order to gain a fuller impression of what the text is trying to tell its readers.

D. Expansion

The final type of meaning we will examine in this paper is what can be termed "expansion." This type of meaning occurs when the Doctrine and Covenants alludes to a passage from the Old Testament in a way that expands or diverts from the original context, essentially creating a new context or frame of interpretation. A significant example of expansion occurs in D&C 45:48–52:

> And then shall the Lord *set his foot upon this mount,* and it *shall cleave in* twain, *and the earth shall tremble,* and *reel to and fro,* and the heavens also shall shake. And the Lord shall utter his voice, and all the ends of the earth shall hear it; and the nations of the earth shall mourn, and they that have laughed shall see their folly. And calamity shall cover the mocker, and the scorner shall be consumed; and they that have watched for iniquity shall be hewn down and cast into the fire. And then shall the Jews look upon me and say: *What are these wounds in thine hands* and in thy feet? Then shall they know that I am the Lord; for I will say unto them: *These wounds are the wounds with which I was wounded in the house of my friends.* I am he who was lifted up. I am Jesus that was crucified. I am the Son of God. (D&C 45:48–52)

D&C 45:48, 51, and 52 contain allusions to two verses from Zechariah:

> And *his feet shall stand* in that day *upon the mount* of Olives, which is before Jerusalem on the east, and the mount of Olives *shall cleave in* the midst thereof toward the east and toward the west, and there shall be a very great valley; and half of the mountain shall remove toward the north, and half of it toward the south. (Zechariah 14:4)
>
> And one shall say unto him, *What are these wounds in thine hands?* Then he shall answer, *Those with which I was wounded in the house of my friends.* (Zechariah 13:6)

Significantly, while the two passages from Zechariah have been combined to form one (inverted) allusion in D&C 45:48–52, the two Zechariah passages actually originate in two separate prophecies.

The first one, Zechariah 14:4, is an eschatological prophecy of a time in the future where Yahweh will descend from heaven and stand as a warrior upon the Mount of Olives. The result of his arrival will be the cataclysmic splitting of the mount in half, creating a valley of refuge for Israel. This eschatological arrival of Yahweh "stresses Yahweh's power over history and the peoples of the world. He will fight against the nations. The nations are undifferentiated here. The Mount of Olives will split and a valley will be formed across it from east to west so that the rest of the people in Jerusalem can find refuge and a way of escape."[31]

The second prophecy, Zechariah 13:6, is also likely eschatological but is a difficult passage to contextualize. The chapter begins with a general denunciation of false prophets and shifts to a farmer who explicitly claims, "I am no prophet," apparently seeking to distance himself from the group of false prophets condemned in the previous verses. The farmer is then asked about wounds that he has received, wounds that could identify him as a prophet, since self-flagellation and cutting were often signs of non-Israelite prophets.[32] The farmer responds that he "was wounded in the house of my friends," claiming that his wounds were received in a setting other than a prophetic setting.[33] The point of Zechariah's prophecy seems to be that at some future time, false prophets will be sought out and condemned, driven to offer alternative explanations for their prophetic marks.[34]

One of these prophecies from Zechariah seems to refer to the future coming of Yahweh, and one seems to refer to a future rejection of false prophets. In D&C 45, these two verses are skillfully appropriated and woven together into a description of the eschatological appearance of Jesus to the Jews gathered in Jerusalem. The Book of Mormon teaches that the era of the Gentiles will end when the Gentiles have heard the restored message of the gospel but then "shall sin against my gospel, and shall reject the fulness of my gospel, and shall be lifted up in the pride of their hearts above all nations"

(3 Nephi 16:10). At this point, the fulness of the gospel will be taken away from the Gentiles, "and then will I remember my covenant which I have made unto my people, O house of Israel, and I will bring my gospel unto them" (3 Nephi 16:11). D&C 45 describes how Jesus's appearance on the Mount of Olives and his revelation that he, the crucified Jesus, is the long-awaited Messiah, the warrior of Zechariah 14, will be a major step in the commencement of the gathering of the Jewish nation. What D&C 45 does is expand upon Zechariah 13:6 and 14:4 by maintaining the language but drastically shifting the context so that Zechariah's words have a new application and meaning.[35]

A second example of expansion in the Doctrine and Covenants' use of the Old Testament is found in three verses from the Doctrine and Covenants:

> And to none else will I grant this power, to receive this same testimony among this generation, in this the beginning of the rising up and the coming forth of my church out of the wilderness—*clear as the moon, and fair as the sun, and terrible as an army with banners.* (D&C 5:14)
>
> But first let my army become very great, and let it be sanctified before me, that it may *become fair as the sun, and clear as the moon, and that her banners may be terrible unto all nations;* (D&C 105:31)
>
> That thy church may come forth out of the wilderness of darkness, and shine forth *fair as the moon, clear as the sun, and terrible as an army with banners;* (D&C 109:73)

All three of these verses are alluding to a passage from the Song of Solomon:

> Who is *she* that *looketh forth as the morning, fair as the moon, clear as the sun, and terrible as an army with banners?* (Song of Solomon 6:10)

The Song of Solomon, while largely ignored by Latter-day Saints, is a beautiful and moving series of exchanges between two lovers.[36] In Song of Solomon 6:10, the verse cited above, the man[37] is describing the woman using celestial imagery, comparing her beauty to the grandest objects in the universe—the sun, the moon, and the stars.[38] In his mind, she has no equal. Interpretations of the Song of Solomon tend to fall into two camps: literal and allegorical. Those who see the Song of Solomon as literal read it as the actual expression of love between two lovers, perhaps Solomon and the Shulamite woman explicitly named in the text. For those who seek an allegorical interpretation, the most common theories are that the text symbolically refers to the relationship between Yahweh and Israel or the relationship between Jesus Christ and his church.[39]

This later allegorical interpretation, that of the relationship between Jesus Christ and his church, appears to be the interpretation taken by the Doctrine and Covenants as well. In D&C 5, a revelation given to Joseph Smith that addresses Martin Harris and his lack of faith, the allusion to Song of Solomon 6:10 appears in verse 14: "The coming forth of my *church out of the wilderness.*" This application is similar to what readers encounter in D&C 109, the dedicatory prayer for the Kirtland Temple. There again the passage from Song of Solomon follows the line "that thy *church may come forth out of the wilderness of darkness*" (D&C 109:73). D&C 105 seems to give Song of Solomon 6:10 a slightly different application, although still within the allegorical vein of D&C 5 and 109. In D&C 105, Joseph is told to disband Zion's Camp and to begin looking ahead to the building up of the kingdom of Zion upon the Earth through the construction of the Kirtland Temple. The redemption of Zion, the Lord said, would come after "a little season" (D&C 105:9). The Saints should also seek to legally purchase land in Missouri, after which "I will hold the armies of Israel guiltless in taking possession of their own lands" (D&C 105:30). Likely playing off of the word "armies," the inverted allusion to Song of Solomon 6:10 follows in the next verse: "But first let my *army* become very great, and let it be sanctified before me, that it may become fair as the sun, and clear as the moon, and that her banners may be terrible unto all nations." In this context, it is not the church but the "army of Israel" that is described by Song of Solomon 6:10. In all three cases, the Doctrine and Covenants has taken the language of the Old Testament and expanded upon its context, bestowing meanings beyond what the original text had allowed.

Conclusion

The use of the Old Testament through the revelations and other texts canonized as the Doctrine and Covenants goes beyond simply inserting phrases or passages into the middle of new texts. Structurally, the phrases from the Old Testament that are appropriated into the text of the Doctrine and Covenants can sometimes follow nearly word-for-word what is in the Old Testament, but at other times the Old Testament text can be condensed, expanded, or inverted into a new text, one that is recognizable as an Old Testament passage but that contains enough innovation to establish itself as a new text. This innovation carries over to the meaning of the appropriated allusions. The Old Testament allusions are often recast in a way that modernizes the archaic and clarifies the enigmatic. The Doctrine and Covenants text can reflect the context of the Old Testament passages in a way that can allow them to inform one another; they also expand upon Old Testament contexts to such an extent that the reader is encouraged to study both texts as a means of deriving possible meanings. However, it is important to remember that while the Doctrine and Covenants may offer an alternative perspective on an Old Testament passage, this does not mean that the original Old Testament context can be dismissed or ignored. Restoration scripture does not supersede the Bible; rather it offers the alternative perspective of those who read it from a different vantage point.

But the presence of the Old Testament in the Doctrine and Covenants also reflects a broader trend that can be seen throughout the Restoration, namely a serious engagement with Israelite scripture. Because the restored gospel is often represented as a restoration of the primitive New Testament church, the Old Testament is often forgotten or gently pushed aside. But the language of the Old Testament runs through critical periods of the Church's Restoration. When Moroni appeared to Joseph Smith to introduce the Restoration, he quoted heavily from Old Testament texts such as Isaiah and Malachi. The language of the Old Testament courses through the Book of Mormon and, as we have seen, the Doctrine and Covenants. Isaiah, not surprisingly, appears to be the author alluded to the most in the Doctrine and Covenants, while Malachi 4 is the chapter alluded to the most (a topic worthy of a full-length paper in its own right). But the Doctrine and Covenants also quotes from Genesis, Job, 2 Kings, Zechariah, and even the Song of Solomon. Through the various ways the Doctrine and Covenants deconstructs and reconstructs the language and meaning of the Old Testament, it begs readers to engage in a serious study of these holy and sacred writings. This is a daunting project that may require us to stretch a little bit more than we are often comfortable doing, but one that in the end will help us understand Restoration scripture on a deeper and more profound level.

Notes

1. The term "allusion" is notoriously difficult to define among scholars of intertextuality. Often it is positioned as less defined and harder to identify than a "quotation" but more defined and identifiable than an "echo." For the purpose of clarity, this paper will use "allusion" to refer to any instance where the Doctrine and Covenants adopts the language (usually phrasal) of the Old Testament in a manner that is clear and identifiable.

2. The technical name for the study of how two or more texts interact is called "intertextuality." It has become common in biblical studies to use intertextuality in studying the impact of the Old Testament on the New Testament. Important to this type of intertextual study are the works of Richard Hays *Echoes of Scripture in the Letters of Paul* (New Haven, CN: Yale University Press, 1989) and *The Conversion of the Imagination: Paul as Interpreter of Israel's Scripture* (Grand Rapids, MI: William B. Eerdmans, 2005), as well as the recent publication of G. K. Beale's and D. A. Carson's massive work, *Commentary on the New Testament Use of the Old Testament* (Grand Rapids, MI: Baker Academic Books, 2007). The standard work analyzing the role of the Bible and Mormon scripture is Philip Barlow, *Mormons and the Bible: The Place of the Latter-day Saints in American Religion*, 2nd ed. (Oxford: Oxford University Press, 2013). In Mormon scripture, intertextuality has most often been used to study the impact of the Bible on the Book of Mormon, such as Donald W. Parry and John W. Welch, eds., *Isaiah in the Book of Mormon*, (Provo, UT: FARMS, 1998); Victor L. Ludlow, *Unlocking Isaiah in the Book of Mormon* (Salt Lake City: Deseret Book, 2003); David P. Wright, "Isaiah in the Book of Mormon: Or Joseph Smith in Isaiah," in *American Apocrypha: Essays on the Book of Mormon*, ed. Dan Vogel and Brent Lee Metcalfe (Salt Lake City: Signature Books, 2002), 157–234; Krister Stendahl, "The Sermon on the Mount and Third Nephi," in *Reflections on Mormonism: Judaeo-Christian Parallels*, ed. Truman G. Madsen (Provo, UT: Religious Studies Center, 1978), 139–54; John W. Welch, *The Sermon at the Temple and the Sermon on the Mount* (Salt Lake City: Deseret Book; Provo, UT: FARMS, 1990); Daniel L. Belnap, "The King James Bible and the Book of Mormon," in *The King James Bible and the Restoration*, ed. Kent P. Jackson (Provo, UT: Religious Studies Center, 2007), 162–81; David P. Wright, "'In Plain Terms That We May Understand': Joseph Smith's Transformation of Hebrews in Alma 12–13," in *New Approaches to the Book of Mormon: Explorations in Critical Methodology*, ed. Brent Lee Metcalfe (Salt Lake City: Signature Books, 1993), 165–229; and Julie M. Smith, "So Shall My Word Be:

Reading Alma 32 through Isaiah 55," in *An Experiment on the Word: Reading Alma 32*, ed. Adam S. Miller (Salem, OR: Salt Press, 2011). As for intertextual work involving the Doctrine and Covenants, less has been done. Two important master's theses exploring the textual connections are Ellis T. Rasmussen, "Textual Parallels to the Doctrine and Covenants and Book of Commandments as Found in the Bible" (master's thesis, Brigham Young University, 1951), and Lois Jean Smutz, "Textual Parallels to the Doctrine and Covenants (Sections 65 to 133) as Found in the Bible" (master's thesis, Brigham Young University, 1971). Other works include Eric D. Huntsman, "The King James Bible and the Doctrine and Covenants," in *The King James Bible and the Restoration*, 182–96; Terry B. Ball and Spencer S. Snyder, "Isaiah in the Doctrine and Covenants," in *You Shall Have My Word: Exploring the Text of the Doctrine and Covenants*, ed. Scott C. Esplin, Richard O. Cowan, and Rachel Cope (Provo, UT: Religious Studies Center; Salt Lake City: Deseret Book, 2012), 108–33; and Lisa Olsen Tait, "Gathering the Lord's Words into One: Biblical Intertextuality in the Doctrine and Covenants," in *You Shall Have My Word*, 92–107. For a general introduction to intertextuality as a methodology, see Nicholas J. Frederick, "The Use of the Old Testament in the New Testament Gospels," herein.

3. While I will briefly discuss the context of some of the Old Testament passages analyzed in this section, the majority of contextual analysis will be done in the second section, "Meaning." In this first section, the focus will be primarily on an evaluation of text more so than context.
4. Isaiah 35 represents the apex of Isaiah's "eschatological vision." John Oswalt, *The Book of Isaiah, Chapters 1–39* (Grand Rapids, MI: William B. Eerdmans, 1986), 626.
5. The context of Isaiah 28:10 is interesting, especially as the phrase "line upon line, precept upon precept" has become a common part of LDS discourse. In Isaiah 28:10, the religious leaders of Israel, who are represented as drunk to the extent that they are vomiting onto their tables, are chastising the prophets for teaching the people in such a simplistic fashion, as you

would teach a young child the alphabet or repeat a simple phrase over and over again until their young minds grasp your message. It is this style of teaching that is represented by the phrase "precept upon precept, line upon line." Isaiah will cleverly turn this insult back upon the drunkards in 28:13. See discussion in Oswalt, *Isaiah 1–39*, 511–14. See also the discussion in John D. W. Watts, *Word Biblical Commentary: Isaiah 1–33*, rev. ed. (Nashville: Thomas Nelson Publishers, 2005), 430–32, and Joseph Blenkinsopp, *Isaiah 1–39: A New Translation with Introduction and Commentary* (New York: Doubleday, 2000), 387–90.

6. According to John Oswalt, "the prophet promises a day when true values are seen and true guidance is received. In short, in this context, they will cease to trust the nations and begin to trust God" (Oswalt, *Isaiah 1–39*, 624). Blenkinsopp sees Isaiah as speaking of "a visionary future of the transformed land and saved people." Blenkinsopp, *Isaiah 1–39*, 456.
7. One approach to this method of editorial inversions is what has become known, after its discoverer, as Seidel's Law. Seidel argued that quotations of earlier Old Testament texts by later authors were marked by a reversal of the source text by the newer text. See M. Seidel, "Parallels between Isaiah and Psalms," *Sinai* 38 (1955–56): 149–72. A more specific approach to Old Testament quotations is found in Shemaryahu Talmon, "The Textual Study of the Bible—A New Outlook," in *Qumran and the History of the Biblical Text*, ed. Frank Moore Cross and Shemaryahu Talmon (Cambridge: Harvard University Press, 1975), 321–400.
8. For more on the context of this letter, see Andrew H. Hedges, "'They Pursue Me without Cause': Joseph Smith in Hiding and D&C 127, 128," *Religious Educator* 16, no. 1 (2015): 43–59.
9. Contextually, there is something interesting at work behind this combination of phrases. The first two phrases, "the weak shall confound the wise" and "the little ones become a strong nation," both refer to the eventual influence of the remnant of Israel. However, the third phrase, "two shall put their tens of thousands to flight," is a phrase that functions in exactly the opposite way. In this passage, the Lord is predicting what will happen

to those who put their trust in themselves and not in him, namely that an army with greater numbers will be easily vanquished without the assistance of Yahweh. Yet in D&C 133:58, all three phrases have been united under a single context (cf. Isaiah 30:17).

10. Joseph M. Blenkinsopp, *Isaiah 56–66* (New York: Doubleday, 2003), 249–50. See also John D. W. Watts, who adds, "The blood-spattered clothes are unmistakable. First comes the confession: 'I did it, alone and in anger.' Then comes the justification: it was an act of vengeance. That is, the enemy had done something first that created an unjust situation. This had to be answered and put right. So this was done to redeem something or someone. It freed someone from bondage, and it allowed healthy progress and life to return to the communities and societies of the land." John D. W. Watts, *Word Biblical Commentary: Isaiah 34–66*, rev. ed. (Nashville: Thomas Nelson Publishers, 2005), 891.
11. Watts, *Isaiah 34–66*, 887.
12. This interpretation appears to be the one followed by John the Revelator. See Revelation 19:13–15.
13. John N. Oswalt, *The Book of Isaiah: Chapters 40–66* (Grand Rapids, MI: William B. Eerdmans, 1998), 596.
14. Blenkinsopp, *Isaiah 56–66*, 249.
15. Note as well the insertion of "And he shall say" into D&C 133:47 (not in Isaiah 63:1) in order to help the reader understand they have suddenly entered into a dialogue, a point that could be confusing without the context of Isaiah 62–63.
16. See the discussion in John E. Goldingay, *Word Biblical Commentary: Daniel* (Dallas: Word Books, 1982), 49–61.
17. See the discussion in Goldingay, *Daniel*, 49–61.
18. For a discussion of the various viewpoints regarding the stone, in particular the early Christian interpretation, see Gerhard Pfandl, "Interpretations of the Kingdom of God in Daniel 2:34," *Andrews University Seminary Studies* 34, no. 2 (1996): 249–68.
19. Henry William Bigler, Journal, February 1846–October 1899, Church History Library, Salt Lake City, as cited in Steven C. Harper, *Making*

Sense of the Doctrine and Covenants: A Guided Tour through Revelation (Salt Lake City: Deseret Book, 2008), 227.

20. Watts, *Isaiah 34–66,* 321. But see also Blenkinsopp, who argues that the soldier is Yahweh: "What is emphasized in the reply to the second question is that in executing judgment YHVH acted alone" (Blenkinsopp, *Isaiah 56–66,* 250).
21. For a discussion of multiple fulfillments of prophecy as well as other types of prophetic interpretation, see the useful discussion in David L. Turner, *Matthew* (Grand Rapids, MI: Baker Academic Books, 2008), 68–73.
22. John Walton, "The *Anzu* Myth as Relevant Background for Daniel 7?," in *The Book of Daniel: Composition and Reception,* ed. John J. Collins and Peter W. Flint (Leiden: Brill, 2001), 1:79.
23. For background on both the "Ancient of Days" and the "Son of Man," see Karel van der Toon, Bob Becking, and Pieter W. van der Horst, eds., *Dictionary of Deities and Demons in the Bible,* (Leiden: Brill, 1999).
24. A year later, Joseph Smith taught: "Dan VII Speaks of the Ancient of days, he means the oldest man, our Father Adam, Michael; he will call his children together, & hold a council with them to prepare them for the coming of the Son of Man. He, (Adam) is the Father of the human family & presides over the Spirits of all men, & all that have had the Keys must stand before him in this great Council. This may take place before some of us leave this stage of action. The Son of Man stands before him & there is given him glory & dominion.—Adam delivers up his Stewardship to Christ, that which was delivered to him as holding the Keys of the Universe, but retains his standing as head of the human family." Andrew F. Ehat and Lyndon W. Cook, eds. *The Words of Joseph Smith* (Orem, UT: Grandin Book Company, 1991), 8–9.
25. "Since the writings of Luther and Calvin, most Protestant commentators have figuratively interpreted the Elijah figure as 'a prophet in whom the spirit and power of Elijah are revived'—not the prophet Elijah reincarnate or resurrected." Andrew H. Hill, *Malachi* (New York: Doubleday, 1998), 383.
26. Hill, *Malachi,* 386.

27. In Job, "Satan" is more literally "the Satan," likely meaning "the accuser." It is difficult to fully grasp his relationship with Yahweh and the "sons of God," whether he is intruding upon their council or whether he is a member of it himself. David J. A. Clines describes the enigmatic relationship between Yahwah and "the Satan" in the following way: "There are two heavenly personalities in uneasy confrontation; two personalities who are not equals but able to converse freely, who are neither enemies nor conspirators, neither friends nor rivals." David J. A. Clines, *Job 1–20: Biblical Word Commentary* (Dallas: Word Books, 1982), 22. For more on the origin and development of Satan in the Judeo-Christian tradition, see van der Toon, Becking, and van der Horst, *Dictionary of Deities and Demons*, 726–32.
28. The experience Joseph is referencing likely would have occurred before the reception of D&C 49, the revelation that answered Joseph's inquiry. See discussion in Stephen E. Robinson and H. Dean Garrett, *A Commentary on the Doctrine and Covenants* (Salt Lake City: Deseret Book, 2005), 4:227.
29. Moshe Weinfeld, *Deuteronomy 1–11* (New York: Doubleday, 1964), 189.
30. Duane L. Christensen, *Word Biblical Commentary: Deuteronomy 1:1–21:9* (Dallas: Word Books, 1991), 69. The NIV translates the Lord's rebuke as "That is enough. . . . Do not speak to me anymore about this matter."
31. Ralph L. Smith, *Word Biblical Commentary: Micah–Malachi* (Dallas: Word Books, 1984), 286. See also Carol L. Meyers and Eric M. Meyers, who write that this event provides "a final resolution to Jerusalem's centuries-long history of being threatened or subjugated by other nations. . . . Here God's fight against the nations involves a cataclysmic reordering of the natural world in order to achieve security for the people." Carol L. Meyers and Eric M. Meyers, *Zechariah 9–14* (New York: Doubleday, 1993), 421.
32. "Like special clothing, certain modes of activity characterized the professional identity of prophetic figures. Dancing, eating or imbibing certain foods or liquids, and chanting were such activities; flagellation or wounding by one's own hand or by that of an associate was apparently another." Meyers and Meyers, *Zechariah 9–14*, 382. See also Ralph L. Smith, who writes, "The wounds between the prophet's hands were probably wounds

made in an ecstatic orgy (1 Kgs 18:28). The wounds or scars would have been visible in the summer. Such a prophet would deny that they were the marks of a prophet." Smith, *Micah–Malachi*, 281.

33. "Anyone prophesying was to be accused of lying in the name of Yahweh and put to death (v 3). Consequently any prophet would be ashamed of his vision and not put on the hairy mantle in order to deceive (v 4). He will deny that he is a prophet and claim to be a farmer instead." Smith, *Micah–Malachi*, 281.

34. As Meyers and Meyers note, the wounds "could have been received in a household accident or in a quarrel with these friends—but we are left wondering, a fact that makes us suspect that this disclaimer is a cover-up. That is, the bruises may in fact be flagellation wounds of a professional prophet who now, in the eschatological future, renounces his profession and thus must find an explanation for the physical signs of his former role." Meyers and Meyers, *Zechariah 9–14*, 384.

35. F. F. Bruce, quoting T. V. Moore, wrote that "No New Testament writer tries to interpret this utterance as a prophecy of the nail-wounds in our Lord's hands, 'in the grossest misapprehension of its meaning." F. F. Bruce, *New Testament Development of Old Testament Themes* (Grand Rapids, MI: William B. Eerdmans, 1968), 114.

36. The Joseph Smith Translation includes the description that "the Songs of Solomon are not inspired writings." Elder Bruce R. McConkie referred to the Song of Solomon as "biblical trash." "The Bible—a Sealed Book" (Church Education Symposium, BYU, 17 August 1984). In contrast, the Mishnah includes the following: "Said R. Aqiba, 'Heaven forbid! No Israelite man ever disputed concerning Song of Songs that it imparts uncleanness to hands. For the entire age is not so worthy as the day on which the Song of Songs was given to Israel. For all the scriptures are holy, but the Song of Songs is holiest of all." Mishnah, *Yad.*, 3:5. For an article advocating a healthy, positive Latter-day Saint view of the Song of Solomon, see Dana M. Pike, "Reading the Song of Solomon as a Latter-day Saint," *Religious Educator* 15, no. 2 (2014): 91–113.

37. The other possibility is that the question is posed by a choral group observing the interplay between the two lovers. In this case, the question would likely be posed interrogatively rather than the rhetorical sense of the man's question.
38. That the phrase "an army with banners" refers to heavenly stars is argued by Duane Garrett, who says that "the בדגלות must be the stars, here personified as heavenly armies, 'awesome as the panoply of heaven.'" Duane Garrett and Paul R. House, *Word Biblical Commentary: Song of Songs/ Lamentations* (Nashville: Thomas Nelson Publishers, 2004), 229. He continues: "Where v4 had described the woman's awesome beauty under the metaphor of the fortified cities, this text describes her as splendid under the metaphor of heavenly bodies." The NIV translation follows this interpretation: "Who is this that appears like the dawn, fair as the moon, bright as the sun, majestic as the stars in procession?"
39. See discussion in Marvin H. Pope, *The Song of Songs* (New York: Doubleday, 1977), 89–229.

Index

K

L

M

N

O

P

R

S

T